T0305676

The Complete Guide
to Cybersecurity
Risks and Controls

Internal Audit and IT Audit

Series Editor: Dan Swanson

PUBLISHED

Leading the Internal Audit Function
by Lynn Fountain
ISBN: 978-1-4987-3042-6

Securing an IT Organization through Governance, Risk Management, and Audit
by Ken Sigler and James L. Rainey, III
ISBN: 978-1-4987-3731-9

A Guide to the National Initiative for Cybersecurity Education (NICE) Cybersecurity Workforce Framework (2.0)
by Dan Shoemaker, Anne Kohnke, and Ken Sigler
ISBN: 978-1-4987-3996-2

Operational Assessment of IT
by Steve Katzman
ISBN: 978-1-4987-3768-5

The Complete Guide to Cybersecurity Risks and Controls
by Anne Kohnke, Dan Shoemaker, and Ken Sigler
ISBN: 978-1-4987-4054-8

Software Quality Assurance: Integrating Testing, Security, and Audit
by Abu Sayed Mahfuz
ISBN: 978-1-4987-3553-7

FORTHCOMING

Practical Techniques for Effective Risk-Based Process Auditing
by Ann Butera
ISBN: 978-1-4987-3849-1

Internal Audit Practice from A to Z
by Patrick Onwura Nzechukwu
ISBN: 978-1-4987-4205-4

The Complete Guide to Cybersecurity Risks and Controls

Anne Kohnke • Dan Shoemaker • Ken Sigler

CRC Press
Taylor & Francis Group
Boca Raton   London   New York

CRC Press is an imprint of the
Taylor & Francis Group, an **informa** business
AN AUERBACH BOOK

CRC Press
Taylor & Francis Group
6000 Broken Sound Parkway NW, Suite 300
Boca Raton, FL 33487-2742

First issued in paperback 2022

Version Date: 20160205

ISBN 13: 978-1-4987-4054-8 (hbk)
ISBN 13: 978-1-03-240255-0 (pbk)

DOI: 10.1201/b19631

Library of Congress Cataloging-in-Publication Data

Names: Kohnke, Anne, author. | Shoemaker, Dan, author. | Sigler, Kenneth, author.
Title: The complete guide to cybersecurity risks and controls / Anne Kohnke, Dan Shoemaker, Ken Sigler.
Description: Boca Raton, FL : CRC Press, [2016] | Series: Internal audit and IT audit | Includes bibliographical references and index.
Identifiers: LCCN 2015050140 | ISBN 9781498740548
Subjects: LCSH: Computer security. | Computer networks--Security measures. | Information technology--Security measures.
Classification: LCC QA76.9.A25 K6346 2016 | DDC 005.8--dc23
LC record available at http://lccn.loc.gov/2015050140

Visit the Taylor & Francis Web site at
http://www.taylorandfrancis.com

and the CRC Press Web site at
http://www.crcpress.com

Contents

Preface

Controls and Trust

This book presents the fundamental concepts of information and communication technology (ICT) governance and control. In this book, you will learn how to create a working, practical control structure, which will ensure the ongoing, day-to-day trustworthiness of ICT systems and data. The book will explain how to establish systematic control functions and timely reporting procedures within a standard organizational framework as well as build auditable trust into the routine assurance of ICT operations. However, before you can select an appropriate framework, this book provides an overview of the most widely adopted frameworks that are in use.

The overall aim of the ICT governance and control process is to establish a complete set of managerial and technical control behaviors that will ensure reliable monitoring and control of ICT operations. The body of knowledge for doing that is explained in this text. This body of knowledge process applies to all operational aspects of ICT responsibilities ranging from upper management policy making and planning, all the way down to basic technology operation. The details of this process are itemized in very well-known and widely accepted professional standards for best practice. We have adopted a representative set of these standards from industry and government. Accordingly, the knowledge contained in this book is authoritative as well as part of commonly agreed on best practice. The standards we have adopted to underwrite this text are global in scope. As a consequence, they provide an ideal platform for illustrating and discussing the practical application of governance-based control in all ICT organizations.

This book is based around the belief that ICT operation is a strategic governance issue rather than a technical concern. The purpose of adopting that point of view is to avoid implementing piecemeal control over ICT work. With the exponential growth of security breaches and the increasing dependency on external business partners to achieve organizational success, the effective use of IT governance and enterprise-wide frameworks to guide the implementation of integrated security controls is critical in order to mitigate data theft. Surprisingly, many organizations do not have formal processes or policies to protect their assets from internal or external threats.

Every ICT enterprise is managed by its common practices. These are typically based on some individual unit's or manager's appreciation of the proper way to do the work. These practices tend to embed themselves in the organization over time, without any particular logic. And, the end result is dangerously flawed management control. That is because the management of the operation does not embody or address all necessary and relevant practices for ensuring comprehensive and coordinated control over all aspects of ICT operation. The solution is to impose a formally defined and implemented infrastructure of best practice controls that are specifically aimed at optimizing the coordinated day-to-day functioning and assurance of the *entire* ICT function. As with any complex deployment, the creation and everyday application of these controls have to be managed through a rational and well-defined process, made up of commonly understood best practice procedures. The standard approach that can be used to create, coordinate, ensure, and deploy those procedures is what we are presenting here.

Justification and Objectives of the Book

In more than 1,300 data breaches and 63,400 security incidents in 95 countries, a 2014 Data Breach Investigations Report found basic lapses at the heart of many of them such as employee mistakes, the use of weak and default passwords, system configuration issues, and inadequate system monitoring (Verizon, 2014). And according to the Privacy Rights Clearinghouse (PRC), over one billion records have been lost during the previous 10 years (PRC, 2013). This number is not entirely accurate because it only includes breaches that were reported and many organizations do not always publicize their security failures. The number of reported breaches has risen annually from 136 breaches in 2005 to 623 in 2013 (PRC, 2013) and certainly suggest that an effective and continuously evolving cyberdefense program is an absolute imperative.

However, many organizations do not structure or conduct their ICT management and risk processes in a systematic way. This is a direct consequence of the people at the top of the organization not taking the necessary steps to ensure across-the-board coordination and control over the process of overseeing and governing risk and information assets. One logical explanation for the unwillingness of the C-level executives to get involved with ICT governance and risk management is that they have neither the background nor the time to organize and manage an organization-wide oversight and governance effort. That is the reason why the all-in-one approach that we provide in this book will aid the organization as a whole and upper managers in particular in sponsoring and creating a trustworthy oversight control system over ICT work. Comprehensive ICT oversight and control require the everyday use of an established collection of common practices, which are meant to work together to produce an optimum solution. The corporate effort to ensure effective governance control over its ICT operations can be understood in terms of those fundamental components and their logical interactions.

Chapter 1: Why Cybersecurity Management Is Important?

This book will detail why governance-based control infrastructures are valuable. Readers will see how they provide the basis for the most effective control over ICT resources. Readers will discover the importance of best practice standardization as well as the most widely accepted models for best practice in this area.

Chapter 2: Control-Based Information Governance, What It Is and How It Works

The reader will learn why a formal, comprehensive, standards-based control framework is a critical asset for ICT management and oversight. The aim of this chapter is to demonstrate how to utilize a complete governance framework that will effectively control the activities of all members of the organization.

Chapter 3: A Survey of Control Frameworks, General Structure, and Application

The term *information governance* was coined to describe the strategic function that underwrites due professional care in the management of an organization's information resources. Information governance accomplishes these aims by building a comprehensive structure of rational procedures and relationships that can be employed to direct and control information assets.

Chapter 4: What Are Controls and Why Are They Important?

This presents a complete discussion of management and behavioral controls, including what they are and how they are formulated and audited. The entire control creation and use discussion will be presented here. At the end of the chapter, the reader will understand what a control is and how they are aggregated into an everyday system of integrated security activities.

Chapter 5: Implementing a Multitiered Governance and Control Framework in a Business

This is the chapter that illustrates how to implement control frameworks in practical settings. This will be end-to-end from concept of need to the actual auditing reports. It will include gap analyses and implementation of controls and corrective actions.

Chapter 6: Risk Management and Prioritization Using a Control Perspective

The aim of this chapter is to ensure that the reader can move from an identification of risk to the development of a targeted control set. This is where the deployment of controls is hooked to the body of knowledge of risk management and incident response.

Chapter 7: Control Formulation and Implementation Process

This chapter provides a walkthrough of the discrete control formulation process from identification of threat to deployment and maintenance of control effectiveness. The aim is to instill a sense of practical controls for various aspects of the business; every common aspect of doing business will be illustrated with some model control set.

Chapter 8: Security Control Validation and Verification

This explains assurance of control performance and explains how to maintain an operational process that will carry out the necessary tests and reviews on a regular basis. That includes static reviews and dynamic control test processes and protocols as well as the various forms of auditing.

Chapter 9: Control Framework Sustainment and Security of Operations

This explains sustainment. It will show how the control set will be maintained under configuration management as a way of ensuring long-term security of operations. The aim is to ensure that the reader knows how to make the control process long-term, reliable, and systematically sustainable.

Readership Requisite Skills and Experience

This book presents the concepts of the audit and control process for ICT operations as an all-in-one concept. As such, there is no assumption about specialized knowledge. All readers will learn how to create a systematic risk-based control structure for ICT work, establish systematic accounting and control procedures for this structure, and build systematic control assurance capability into the IT function.

At the end of this book, the reader will be able to

■ Implement formal, organization-wide, standards-based security control over a given aspect of organizational functioning.
■ Define comprehensive control mechanisms to ensure adequate monitoring and assurance capability within that framework.

■ Create an auditable security control process that is built on tangible control objectives.

The aim is to provide sufficient comprehensive knowledge to allow a reader to integrate a complete oversight and control solution in a typical organization that has mission-critical data assets they must protect.

This book was written to provide a survey of the field of control-based governance of risk, information, and communication technology work. Thus the audience for this material could be anyone who wishes to acquire security knowledge and competencies appropriate to their personal, career, or disciplinary area of interest. Individuals who might benefit from this knowledge in the practical world range from managers through all types of technical workers, specialists such as auditors, physical security practitioners, and ICT users.

References

Privacy Rights Clearinghouse. (2013). *Chronology of Data Breaches Security Breaches 2005–Present.* PRC.

Verizon Enterprise Solutions. (2014). *Verizon Data Breach Investigations Report.* www .verizonenterprise.com/DBIR/2014/.

Chapter 1

Why Cybersecurity Management Is Important

At the conclusion of this chapter, the reader will understand:

- The importance of cybersecurity in today's life
- The issues associated with an emerging discipline
- The form and content of a governance solution
- The general structure and intent of controls-based frameworks
- The general application and development of a controls-based solution
- The elements of audit and control, and why they are important

Computing and Culture Shock

Commercial computing has been with us for slightly over 50 years, which means that the entire computer age has passed within the lifetime of the average Baby Boomer. Nevertheless, within the period of a single generation, information technology (IT) has radically changed every aspect of our society, economy, and culture (Figure 1.1).

For perspective, think about how people communicated in the 50 years prior to 1958. Notwithstanding improvements in radios and telephones, our society used the same technology to transact its business in 1910 as it did in 1960. On the other hand, this cannot be said for the most recent 50-year period. Now thanks to computers, business and government entities interact across multiple continents as if

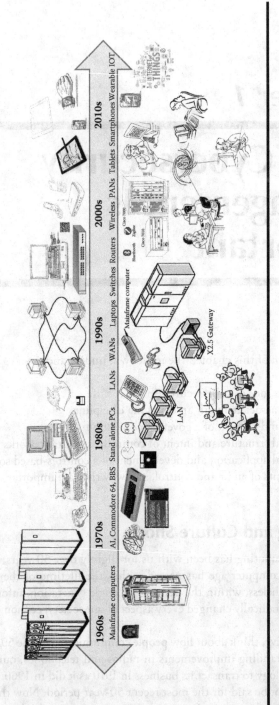

Figure 1.1 How IT has radically changed.

all of the participants were in the same room. That creates a splendid set of new opportunities. But it also places an inconceivable set of new demands on traditional organizations and their people.

The World Wide Web has various birthdays but it is generally acknowledged that the mid-1990s popularized it. So in effect, the average 30-year old probably does not remember a time when people were not electronically linked. This in effect means that a significant proportion of the population does not recall an era when the whole world was not plugged into a global information grid.

Consequently, within the scope of this very short space, the pervasive influence of IT and the scope of the Internet have made computers and electronic information a very significant element of our society. It is information that enables our national defense. It is information that powers our national economy. It is information that ensures that we get the goods and services that we need, and it is information that informs and entertains us.

At the same time, this inconceivably rapid evolution has caused a problem of perception, in the sense that the average person's grasp of the role that computers and IT play in society has not kept up with the facts of the situation. In essence, for most people information-processing equipment is just a part of their daily life. Like the weather, it is just *there* and like the weather, people never think in personal terms about what a compromise of that technology, or the information it might contain, could mean.

It is a fact that information and IT have become so tightly woven into our social fabric that its fundamental trustworthiness determines whether we are able to have such necessities as electric power, telecommunications, and energy. One only needs to ponder the impact of a malicious adversary hacking into the technologies that control our national defense to understand how dependent we are on properly functioning computers.

While at the same time, the information that resides in those computers defines us to the external world. Just consider the tangible costs of identity theft if you want to get a sense of the impact of information on any given person's life. Still, it is hard for the average individual to understand any of this.

The root of the misunderstanding lies in the fact that information has no tangible form. So, even though information has value and real impact on lives, it is hard to visualize exactly what it is, where it resides, and how it can be threatened. Accordingly, in order to assure information's confidentiality, integrity, and availability it is essential to find out all of the ways that it might be compromised and then to develop concrete protection measures. That is the role of the newly emerging field of cybersecurity.

Six Blind Men and an Elephant

The present challenge to generating comprehensive and sustainable solutions stems from the fact that the field of cybersecurity suffers from a "Six Blind Men and an Elephant" syndrome. In that old story, six blind men are asked to describe an elephant based on what they are touching. So to one, it is a snake, another, a wall, and to another, a tree, and so on. In the end, "Though each was partly in the right, all were entirely wrong" (Figure 1.2).

We have the same problem with knowing what to do in order to protect our system and information assets. There are established elements of the field that know how to secure the part of the elephant that they touch. But until we are able to amalgamate that knowledge into a single coordinated solution, we cannot realistically say we are protected. It should be obvious that highly complex problems cannot be solved piecemeal. Effective solutions can only be based on whole system approaches. Or in simple terms, "You are not secure if you are not *completely* secure."

Those solutions have to encompass the entire security challenge. And they have to be approached as a coherent entity within a comprehensive framework or properly designed and arrayed security controls. Needs may vary in their particulars within the overall scope of the problem. But it is important to keep in mind that the elephant is a lot bigger than its individual parts. So we have to address the beast as a comprehensive entity in order to master it.

Figure 1.2 Blind men and an elephant syndrome.

What Is Cybersecurity?

The Internet age has produced a lot of jargon. One of those is the term "cybersecurity." The following are a few of the current examples of dictionary attempts to define cybersecurity:

- The state of being protected against the criminal or unauthorized use of electronic data, or the measures taken to achieve this (Oxford English Dictionary)
- Measures taken to protect a computer or computer system (as on the Internet) against unauthorized access or attack (Merriam-Webster)
- The body of technologies, processes, and practices designed to protect networks, computers, programs, and data from attack, damage, or unauthorized access (WhatIs.com)
- Refers to preventative methods used to protect information from being stolen, compromised, or attacked (Technopedia)

These definitions have commonality in that their target is clearly data and the aim is protection. The measures themselves are undefined but their purpose is clear, which is to prevent loss, or harm to information that is stored on an electronic device. Therefore, it might be safe to conclude that the field of cybersecurity embraces any appropriate measure to ensure that electronic data are kept safe from unauthorized access, or harm. Or in simple terms, cybersecurity safeguards the information that is stored on computers and other types of electronic-processing equipment.

The processes, technologies, and practices in the field of cybersecurity are all developed in service of that purpose. That includes the efforts of professionals in the field to create unbreakable defenses against penetration of the electronic perimeter. Those types of attacks go by the common, if slightly inaccurate, term of "hacking." Additionally, should that electronic boundary be breached, a good cyber-defense should contain controls sufficient to detect and defend against intrusions, by preventing loss, or harm to the data. Done properly, an effective set of cybersecurity controls should

- Accurately identify and authenticate all entities seeking access to a system
- Authorize access to only those objects that the entity's level of trust permits
- Monitor and control activities during the time that the entity is granted access
- Ensure against unauthorized access, or manipulation of data
- Ensure against unauthorized manipulation of system objects

The Growing Pains of an Emerging Discipline

The need for cybersecurity is a rapidly emerging condition. Fifteen years ago, the notion of a national level effort that was entirely dedicated to the protection of cyber-assets might be considered to be an oddity. Now, with the critical role, that information plays in every aspect of our society, the specific study of ways to assure it in all of its forms has moved to center stage.

Even with its new central role, however, the reality is that until recently the field of cybersecurity did not have a single, commonly accepted approach to the entire problem. Accordingly, the entire profession is just beginning to materialize.

Nonetheless, in the 20-year period since the emergence of the commercial Internet cyber-crime, cyber-espionage and even cyber-warfare have become visions with real consequences. Consequently, it is unrealistic to assume that our way-of-life is adequately protected until substantive methods are utilized to secure every element of our national infrastructure.

The problem is that, even with its newfound national prominence, there is still a lot of disagreement about what legitimately constitutes the right set of actions to prevent harmful or adversarial actions. That disagreement was captured in a 2013 report sponsored by the National Academy of the Sciences (Bishop and Burley, 2013).

The report asserts that cybersecurity is at best an ill-defined field, which is subject to a range of interpretation by numerous special interest groups. Since there has been heretofore no clear definition of the field, the profession, and the actual protection of computers and information tends to be characterized by a long track record of hit-and-miss failures.

The confusion about what constitutes the proper elements of the field originates in the fact that the profession of cybersecurity could potentially comprise concepts from a number of disciplines. Some content from all of these disciplines might reasonably fall within legitimate boundaries. That includes such diverse areas as the following:

- Business management—which contributes concepts like security policy and procedure, continuity planning, personnel management, contract, and regulatory compliance to the cause.
- The traditional technical studies of computer security, such as computer science, contribute knowledge about ways to safeguard the processing of information in its electronic form.
- Likewise, knowledge from the field of networking adds essential recommendations about how to safeguard the electronic transmission and storage of information.
- Software engineering adds the necessary system and software assurance considerations like testing and reviews, configuration management, and lifecycle process management.
- Law and law enforcement contribute important ideas about such topics as intellectual property rights and copyright protection, privacy legislation, cyber-law and cyber-litigation, and the investigation and prosecution of computer crimes.
- Behavioral studies address essential human factors like discipline, motivation, training, and certification of knowledge.

■ Even the field of ethics, with its consideration of the personal and societal implications of information use and information protection, as well as codes of conduct contribute to the discussion.

All of these areas potentially bring something to the overall aim of information protection. As such, it would seem logical to incorporate the principles and methods from each area into the total body of best practice for cybersecurity. Nonetheless, at this point there is still discussion about where the line ought to be drawn, or where the focus within those boundaries ought to be. That is where two simple common sense principles come into play, integration, and control.

To achieve that purpose, cybersecurity encompasses approaches from a large and diverse range of disciplines. For instance, obviously relevant areas like business contribute elements such as security policy and procedure, continuity planning, personnel management, contract, and regulatory compliance. While the technical areas, such as computer science, contribute knowledge about ways to safeguard the processing of information in its electronic form. Likewise, networking adds know-how about how to safeguard the electronic transmission and storage of information and even software engineering adds process considerations like configuration management and lifecycle process security.

And at the same time, ostensibly unrelated areas such as law and law enforcement contribute such important considerations as intellectual property rights and copyright protection, privacy legislation, cyber-law and cyber-litigation, and the investigation and prosecution of computer crimes. Finally, behavioral studies, like education address necessities like motivation, training, and certification of knowledge. Even the field of ethics, with its focus on cyber-rights, contributes and are all shown in Figure 1.3 in its entirety.

All of these fields add important aspects to the overall goal of information protection. As such, principles and methods from each area must be integrated into a complete and cohesive body of knowledge. The aim of that body of knowledge should be comprehensive security management. Or in simple terms, all of the relevant elements of each contributing discipline need to be evaluated for their contribution to overall security assurance. And then the appropriate methods, techniques, and behaviors that contribute to the overall goal of managing and securing information and communication technology assets must be applied to the problem.

Understanding the Costs and Benefits to an Organization

The problem is that correct and proper strategic application of these principles centers on the issue of deciding what is required to determine security's worth to an organization. In a profit-driven world, it is hard for the leaders in the public and private sectors to justify the tangible expense of protecting virtual assets like computers and networks, and their contents. As a result, even though the constituent elements of cyber-space have real value and can directly impact people's lives,

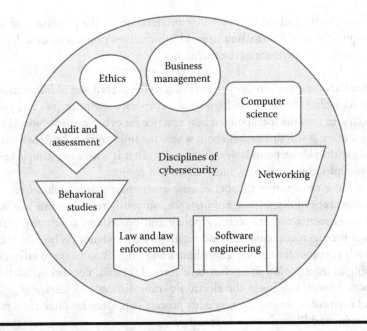

Figure 1.3 The disciplines of cybersecurity.

it is hard for the people who are putatively responsible for the protection of those contents to understand how the ways that the theft or destruction of a computer or its information might affect them personally.

Equally as important, it is exceedingly difficult and very costly for any organization to ensure reliable and systematic protection for an asset that is as dynamic and abstract as its IT systems and information. In essence, the processes and technologies that are required to assure reliable and consistent protection of cyber-assets change as rapidly as the technology evolves. As a result, most people view the steps involved in ensuring cybersecurity as an opaque set of activities and requirements that nobody outside the elected few can truly understand or apply.

As a consequence, America's electronic infrastructure is riddled with vulnerabilities that have underwritten an outrageous number of criminal and national security exploits over the past decade. For instance, according to the nonprofit Privacy Rights Clearinghouse (PRC), we have lost over one *billion* records in the past 10 years (PRC, 2014). And you should keep in mind that those losses only comprise the outcome of breaches that were *reported*. Since most companies do not like to publicize their security failures that number could be, and probably is, much higher.

The running average of 100 million records reported lost per year has been subject to some variation over time and the source of breach has changed in logical ways. But, the number of reported incidents rose annually from 108 in 2005 to 607 in 2013. And you should still keep in mind that these are only the ones that were *reported*. So, it would be unrealistic to conclude that we have been getting *better* at protecting information.

Each of these incidents represented a discrete event that entailed one of four attack types: unauthorized access, malicious code, denial of service, and inappropriate usage (PRC, 2014).

There are probably a lot of factors that underlie these statistics, but the direction is clear. An effective and continuously evolving cyber-defense is an absolute imperative.

The US General Accounting Office (GAO) has done one of the most thorough studies of that question. It found significant weaknesses in the national information infrastructure. Moreover, it hypothesized that, as the body of audit evidence grows it is likely that "Additional significant deficiencies will be identified" (GAO, 2013). The six major findings of the GAO study were (GAO, 2013) as follows:

1. Risk-based security plans not developed for major systems
2. Security policies not documented
3. Programs for evaluating the effectiveness of controls not implemented
4. Controls for application development and change control not implemented
5. Inadequate control over the implementation and use of software products
6. No expertise to select, implement, and maintain security controls

The overall problem highlighted by the GAO is that protection of our electronic infrastructure is not a simple issue of computer security. Breaches that fall under the domain of traditional computer security, such as network and operating system assurance, comprise only 29% of the total source of breaches. The other 71% can be attributed to attacks that exploit human behavior, commonly called "social engineering" and outright physical attacks, such as loss or theft of laptops, personal devices, or media (PRC, 2014).

What these statistics imply is that, until all avenues of attack have been safeguarded and controlled, we will never be able to realistically say that our electronic infrastructure is protected. So, the challenge is clear: we have to adopt better and more effective methods and models to protect our information. This book will present the fundamental concepts of how to do that. This approach is termed "controls," or "governance" based, and it is supported by a detailed framework of best practices and a rigorous audit process to confirm compliance.

The framework is strategic in orientation. And it enforces comprehensive protection from all forms of cyber-attack, both electronic and behavioral. When reading this keep in mind that we are taking an inclusive view, rather than diving down into some specific area. Thus, the concepts in this book constitute an all-in-one overview rather than a specific listing of all potential controls in every area of the field. That having been said, we start where every other discussion of cybersecurity begins. That is, with the focus of the process.

Two Absolute Rules for Cybersecurity Work

The assurance of systems and information in cyberspace is governed by two absolute principles for control. The first is the "complete protection" principle. It simply states a common sense proposition that in order for information assets to be secure, every instance in every repository has to be protected at all times. This is a difficult task, because in order for it to be useful, information has to be available, which means that the same item of information has to be kept in many different places at the same time. The problem is that every one of those places has to be secured. Or a compromise of information in one place will compromise all other instances of the same item.

However, it is the second principle that defines the down-to-earth practice of control-based cybersecurity. This is the "organizational governance" principle. That principle establishes the basis for how the cybersecurity functions should be organized and conducted. In its practical embodiment, organizational governance simply means that it must be possible for the company to systematically control and coordinate the assurance of all of its activities as a single organization-wide function.

Why Complete Protection Is Important

It goes without saying that in order for any defense to be effective, every requisite control and countermeasure has to be identified, properly designed, and put in place. This might seem self-evident, but the typical cybersecurity scheme tends to include only those countermeasures and controls that fall within the specific area of responsibility of the designers of the approach.

For instance, IT installs technical countermeasures but it rarely deploys an accompanying set of physical security controls. While physical security might deploy a complete set of physical protection controls, these are rarely coordinated with the electronic protection controls utilized by IT. In most organizations physical and electronic security involves two entirely separate and independent areas. As a result, the assurance scheme has holes in it.

This lack of a comprehensive approach to the deployment of controls is understandable given the focus, interest, and responsibilities of each of those functional areas. However, it can be a fatal flaw for any organization since any competent attacker will scout around for the holes in the defense. For instance, it would not be reasonable to assume that the typical successful attack on a robust electronic defense would be through the robust firewall. Instead, it is more sensible to attack a well-protected system through social engineering or a physical exploit.

Accordingly, in order to ensure effective cybersecurity it is necessary to maintain a comprehensive framework of mutually supporting controls and countermeasures. These measures have to be integrated into a single coherent framework that addresses every potential area of exploitation. It should be obvious that in order to devise such a scheme, the designer will have to consider all relevant principles for building effective protection.

Nevertheless, there are challenges to complete protection because information, unlike any other resource, is both invisible and dynamic. And to make matters worse, most instances of information can exist simultaneously in more than one form. Information can be kept electronically, or it can also be written down. In fact, valuable information can even reside in a person's head, which is the reason for the "need to know" principle. So in essence, information is hard to manage because it is hard to keep track of.

Because information exists in so many forms, all of which are hard to monitor, a comprehensive solution has to incorporate all necessary procedural, environmental, technical, and human controls across all relevant parts of the organization. To be effective, these controls have to be embodied in a single reliable organization-wide system that is capable of ensuring total protection of all information assets of value to the organization.

Moreover, this system also has to be practical, meaning it has to operate within a well-defined, complete, and economically feasible infrastructure that accurately reflects the business case for that particular organization. And that infrastructure has to safeguard against all threats and be able to respond to all incidents. Furthermore, it must be possible to demonstrate in a concrete and objective way that protection remains trustworthy over time. The latter condition lets the organization manage and evolve its cybersecurity system as the asset base and the specific threat environment changes.

The Problem of Diversity and Dispersion

The classic purpose of cybersecurity is to ensure the continuing secure status of all information assets during their deployment and use. Operationally though, this is an impossible task, because all information resources are both diverse and dispersed. For instance, potential targets for control include any resource that might be an organizational asset. That includes hardware and system assets, applications, facilities, personnel, the actual information in the form of assets, even the various organizational interfaces, such as business relationship plans and contracts.

With the exception of hardware, personnel, and facilities, none of these are easily accounted for due to them also being dynamic or intangible. Thus, the organization cannot directly control its investment in applications, the actual information they process, or the various organizational interfaces.

In addition, information flows back and forth over all of the organization's boundaries, both virtual and physical. The problem is that some, or perhaps even many, of these flows are either not known or not controlled. It is easy to account for the flow of financial assets because they are tangible. The same is true with other material assets such as equipment. Information assets, even the tangible ones, are dispersed as part of their basic purpose. For instance, the whole point of a network is remote access for the users. So, in order to be useful, information assets by definition have to be widely accessible from dispersed locations and that makes them hard to secure.

As a result, cybersecurity requires the ability to explicitly identify, classify, and label all information of any value, and then manage those assets within a tangible framework. This framework is operationalized through explicit objectives and rules for control. Accordingly, the function responsible for protecting information has to be governed as a single, comprehensive, well-coordinated organization-wide system.

Introduction: Why Formal Organizational Control Is Crucial

The concept of audit and control for IT operations is rooted in several standard bodies of knowledge. The purpose of each of these is to establish the exact status of some aspect of IT functioning for the purposes of control assurance. Nonetheless, the ideas in this book center directly on the creation and maintenance of an audit-based control structure for IT as well as the establishment of systematic accounting and control procedures within this structure that allow the organization to build auditable security assurance capability into the IT function.

The body of knowledge for control formulation and deployment involves steps to adapt a comprehensive control framework and the attendant control objectives to a given problem. As well, it is supported by an evidence-based reporting system. The approach that we will be discussing in this book applies to operational aspects of IT work ranging from process control to security. And guidance for carrying it out is fully supported by authoritative standards for best practice published by two national standards bodies and an influential standard organization.

The first of these is the International Organization for Standardization (ISO) 27000 Information Security Standard. This is one of the world's standard for information security management (ISO, 2012). The second is the National Institute for Standards and Technology (NIST) and its Federal Information Processing Standards (FIPS) 200 Framework, as implemented by NIST 800-53. The third and perhaps more influential are the Information System Audit and Control Association (ISACA) and its Control Objectives for IT (COBIT) Model (ISACA, 2013). An overview of the various frameworks will be discussed in more detail in Chapter 3.

The intention is to help the reader to understand how to adapt a formal, organization-wide, standards-based control framework for a given aspect of organizational functioning using one of these models. In addition, we will discuss the approach to defining comprehensive control mechanisms for information and IT asset accounting and assurance within that framework. And create an audit control process for a specific area of IT work, which will be built on those detailed control objectives.

More importantly, you will see why governance-based control infrastructures are valuable. And you will see how they provide the basis for the most effective control of IT and information resources. You will also discover the importance of expert advice about the best practices for building them. And, since the need for uniform understanding of best practice implies standardization, you will also examine the most widely accepted standards in this area. The goal is to demonstrate how authoritative best-practice frameworks can be used to ensure comprehensive control over IT assets and information resources.

The key concept here is "comprehensive." Expert advice and a standard point of reference are necessary to establish full accountability since **all** of the potential issues must be identified, assessed, and responded to. The ability to reach a sufficient level of comprehensiveness is conceptually difficult without a framework model. That is because the average manager or academic cannot be expected to identify every potential area of concern, let alone devise foolproof ways to control it.

Nevertheless, as mentioned previously, at a given level of sophistication of malicious agents, a control system with even one hole is a business catastrophe waiting to happen. A formal IT control system is an important asset, because business has developed a growing dependence on technology. And an increased need to ensure that the IT function is responsibly run and properly protected comes with that increasing reliance. So, as business organizations grow and diversify progressively, more powerful IT management measures are necessary.

Cybersecurity, as a basic condition, is far too broad and far too important to be a simple technological problem. Therefore, the cybersecurity process can only be founded and sustained by means of an organizational governance process. The goal of that process is to develop and integrate every necessary technology and management control into an organization-wide and sustainable system, which is able to meet the precise assurance needs of each immediate situation.

In practical terms, a tangible and coherent structure of technical and managerial controls is necessary to achieve an adequate level of comprehensive assurance. In their real-world incarnation, these controls are typically arrayed within a governance structure. Ideally, this structure will ensure that all of the actions that the organization takes to protect its information assets are comprehensive, correct, and fully coordinated and demonstrate due professional care in safeguarding the organization's information resources.

It should be noted that this requires an entity that operates at the strategic level, which is why cybersecurity is termed a governance process. Cybersecurity has traditionally not been seen as a responsibility of conventional strategic governance. So, the idea of the people responsible for planning cybersecurity functioning and operations at that level is an innovative one. Nonetheless, in a world where there is increasing concern about cyber-disasters, due diligence alone requires organizations to have a strategic management function in place that is dedicated to building a comprehensive structure of rational procedures and relationships to control access to information assets.

In that respect, the cybersecurity profession forges a tangible link between information and business strategy. Ideally, this occurs in such a way that it adds value to the enterprise's purposes.

One of the common complaints about the measures that are required to ensure proper cybersecurity is that they adversely impact business processes. The role of cybersecurity as a governance function is to ensure effective and efficient access to information, as well as its confidentiality, integrity, and availability. The idea is to ensure an optimum relationship between the business and the measures taken to secure it. That condition is termed "alignment." In practice, proper alignment is enabled by specification of policies, organizational structures, practices, and procedures designed to achieve particular ends. Operationally, it involves the definition of explicit procedural and technical control elements for any given requirement. Properly stated, these controls should ensure that due professional care has been displayed in the management, use, design, development, maintenance, or operation of cybersecurity processes. The overall aim of the information governance process is to maintain a tangible control and accountability structure that will establish exact organizational accountabilities for specific business functions.

The organizational control structure, which is an outcome of the process, is always complete and consistent for the aspect being controlled. As such, this structure embodies a set of carefully designed and explicit electronic and managerial control activities, the outcomes of which can be observed and documented. Those controls are rarely standalone. They are typically integrated with a range of other controls to produce a verifiable state of assurance. The general aim is to create and enforce ongoing organizational accountability for the security of information within a well-defined framework.

The function of the governance framework then, is to explicitly account for and manage an identified information resource. This is always operationalized as a systematic and ongoing process. This implies that the control framework must always ensure that the precise status of an information asset is known and under control at all times.

In order to make that happen, the coordination and management of the activity have to be located with the people who establish and enforce organization wide policy. In that respect, the cybersecurity function must always be planned for and administered from the top of the organization. That level of involvement is essential because the executive level decision makers are the only people who have the authority to create and enforce policies and procedures across the organization.

Implementing a Strategic Response

The real-world mechanism that is employed to implement and enforce cybersecurity governance is a formal, organization-wide strategic planning process. To be effective, the planning process must involve every part of the organization and it must provably address all known security exposures, not just the ones that are interesting or convenient for the organization. Moreover, the strategic planning process must be sustainable in the long term. That means that the process itself must directly support and be traceable to the overall strategic planning function for the entire organization.

Because cybersecurity is a planned process, the people at the top have to be engaged in strategic planning for cybersecurity. The problem is that most top executives do not think that cybersecurity is their problem, so they shift that responsibility down to the managers of the functional areas. That is a mistake since nobody at the managerial level has the authority to maintain security outside of their own area of responsibility and as a result, the assurance measures that are implemented are likely to be deployed piecemeal and in an uncoordinated fashion.

That creates gaps in the protection scheme that can be easily exploited by any determined adversary. For instance, the steps that are taken to ensure that the organization's workers are properly authorized are rarely in synch, with the measures that provide electronic security. So passwords are too simple, or never changed. People retain access to their old e-mail accounts after they have left the company and individuals who have become disciplinary problems over time retain all of their old privileges.

The current data bear out the conclusion that we are not approaching the problem in a comprehensive enough or realistic fashion. The most recent Ponemon/ HP annual report, estimates that the average annual loss to US companies was $350,424 (Ponemon Institute Research Report, 2013).

More importantly, 71% of the losses were due to either physical theft or insider malfeasance (PRC, 2014). Neither of these two can be prevented by electronic means. Instead, they have to be addressed by specific organizational controls that regulate human behavior, which is not in the traditional repertoire of the technical units, or IT. Quite often, most of the cybersecurity problems facing organizations are managerial rather than technical.

Nonetheless, because of our inability or unwillingness to deal with the entire problem, common sense prerequisite conditions such as simply knowing what information the organization possesses, or where it is kept can become major sources of breach. For instance, according to Verizon, nine out of ten breaches, involved cases where the data that were compromised were not known to be on the system (Verizon, 2015). Therefore, "most breaches go undetected for quite a while until they are discovered by a third party rather than the victim organization" (Verizon, 2015). According to Verizon, these attacks tend to be largely opportunistic in nature rather than targeted, which led them to conclude that:

> Given the opportunistic nature of attacks leading to data breaches, organizations are wise to focus on ensuring essential controls are met across the organization and throughout the extended enterprise. This includes following through on security policies so they are actually implemented and ensuring that a basic set of controls is consistently met across the organization.
>
> **(Verizon, 2015)**

Up to this point, the lack of demonstrated due care in the design and deployment of cybersecurity processes has not resulted in specific consequences for organizations. However, this will change, as the legal system begins to address negligent practices in information protection.

One of the likeliest outcomes, however, will be the outright regulation in terms similar to several European approaches to data protection, such as the United Kingdom's Data Protection Act of 1998, or Germany's Federal Data Protection Act of 2006. In the United States, several states are beginning to move in the direction of regulated identity protection, the California Identify Information Protection Act of 2007 being one example of this trend.

Nevertheless, whether the eventual outcome is simply a loss of reputation or whether the consequences fall into the legal and regulatory domain it is likely that all organizations will eventually have to demonstrate that they have exercised due professional care in the protection of personal information. So the important question becomes, is there a standard mechanism already available for establishing and documenting due professional care?

Frameworks for Ensuring Due Care

Due professional care in cybersecurity implies the performance of all reasonable practices necessary to meet a minimum standard of due diligence. That minimum standard must embody all of the practices required to ensure reliable long-term security performance. If these practices are performed properly then the organization can be said to have met all of its legal and ethical obligations for information protection.

In practice, the standard of care adopted must embody all known elements required to address all likely threats and incidents. And since the practical consequences of failure are real and can be drastic, ignorance of what to do is no defense against liability. All the same, it is a lot to expect cybersecurity professionals to know about and be able to satisfy the requirements of due professional care. Therefore, it would be helpful to have a general model of good cybersecurity practice available to aid that understanding. Ideally, this model should be universal in its application and commonly accepted as correct within the practitioner community.

The model's recommendations should embody all of the currently understood best practices for ensuring the confidentiality, integrity, and availability of information. Moreover, those recommendations should be expressed in a form that allows a competent practitioner to evolve a concrete set of countermeasures to protect the information under their care.

In application, that is the role of three authoritative and commonly accepted compendiums of best practices mentioned earlier: the ISO 27000, "Information System Management Standard (ISMS)," The ISACAs, "COBIT," and the NISTs "FIPS 200/NIST 800-53." All of these large strategic frameworks make an authoritative, formal statement about what an individual organization has to do in order to fulfill the requirements of best practice in cybersecurity. And all of them are governance and controls based in their recommendations. There are other bodies of knowledge and frameworks in the field but the advantage of these three is that all of the sponsoring agencies are considered to be influential in the overall field of computing. And so, the recommendations contained in them are as legitimate as possible.

The ISO 27000 suite of standards provides the world's categorization of the types of threats to information systems (ISO, 2012). The standard was developed by the ISO over an extended period of time culminating in its initial publication in 2005. The current 27000 is the 2014 version. It specifies 14 areas of control which can be considered to be a classification of the general types of threats. There are 135 explicit controls specified within these areas and the process for defining additional controls is also provided.

The United States has its own model which was developed in response to the Federal Information Security Management Act (FISMA, [2015], 44 U.S.C, 3541 *etseq*). That is the FIPS 200 Framework. FIPS 200 describes the steps needed to satisfy the requirements of FISMA. This model serves the exact same purpose as 27000 in that it describes areas of threat and common control practices to meet those threats. There are 17 specific categories of threat specified in FIPS 200. The recommended practices for dealing with those threats are contained in NIST 800-53 (NIST, 2013). That is an extensive document containing over 100 pages of controls.

For comparative purposes, Figure 1.4 shows there is a 93% overlap between these two standards which rather persuasively indicates that all of these frameworks target the same general set of issues.

To simplify the terminology, the areas of common threat that might require some form of control or countermeasure lie in the following:

1. Policy
2. Governance control
3. Personnel security
4. Physical and environmental security
5. Asset management
6. Access control
7. Security of operations
8. Network security
9. Computer security
10. Software development and maintenance security
11. Acquisition
12. Incident management
13. Compliance
14. Continuity
15. Elements of human factors such as training and education

	ISO 27002:2013 Framework Components
1	Information Security Policies (A.5)
2	Organization of Information Security (A.6)
3	Human Resource Security (A.7)
4	Asset Management (A.8)
5	Access Control (A.9)
6	Cryptography (A.10)
7	Physical and Environmental Security (A.11)
8	Operations Security (A.12)
9	Communications Security (A.13)
10	System Acquisition, Development, and Maintenance (A.14)
11	Supplier Relationships (A.15)
12	Information Security Incident Management (A.16)
13	Information Security Aspects of Business Continuity Management (A.17)
14	Compliance (A.18)

	FIPS 200 Framework Components
1	Planning (PL)
2	Audit and Accountability (AU)
3	Personnel Security (PS)
4	Identification and Authentication (IA)
5	Access Control (AC)
6	Physical and Environmental Protection (PE)
7	System and Information Integrity (SI)
8	System and Communications Protection (SC)
9	Maintenance (MA)
10	System and Services Acquisition (SA)
11	Incident Response (IR)
12	Contingency Planning (CP)
13	Certification, Accreditation, and Security Assessments (CA)
14	Risk Assessment (RA)
15	Awareness and Training (AT)
16	Media Protection (MP)
17	Configuration Management (CM)

Figure 1.4 ISO 27002 framework components versus the FIPS 200 framework.

This might be considered to be a summary of the potential threat vectors in any cybersecurity control situation. Any or all of these areas must have effective countermeasures in place in order to protect against the types of threats that might be identified for each category.

The controls suggested by each of these standards can serve as a point of reference for developing a tailored cybersecurity response. However, none of these will be effective unless the organization undertakes a comprehensive analysis of the threat environment using some form of checklist or other standard guidance that is normally developed from the recommended control set.

The term that is normally used to describe frameworks like this is "umbrella model," in the sense that its purpose is to define the complete set of competencies associated with cybersecurity work. The use of any of these models is to standardize concepts and terms into a set of recommended professional practices. That standardization then focuses the formulation of control practices on specific control targets that exist within each of the standard categories.

Process Implementation

The application of any of these models in a practical setting is enabled and sustained through a strategic cybersecurity management plan. This plan enumerates in totally unambiguous terms the general areas for control and the control activities that will constitute the overall cybersecurity governance process. That includes the itemization of specific procedures that will be followed to perform the work. Furthermore, all organizational roles, responsibilities, and interrelationships must be explicitly defined and assigned by this plan. The end product of this process is a complete and fully documented strategic approach to information security.

The first step is to establish the formal asset identification scheme. This is a critical stage because it defines the tangible form of the information asset, which is used in every other aspect of the control formulation process. This scheme integrates all of the organization's information assets into a coherent baseline representation for control assignment. In essence, it comprises everything considered worth managing and protecting.

Because of that practical requirement, this part of the process is almost always guided by the business case. The baseline control identification scheme is crucial for two reasons. First, because the specific controls are directly referenced to the structure, the asset being managed, this essentially defines and targets the assignment of those controls. Second, because the identification scheme is the documentation of the target for control itself, it serves to define the form of the operational governance system for cybersecurity management.

There are two separate steps involved in creating this identification scheme. First, the criteria that will be used to identify the asset items must be agreed on and made explicit. This includes an itemization of all of the decision criteria that will be employed to define the various qualities of the asset. For instance, statements like "The information item must be directly traceable to and support a business process" could be utilized as a basis for deciding whether an information item was of any value to the organization.

Then, it is important to have a procedure that will ensure that people responsible for the actual labeling process follow these criteria. Following this, each information asset is identified and appropriately labeled. That is essentially a documentation process and it is always associated with the business case. The overall description of the targets for protection and control, their purpose, and general use are defined in detail and labeled.

This process involves two iterations. First, a high-level baseline of items is described. This baseline itemizes the items that are the large components of a given real-world function, such as the invoices and accounts that are part of the general ledger. These high-level baselines are more descriptive than detailed and they are focused at the level of managers and users.

Then, all of the individual items that comprise each of the large elements in the high-level baseline are itemized. Each of these component data items is also individually identified and uniquely labeled. This activity is based on and guided by the components in the high-level baselines.

The outcome of this second pass is a very detailed description of all of the items that constitute a given real-world process and which require control. Since control behaviors vary in their purpose and effect, it is important that each control target be assigned a carefully crafted set of behavioral controls.

The labeling for this representation reflects the structure. In actual application, the labels employ mnemonics that are unique to each item. Those always correlate to the individual element's location in the identification scheme. Furthermore, this is represented in such a way that the hierarchy of links between entities can be established and followed.

Then, the entire array of control targets and their associated controls is kept under rigorous configuration management. Configuration management is primarily an analysis and authorization function. A comprehensive configuration management process is necessary because control targets are always evolving. Controls are continuously added to baselines, and the form and content of individual elements change as the business model evolves.

Moreover, the control structure also changes in accordance with alterations in policy as well as to the form of the asset itself. So, there has to be a formal organizational process available to rationally manage that natural evolution, or control of the asset base will quickly move out of the grip of the organization. And for that reason alone, effective control-based governance depends on rigorous change control.

All of these functions are interrelated in the sense that the ability to conduct effective configuration management is dependent on identification. That is true because changes to formally defined baselines are what are managed in this process.

So, at its very essence security governance includes a documentation management function. Any change to a baseline is

- Brought forward through a proper channel
- Recorded in a ledger
- Then the change is analyzed for its impacts

Although that might seem like an excessive bureaucratic exercise, this is an important part of the overall process of control-based cybersecurity. The information assets of any organization are intangible, so they can change on a whim. As a consequence, the ability to warrant that the form of the information base was known would quickly disappear without configuration management and thorough documentation. And all formally instituted assurance would be pointless because what was being protected would not be known.

There are substantial resource implications involved in maintaining the known status of the asset baselines. As a result, the appropriate stakeholder has to authorize all alterations to the form of a baseline. It is important to ensure stakeholder control over change because the baselines and their associated controls constitute the assurance system.

This decision-making process must be supported by an appropriate degree of analysis of the implications of that change. This analysis should consider such things as how the changed item will now interface with the old assurance system as well as an estimate of the anticipated impacts and resource commitments requisite to change the form of the protection.

Monitoring and Accounting for Control Status

The point of the prior two functions is to establish and maintain a correct and continuously evolving picture of the form of the control targets and their associated controls. That representation is documented and maintained by a baseline monitoring and accounting function. Baseline monitoring and accounting maintain evidence-based understanding of all control target and control baselines. This record is normally maintained in some sort of electronic repository, or "ledger." The ledger is utilized by the control baseline monitoring and accounting function to perform the impact analysis prior to the change authorization. It is updated in a timely fashion once a change has been approved and implemented.

The process of maintaining the control set extends throughout the rest of the cybersecurity process. It demands a step-by-step analysis of the precise security requirements. To do this, the organization moves item-by-item through the baseline and decides what control behaviors are appropriate and feasible to protect the integrity and availability of the information components.

This activity is always based on the degree of estimated risk. The risk assessment can be either formal or informal, but the idea is to identify all logical weaknesses.

These are assessed and classified in the form of a two-dimensional table because threat types are either physical or logical and they can only originate from internal or external sources. The next step in the process is to assess the feasibility of each of the controls that will be deployed to respond to each identified threat. The practical outcome of the asset identification and control baseline formulation process is a functioning cybersecurity governance system.

The final requirement is the formulation of a coherent and explicit set of control standards, procedures, or behaviors. These behaviors will dictate precisely *how* the specific cybersecurity controls will interact with each other within the governance scheme. The execution of the required control behaviors for each information item must be spelled out in the form of itemized work practices, which are referenced in the relevant policy and procedure documents.

This specific linkage between work practice and control is necessary in order to avoid any potential misunderstanding in the subsequent practical execution. Steps that need to be taken during this process include the specification of specific behaviors to dictate

- Sequence and timing of control usage
- Specific monitoring practices
- Accountabilities
- Documentation and reporting
- Problem resolution responsibilities

Chapter Summary

The field of cybersecurity embraces appropriate measures to ensure that electronic data are kept safe from unauthorized access, or harm. The processes, technologies, and practices in the field of cybersecurity are all developed in service of that purpose. Done properly, an effective set of cybersecurity controls should accurately identify and authenticate all entities seeking access to a system, authorize access to only those objects that the entity's level of trust permits, monitor, and control activities during the time that the entity's it is granted access, ensure against unauthorized access, or manipulation of data, and ensure against unauthorized manipulation of system objects.

Cybersecurity is a rapidly emerging discipline. Even with its new central role, however, the reality is that until recently the field of cybersecurity did not have a single, commonly accepted approach to the entire problem. Nonetheless, in the 20-year period since the emergence of the commercial Internet cyber-crime, cyber-espionage and even cyber-warfare have become visions with real consequences. Consequently, it is unrealistic to assume that our way of life is adequately protected until substantive methods are utilized to secure every element of our national infrastructure.

The confusion about what constitutes the proper elements of the field originates in the fact that the profession of cybersecurity could potentially comprise concepts from a number of disciplines. To achieve its purposes, cybersecurity encompasses approaches from a large and diverse range of disciplines.

Strategic application of cybersecurity principles centers on the issue of deciding what is required to determine security's worth to an organization. In a profit-driven world, it is hard for the leaders in the public and private sectors to justify the tangible expense of protecting virtual assets like computers and networks, and their contents. As a result, even though the constituent elements of cyberspace have real value and can directly impact people's lives, it is hard for the people who are putatively responsible for the protection of those contents to understand how the ways that the theft or destruction of a computer or its information might affect them personally.

Equally as important, it is exceedingly difficult and very costly for any organization to ensure reliable and systematic protection for an asset that is as dynamic and abstract as its IT systems and information. In essence, the processes and technologies that are required to assure reliable and consistent protection of cyber-assets change as rapidly as the technology evolves.

In order to ensure effective cybersecurity it is necessary to maintain a comprehensive framework of mutually supporting controls and countermeasures. These measures have to be integrated into a single coherent framework that addresses every potential area of exploitation. It should be obvious that in order to devise such a scheme, the designer will have to consider all relevant principles for building effective protection.

Therefore, the cybersecurity process can only be founded and sustained by means of an organizational governance process. The goal of that process is to develop and integrate every necessary technology and management control into an organization-wide and sustainable system, which is able to meet the precise assurance needs of each immediate situation.

In practical terms, a tangible and coherent structure of technical and managerial controls is necessary to achieve an adequate level of comprehensive assurance. In their real-world incarnation, these controls are typically arrayed within a governance structure. Ideally, this structure will ensure that all of the actions that the organization takes to protect its information assets are comprehensive, correct, and fully coordinated and demonstrate due professional care in safeguarding the organization's information resources.

In practice, proper alignment is enabled by specification of policies, organizational structures, practices, and procedures designed to achieve particular ends. Operationally, it involves the definition of explicit procedural and technical control elements for any given requirement. Properly stated, these controls should ensure that due professional care has been displayed in the management, use, design, development, maintenance, or operation of cybersecurity processes. The overall aim of the information governance process is to maintain a tangible control and accountability structure that will establish exact organizational accountabilities for specific business functions.

The real-world mechanism that is employed to implement and enforce cybersecurity governance is a formal, organization-wide strategic planning process. To be correct, the planning process must involve every part of the organization and it must provably address all known security exposures, not just the ones that are interesting or convenient for the organization. Moreover, the strategic planning process must be sustainable in the long term. That means that the process itself must directly support and be traceable to the overall strategic planning function for the entire organization.

The application of any control model in a practical setting is enabled and sustained through a strategic management plan. This plan enumerates, in totally unambiguous terms, the general areas for control and the control activities that will constitute the overall cybersecurity governance process. That includes the itemization of specific procedures that will be followed to perform the assure work. Furthermore, all organizational roles, responsibilities, and interrelationships must be explicitly defined and assigned by this plan. The end product of this process is a complete, fully documented strategic approach to information security.

Key Concepts

- The cybersecurity (information assurance [IA]) process has many facets.
- Cybersecurity centers on devising tangible controls to counter threats.
- Systems and information constitute both an invisible and dynamic resource.
- It is necessary to inventory and label information in order to make it visible.
- Information is actually a proxy for things that have real-world value.
- The cybersecurity process has to be coordinated through governance.
- Coordination involves deploying and then maintaining an appropriate set of technical and managerial controls.
- Effective control ensures trusted access to information.
- Cybersecurity requires formal organization and executive sponsorship.
- Adversaries add a new dimension of threat to information.
- Standard models are important road maps for organizations to follow.
- The standard controls frameworks discussed here are commonly accepted models.
- The controls have to produce evidence that can be used to confirm compliance.

Key Terms

Availability—a state of cybersecurity where all necessary information is accessible at the time it is needed.

Compromise—a breakdown in organizational control leading to the loss or harm to data.

Confidentiality—a state of cybersecurity where information is protected from unauthorized access.

Controls—technical or managerial actions that are put in place to ensure a given and predictable outcome.

Countermeasures—technical or managerial actions taken to prevent loss of a defined set of information items.

Department of Homeland Security—federal agency charged with the overall protection of the national infrastructure.

Information governance—system and information assets have been identified as needing protection and have been placed within a strategic framework of controls in order to manage and secure them.

Integrity—a state of cybersecurity where information can be shown to be accurate, correct, and trustworthy.

NIST—the body responsible for developing and promulgating standards for federal programs and federal government agencies.

Organizational governance—a condition that ensures that all organizational functions are adequately coordinated and controlled by policy, typically enabled by strategic planning. When applied to information protection the term is "information governance."

Strategic planning—the act of translating an organization's intended direction into specific steps along a particular timeline; strategic planning affects the entire organization for a significant period.

Umbrella framework—a comprehensive set of standard activities intended to explicitly define all required processes, activities, and tasks for a given field or application.

References

Bishop, M. and Burley, D. (2013). *Professionalizing the Nation's Cybersecurity Workforce: Criteria for Decision-Making*. Washington, DC: National Academies of Science.

E-Government Act, FISMA. (2015). http://www.gpo.gov/fdsys/pkg/PLAW-107publ347/html/PLAW-107publ347.htm, Accessed July 2015.

General Accounting Office. (2013). *Cybersecurity: A Better Defined and Implemented National Strategy Is Needed to Address Persistent Challenges*. GAO-13-462T. Washington, DC: Author.

Information Systems Audit and Control Association (ISACA). (2013). *Control Objectives for IT (COBIT) v5*. Arlington Heights, IL: ISACA.

International Organization for Standardization (ISO). (2012). *ISO 27000, Information Technology—Security Techniques—Information Security Management Systems—Overview and Vocabulary*. Geneva, Switzerland: ISO.

Mustaka, S. (2014). *Cybercriminals Leverage Recent Chase Data Breach for Phishing Scam*. IT Security News.

National Institute of Standards and Technology. (2013). *NIST Special Publication 800-53 Revision 4: Security and Privacy Controls for Federal Information Systems and Organizations*. Gaithersburg, MD: Computer Security Division, Information Technology Laboratory, NIST. http://csrc.nist.gov/publications/fips/fips200 /FIPS-200-final-march.pdf, Accessed December 2014.

Ponemon Institute Research Report. (2013). *Cost of Cyber Crime Study: United States*. Sponsored by HP Enterprise Security.

Privacy Rights Clearinghouse. (2014). *Chronology of Data Breaches Security Breaches 2005– Present*. San Diego, CA: PRC.

Verizon. (2015). Data Breach Investigations Report (DBIR). New York: Verizon Corporation.

Chapter 2

Control-Based Information Governance, What It Is and How It Works

At the conclusion of this chapter, the reader will understand:

- The importance and value of formal control
- The concept and application of governance infrastructures
- The process approach to information system management
- The general structure and intent of standard models of security control
- The general application and development of a control-based solution
- The elements of the control baseline formulation process
- The elements of the audit process

The Value of Formal Control

In its fundamental day-to-day application, the imperative for better security protection and control requires most companies to understand precisely how they are using their information technology (IT) resources. And given its layers of complexity, this can be a challenging task to perform with IT work. Most IT work is done in multilayered, multivendor, and even multicultural team settings. And all of this must be fully coordinated and controlled in order to ensure effective operation and sufficient security.

Coordination of complex work requires a common and coherent control structure that allows managers to benchmark actions against the policies and procedures of the organization. These policies are dictated by a governance framework (model). The aim is to adapt and implement a governance framework that will effectively control the activities of all members of the organization.

Accordingly, we are operating on the principle requirement that IT control is a strategic governance issue rather than an accounting or a technical concern. The purpose of adopting that stance is to avoid a typical piecemeal management system. That is, whether they are universally standard or documented, every enterprise is managed by its commonly accepted practices.

These practices are usually based on some individual unit or manager's appreciation of the proper way to carry out a specific task. And they tend to embed themselves in the organization over time, without any particular logic. The management model may not fully embody or address all of the security concerns for the entire asset.

The alternative is to formally define and implement a comprehensive infrastructure of best practices aimed specifically at optimizing the management control function. The practical term that is used to describe that activity is IT governance, which we will discuss in the next section.

Governance Infrastructures

The installation of a strategic governance infrastructure will quite often represent a radical change in the way the organization does business. Accordingly, the most straightforward way to overcome that resistance is to initiate the governance from the top. Top-down effectively describes the strategic approach and purposes of information governance. Moreover, it is this strategic concept that drives the deployment of the type of control systems we are discussing in this book. As such, we need to spend some time explaining what the general principles embodied in information governance are and how they work. Figure 2.1 shows all of the responsibilities and functions that define IT governance.

The term information governance was coined to describe the strategic function that underwrites due professional care in the management of the organization's information resources. It is a novel concept in the well-established world of enterprise governance, in that the strategic management of the information and communication system function has traditionally been seen as a corporate side-show with limited strategic relevance when compared with investment or marketing strategies.

However, with the increasing impact of cyber-crime and computers in general, and the overall reliance of business on effective IT functioning information governance, has taken its place as a separate but integral part of the strategic management process (Ponemon Institute Research Report, 2013). This presupposes that the information control function must meet the same expectations and criteria for quality, fiduciary, and operational integrity as every other aspect of the business. It

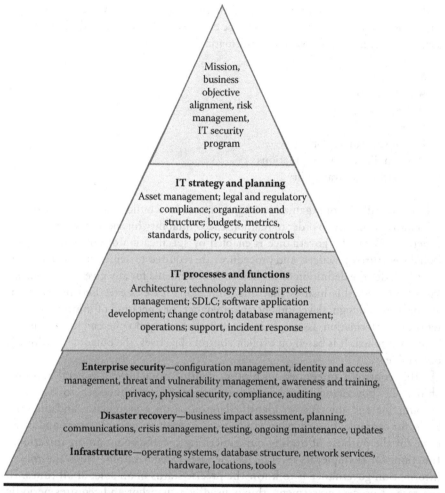

Figure 2.1 IT governance.

also assumes that the business's information and related technology processes must support its larger goals in an explicit and traceable way.

Information technology governance accomplishes its aims by building a comprehensive structure of rational procedures and relationships, which can be employed to direct and control information assets. As a result, IT governance establishes a tangible link between the company's IT resources and its information and business strategy. Ideally, it does this in such a way that it adds value to the enterprise's purposes.

It should be noted that information governance is not the same as enterprise governance. Enterprise governance assures stakeholders that the business will be profitable and productive. It embodies the strategic and tactical means to monitor and assess business performance toward those goals. And it provides the assurance that issues vital to business success will be effectively identified and dealt with. The aim of IT governance is to ensure information's

- Effective use
- Efficient use
- Confidentiality
- Integrity
- Proper distribution
- Compliance with regulations
- Continuous availability

The overall aim of organizational governance is to build a tangible control and accounting structure in order to maintain accountability for specific organizational functions. While IT governance is enabled by specification of policies; organizational structures, practices, and procedures are required to achieve particular ends. That includes the definition of explicit control elements for any given requirement. Properly stated, this insures that due professional care is exercised in the management, use, design, development, maintenance, or operation of information systems and information assets. This is comprehensive and coherent for the aspect being controlled. It is based on explicit control objectives, the outcome of which is observable.

This control is integrated with other controls to achieve a general accountability. IT governance involves a number of related processes to explicitly account for and manage an identified resource on a systematic and ongoing basis, for example, money, parts, and so on. Assessment is exploratory and often done for the purpose of finding out something specific about an organizational function, for example, its level of risk or asset categorization. Thus, the role of information governance is to know the precise status of an asset at all times. In the case of process assessment, this is usually a snapshot and requires periodic reviews.

Organizing Things into a Rational Process

The issue revolves around the need to get IT under control. The question is how do we manage risks and secure the information and IT asset. Since both of these goals are tied directly to best practice, the aim is to utilize a common standard that is generally accepted to define the complete set of controls for effective IT governance. That standard would provide them a generally applicable and accepted basis for judging good IT security and control practice. It would also support the determination and monitoring of the appropriate level of IT security and control for a given organization.

The first criterion for a standard such as this is that it defines an IT governance model/framework that will allow the organization to establish a clear set of policies and best practices for IT control. The aim would be to allow the organization to understand and manage the risks and benefits associated with its IT operation. The practices in the standard need to provide clear proof to the business's stakeholders that their operation is both trustworthy and secure. It would also be helpful if the standard was widely accepted or even established worldwide.

The standard should allow an organization to assess the business risks and assign control objectives to a common set of IT functions. By definition, an IT control objective is a precise statement of the desired result or purpose to be achieved by implementing control procedures within a particular activity. The selected standard should dictate best practice in the accounting and control of IT assets. The best practices should optimize IT governance and represent expert consensus.

The practices should be presented in a logical structure within a domain and process framework. In that respect, as mentioned previously, there are several reference models that can be selected. However, Control Objectives for Information and Related Technology (COBIT), International Organization for Standardization (ISO) 27000, and National Institute of Standards and Technology (NIST) 800-53 are arguably the most frequent models used to judge whether management activities are complete and correct. An overview of the various frameworks will be discussed in more detail in Chapter 3. Whatever the reference, the framework that is utilized should be built around a well-defined and detailed organizational structure, control policies practices, and procedures. COBIT and ISO 27000 are primarily oriented toward conventional business IT in their practical use. NIST 800-53 satisfies the requirements of the Federal Information Security Management Act (FISMA), and is used in all healthcare organizations to substantiate meaningful use with their electronic health records systems.

Security and Control

Risk management and security assurance depend on the ability to apply specific, repeatable management practices. The primary purpose for any of the large-scale control models discussed in this book is to provide a set of these basic recommendations for information technology managers. Every organization has a basic need to understand the status of its own IT systems and to decide the level of security and control they should provide. Neither aspect of this issue—understanding or deciding on the required level of control—is straightforward. Furthermore, it is hard to get an objective view of what should be measured and how.

Besides the need to measure where an organization is at, there is the requirement to ensure continuous improvement in the areas of IT security and control. This implies the need for an array of reporting lines that will allow busy executives to monitor the process by which the general security of its information assets is implemented and maintained. The monitoring process must address management concerns such as

- *Performance measurement*—What are the indicators of good performance?
- *Control prioritization*—What is important? What are the success factors for control?
- *Awareness*—What are the risks of not achieving our objectives?
- *Benchmarking*—What do others do? How do we measure and compare?

The control process formulation must be both direct action oriented as well as generic enough to provide the necessary direction to get the enterprise's information and related processes under control and monitor the achievement of organizational goals. This is done by monitoring the performance within each IT process and benchmarking organizational achievement of those goals over time. Specifically, there must be a means to ensure organizational capability maturity for establishing control over processes in the security and control areas. Ideally, management will be able to map where the organization is today, in relation to the best-in-class ideal.

There is also the need to assess whether the organization is meeting its goals. That assessment needs to be substantiated by explicit measures that will tell management whether an IT process has achieved its security objectives. Those prospective measures should provide a basis for determining how well the IT process is performing. They should address the following types of management concerns:

- How far should we go, and is the cost justified?
- What are the indicators of good performance?
- What are the critical success factors?
- What are risks of not achieving our objectives?
- What do others do?
- How do we compare against best-in-class?

That requires a set of guidelines that are generic in their application and which prescribe a practical set of actions that can be taken to achieve security goals. In order to do this, the manager needs to know what the indicators of good performance are and what is central to control and the attendant success factors as well as the risks and the generalized best practices for addressing them.

The initial requirement for accomplishing these multiple tasks is the existence of a set of generally accepted processes that can be used to rationally manage IT security performance along with a basis for evaluating whether those control practices are effective. The obvious first step in that process is to define the desired outcomes. In essence, companies need to define an explicit link between outcome and strategy at the highest levels of the organization.

Then, they define and monitor the internal assessment processes that have been put in place to achieve that outcome. Critical success factors are also required in order to determine whether the IT process has achieved its goals. These factors can be either

- Strategic
- Technical
- Organizational
- Process
- Procedural

The classic assessment process is based on the presence of defined and documented processes, defined and documented policies, and clear accountabilities. Intangibles such as strong support/commitment of management, appropriate and effective lines of communication, and consistent measurement practices are also involved.

The following are four logical activities that are involved in leveraging current organizational functioning up to higher levels:

1. Stating goals
2. Stating the activities that will be undertaken to achieve each goal
3. Evaluating whether those activities are being accomplished
4. Undertaking corrective action to maintain consistent performance

All of these general requirements belong to the business in that they describe what IT needs to do further to its business objectives and they should always provide a detailed description of the outcome of each required process, in that each activity must be substantially measurable. Ideally, each will be stated in a way that they can be used to determine whether, or when, a process is successfully completed. The description of the control activity should also contain an indication of the impact of not achieving that goal.

The goals must be expressed in precise measurement driven terms, so they should be stated in such a way that the information that is most critical to assessing each process can be identified and collected. These are normally the qualitative maturity measures that assess how well the process is performing. As such they are predictors of success and risk and they provide direction in improving IT processes. Thus, these should be process oriented but driven by common IT principles and security requirements.

Most important is the need for them to be measurable. They need to focus on the resources most important to the process and be driven by generic business needs including:

- Cost efficiency
- Productivity
- Defects

- Cycle time
- Quality and innovation
- Computing performance
- Stakeholder satisfaction
- Staff competency
- Benchmark comparisons

Control Framework Assumptions

It is probably reasonable to assume that managers should be accountable for all aspects of the business process that they direct. This implies that managers must be able to exercise control over their processes. Any audit and control framework is intended to facilitate the execution of those duties. Practically, in order for the organization to achieve its objectives, the manager can ensure that an adequate control system is in place if the right set of control behaviors is available to structure the IT governance activity.

The control framework provides the recommendations for the high-level control objectives which will be used to direct the audit and control process. Thus, the foundation for this activity obviously rests on the detailed control objectives. The basic principle involved here is that control originates from the information that is generated to support business objectives.

As we said earlier, IT governance is the tangible set of actions that links IT processes, IT resources, and business information to enterprise strategies and objectives. The governance model defines the optimal way to plan and organize, acquire and implement, deliver and support, and monitor IT performance. The principal assumption is that IT resources are deployed to produce a given set of desired information outcomes.

In order to effectively and efficiently achieve those outcomes—for example, the desired information—the process has to be rationally and optimally managed. And to satisfy business objectives, the information must directly support the business need. Thus, the following dozen generic requirements tend to appear in most frameworks:

1. Security requirements
2. Quality requirements
3. Confidentiality
4. Integrity
5. Availability
6. Cost
7. Service delivery
8. Fiduciary responsibility
9. Effectiveness and efficiency of operations
10. Reliability of information

11. Compliance with laws and regulations
12. Definition of concepts

These requirements can be factored into the seven distinct outcomes or end-qualities that are the universally desirable characteristics that information should exhibit, as shown in Figure 2.2.

The first of these is "effective." Effectiveness pertains to the relevance and value of the information to the business process. To be effective, the information also must be delivered in a timely, correct, consistent, and usable manner.

The second factor is "efficiency." Efficiency underwrites the provision of information through the optimal, that is, most productive and economical use of resources.

The third factor is "confidentiality." Confidential describes the protection of sensitive information from unauthorized disclosure.

The fourth factor is "integrity." Integrity designates the accuracy and completeness of information as well as to its validity in accordance with business values and expectations.

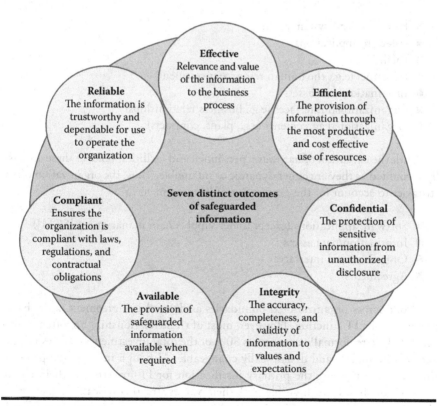

Figure 2.2   The seven distinct outcomes of safeguarded information.

The fifth factor is "available." Availability relates to information being available when required by the business process now and in the future. It also concerns the safeguarding of necessary resources and associated capabilities.

The sixth factor is "compliant." Compliance ensures that the organization complies with those laws, regulations, and contractual arrangements to which the business process is subject, that is, externally imposed business criteria.

The final factor is "reliable." Reliability designates that the appropriate information is trustworthy and dependable enough for management to operate the organization and for management to exercise its financial and compliance reporting responsibilities.

Introduction: The Problem

The classic purpose of controls formulation and use is the responsibility of every organization to account for and ensure its information and communications technology (ICT) resources. Potential targets for control include any resource that might be considered an organizational asset. This includes the following:

- Hardware and system assets
- Software applications
- Facilities
- Personnel (e.g., the human resource investment)
- Information/data assets
- Organizational interfaces (e.g., business relationships)
- Organizational agreements (e.g., plans, contracts)

With the exception of hardware, personnel, and facilities, none of these are easily accounted as they are either dynamic or intangible. Thus, the organization often struggles to account for the exact status of its investment in

- Software applications (except under supply chain management [SCM])
- Information/data assets
- Organizational interfaces
- Agreements

Work across organizational boundaries as defined by agreement is the basic mission of the IT function. However, most of these relationships are often undefined. Software normally constitutes 80% of the total investment in IT resources. Yet, it is intangible and dynamically changeable. Although information production and retention are the primary justification for IT investment, their actual information bases are invisible and their values are theoretical. In fact, it is almost impossible to get an exact definition as to what constitutes the information resource.

It is easy to account for financial assets because they are normally kept in one place. The same is true with other material assets such as parts and tools. The challenge with IT assets is that they have to be dispersed as part of their basic purpose. For instance, the point of a network is remote access, so in order to be useful they, by definition, are difficult to account for and control. Accounting and control of dispersed assets requires an explicit

- Asset identification and labeling scheme
- Asset management framework
- Description of the objectives and rules for control (within that framework)
- Specification of how ongoing audit functions will be conducted

Besides asset control (within IT), there are other definitions/applications for the information governance process including security, software quality assurance (SQA) monitoring and assurance, and quality monitoring and assurance. These other applications also fit the general purposes and mission of audit, which is to create and enforce some type of ongoing operational accountability.

In order to understand the context of its development and use as a concept, information governance became a hot topic because of the Sarbanes–Oxley Act (2002). The act was created to restore investor confidence in US public markets. The Securities and Exchange Commission (SEC) mandated the use of a recognized internal control framework to meet the requirements of this act. For those organizations that had begun the compliance process, it quickly becomes apparent that systems, data, and infrastructure components are critical to the financial reporting process. Thus, the reliability of the financial reporting was heavily dependent on a well-controlled IT environment. Accordingly, there was a general recognition of the need to create a viable set of organizational controls and to accredit those IT controls in a fiscal context.

As information protection became an ever increasing priority throughout the 2000s, the processes that were installed to ensure explicit organizational knowledge and control over the flow of transactions became a vital part of the strategic management process. That included explicit knowledge and control over how all ICT interactions were

- Initiated
- Authorized
- Recorded
- Processed
- Reported

Such transaction flows commonly involved automated processes which supported the high volume and complex transaction processing of modern business.

And reliability of these processes was in turn reliant upon the security of various IT support systems, including networks, databases, and operating systems.

Collectively, these electronic areas constitute the IT systems that underwrote the achievement of business goals. As a result, they became candidates for internal evaluation and explicit internal control. That was vitally important because sufficient and proper control would have a pervasive effect on the security of the organizations physical and virtual IT assets. Nonetheless, this required that the organization pay careful attention to the effectiveness of the internal management control structures meant to ensure effective

- Program development
- Program changes
- Computer operations
- Access to programs and data

While the general need was obvious, substantive principles and practices were still required to determine whether IT controls were properly designed and operating effectively. That was the purpose of several large, strategic IT control frameworks such as ISO 27000 series, NIST 800-53, and COBIT. All or some of these models can be used as the basis for establishing accountability and security control over all forms of IT operation.

Every organization can tailor an IT control approach suitable to its size and complexity by using the explicit controls contained in any one of these popular models. In doing so though, it is expected that the generic controls in these models will be tailored, or adapted, to reflect the specific circumstances of each organization. Specifically the business will tailor out controls to ensure the development process, how changes will be made to programs (patch management), operate and maintain a secure computer environment, as well as to ensure access to programs and data. In that respect, controls will be necessary to ensure the process by which the organization will

- Acquire or develop application software
- Acquire technology infrastructure
- Develop and maintain policies and procedures
- Install and test application software and technology infrastructure
- Manage changes
- Define and manage service levels
- Manage third-party services

The aim is to set up a comprehensive set of controls that will ensure effective corporate governance and security. These standard measures ought to strengthen internal checks and balances and, ultimately, strengthen corporate accountability. However, it is important to emphasize that it is not sufficient to merely establish and maintain an adequate internal control structure. Companies also have to assess its effectiveness on a regular basis. This distinction is significant. It is not sufficient to simply establish a control framework. Its effectiveness has to be routinely validated for the purposes of security, because the situation is always changing in the security universe as new threats emerge. And it is not enough to be partially protected from them.

Thus, it is necessary to conduct a routine formal assessment of the effectiveness of the company's internal security on a regular basis. That assessment must include an explicit evaluation of whether internal control over all priority information assets remains effective. Ideally, this is done on an annual or a semiannual basis. In its most rigorous form, this is a responsibility of the company's internal audit function. If that is the case, the auditors will issue an attestation as to the adequacy of the company's internal control over its IT systems and services.

This is often presented to upper management both as a report on internal control over all IT systems as well as a representation of the general security status of the organization. That conclusion can take many forms. However, management is required to state a direct conclusion about whether the company's internal control over financial reporting is effective. As a consequence of this report all identified material weaknesses in the control set have to be identified. That includes all relevant control sets, as shown in Figure 2.3.

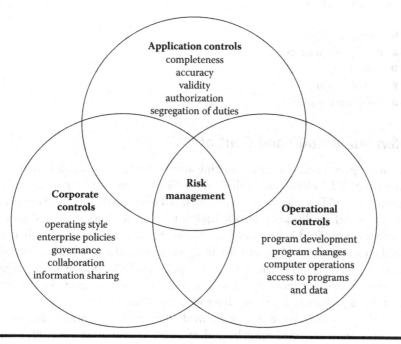

Figure 2.3   Application, general, and corporate controls overview.

Application Controls—Controls embedded in business process applications, which are commonly referred to as application controls. That includes any failures in control

- Completeness
- Accuracy
- Validity
- Authorization
- Segregation of duties

General Operational Controls—Includes any identified weaknesses or absence of management controls designed to ensure the integrity of IT services or the performance of IT operations such as

- Program development
- Program changes
- Computer operations
- Access to programs and data

Corporate-Level Controls—Includes all corporate-level controls embedded in the IT-control environment that is designed to ensure the overall integrity of the IT operation such as

- Operating style
- Enterprise policies
- Governance
- Collaboration
- Information sharing

Information Audit and Control

The investigation and evidence gathering activity that supports this overall control process is called "information audit." Generally speaking, the audit function is well known to most IT managers. It can be conducted both externally (audit) or internally (internal audit). Audits are normally held at preplanned times or at predetermined milestones as specified in a project plan. Audits are performed based on audit criteria, and the company's management has to agree on all outcomes and responsibilities for any action item and closure criteria. The purpose of the audit process is to gather sufficient reliable, pertinent, and practical evidence to demonstrate that the defined security and performance control objectives have been satisfied.

At the point where the audit is deemed completed, any and all objective data and conclusions obtained must be authenticated by means of a suitable analysis, and justified through a careful consideration of the meaning of that evidence. Audits are different from reviews and assessments in that they provide objective third-party certification of conformance to regulations and/or standards. Items that may be audited include

- Plans
- Contracts
- Complaints
- Procedures
- Reports and other documentation
- Deliverables

Audits are normally demanded by external organizations, such as regulatory bodies to verify compliance with requirements. Audits might also be conducted by the organization itself in order to verify compliance with internal plans, regulations, and guidelines, or to do a third-party verification of compliance with external standards or regulations. The auditor is by definition a disinterested third party, even if the actual audit is conducted internally.

Audits are done in order to determine to what extent a given function or system

- Achieves its objectives
- Adheres to corporate requirements
- Complies with regulatory requirements
- Meets customers' contractual requirements
- Conforms to a recognized standard
- Verify that it continues to meet requirements

Audits are always carefully planned. That planning assigns the tasks of the various participants in the audit. There are basically four types of participants as follows:

- Auditee—The organization being audited
- Lead auditor—The chief auditor
- Auditor—Other auditors on the audit team
- Client—The organization that engaged the auditors

Because they are more expensive than reviews and assessments, audits are always carefully planned and resourced. Since they are formal they require careful scheduling, resourcing, and funding assurance. The selection of the auditor and the assignment of roles and responsibilities is also a formal process. The aim is to assure audit integrity.

Reasons for Conducting an Audit

An organization may initiate an audit because a regulatory agency requires an audit. Audits are also conducted because a previous audit indicated that a follow-up audit was needed. Companies will also carry out internal audits on a regular basis to improve system performance or to achieve business objectives.

Information system assurance audits always operate within an explicit asset accounting and control framework that is comprehensive and coherent for the aspect being controlled. They must be based on explicit objectives the outcome of which is observable. Information system security audits are normally based around an accounting and control model such as COBIT or ISO 27000 in the private sector and NIST 800-53 in the public sector.

At the highest level, the general audit approach is supported by the selected control model, especially the process classification and the definition of the requirements for the audit process itself. That includes the guidelines for the conduct of the IT process auditing and the general principles of control, which are normally specified in the model. The detailed audit guidelines for each IT process are typically specified in the main body of the publication.

The guidelines are presented in a standard template form. This template details the generic IT audit guidelines as well as to the detailed audit approach. Using this template, the auditor can tailor the specific audit process to meet local conditions including the selection of detailed control objectives through

- Sector specific criteria
- Industry standards
- Platform specific elements
- Detailed control techniques employed

It is important to note that in its specific application all of the control objectives in the template are not necessarily applicable always and everywhere. Therefore, a high-level risk assessment is often carried out in order to determine which objectives need to be specifically adapted for audit purposes and which may be ignored.

The objectives of the overall auditing and control formulation process are to provide management with reasonable assurance that control objectives are being met and where there are significant vulnerabilities identified, to substantiate the process for addressing the resulting risks and advise management on the corrective actions required. The generally accepted approach to control formulations and conduct of the audit is to (Figure 2.4)

- Identify and document areas for control
- Evaluate control effectiveness
- Undertake compliance testing where appropriate
- Undertake substantive testing of targeted areas where required

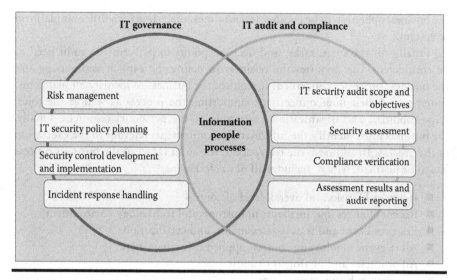

Figure 2.4   IT governance and IT audit.

In order to do this successfully, the organization must obtain an understanding of business requirements related risks and relevant control measures, and then evaluate the appropriateness of stated controls. That might include assessing compliance by testing whether the stated controls are working as prescribed, consistently, and continuously. It also involves substantiating the risk of control objectives not being met. This is done by using analytical techniques and/or consulting alternative sources.

Conducting an Audit

The first step is to determine the correct scope of the audit. This requires investigation, analysis, and definition of the business processes concerned. Platforms and information systems, which are supporting the business process as well as connections with other systems. The IT roles and responsibilities also need to be defined, including what has been in- or outsourced. That connects the audit to all associated business risks and strategic choices.

The next step is to identify the information requirements which are of particular relevance with respect to the business processes. Then, there is a need to identify the inherent IT risks as well as overall level of control that can be associated with the business process. To achieve this, there is a need to identify all recent changes in the business environment having an IT impact and any recent changes to the IT environment, such as new developments. Finally, there is the need to identify all recent incidents relevant to the controls and business environment.

On the basis of the information obtained, it is possible to select and tailor out the relevant control processes from the overall audit template selected as well as to target the business resources that apply to them. This could require certain parts of the business operation to be audited several times, each time for a different platform or system.

Finally, all the steps, tasks, and decision points to perform the audit need to be considered. That requires the business to define the explicit audit scope and the business processes concerned. It requires the business to identify all platforms, systems, and their interconnectivity, supporting the process as well as the roles, responsibilities, and organizational structure of the personnel resources. Finally, the business must identify the information requirements relevant to the execration of the process. In addition, the relevance of the audit target to the business process has to be justified, which includes all of the following:

- Inherent IT risks and overall level of control
- Recent changes and incidents in business and technology environment
- Prior results of audits, self-assessments, and certification
- All relevant monitoring controls applied by management
- All processes and platforms to audit
- All relevant business processes
- Requisite resources
- Controls by risk
- Decision points

Control Principles

The general principles of control can also supply additional insight on how to evolve the organization's response to threat and risk as well as improve operation. These principles are primarily focused on process and control responsibilities, control standards, and control information flows. Control, from a management point-of-view, is defined as determining what is being accomplished. That is, evaluating the performance and if necessary applying corrective measures so that the performance takes place according to plan.

The control process consists of four steps, as shown in Figure 2.5:

1. A standard of desired performance is specified for a process.
2. A means of evaluating what is happening in the process is developed.
3. The auditor compares information obtained with standard requirements.
4. If what is actually happening does not conform to the standard, the auditor directs that corrective action be taken. This is conveyed as information back to the process.

For this model to work, the responsibility for the system process must be clear and that accountability must be unambiguous. If not, control information will not flow and corrective action will not be acted upon. Standards utilized to make the control assessment observations can be of a very wide variety, from high-level plans and strategies to detailed measurable key performance indicators and critical

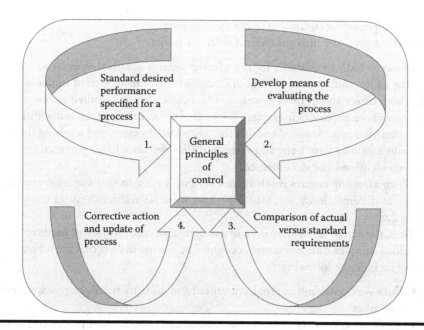

Figure 2.5 General principles of control.

success factors. All of these must be clearly documented, maintained, and communicated. Thus, a defined standard template is a must for the creation and sustainment of a good control process.

The control process must be well documented with clear responsibilities. An important aspect is the clear definition of what constitutes a deviation, that is, what are the limits of control performance. Basic to the good functioning of the control system is the timeliness, integrity, and appropriateness of control information, as well as other information.

Both control information and corrective action information will have requirements as to the evidence that is required in order to establish accountability after the fact. This evidence can be obtained from a number of sources including interviews of appropriate management and staff to gain an understanding of the business requirements and associated risks, the organization structure, the roles and responsibilities, policies and procedures within the audit target, any relevant laws and regulations, and existing control measures in place.

The auditor will document the process-related IT functions that are directly affected by the process under review and confirm the understanding of the process under review. The following types of evidence are collected to evaluate appropriateness of control measures for the process under review:

- Documented processes exist
- Appropriate deliverables exist
- Responsibility and accountability are clear and effective

■ Compensating controls exist, where necessary
■ The degree to which the control objective is met

Direct or indirect evidence for the selected items is obtained in order to ensure that the audit requirements have been complied with for the period under review using both direct and indirect evidence. That might include a limited review of the adequacy of the process deliverables. The level of substantive testing and additional work needed to provide assurance that the control weaknesses, and resulting threats and vulnerabilities have been addressed and that the actual and potential impact has been identified and documented.

When assessing control mechanisms, reviewers need to be aware that controls operate at different levels and that they have intricate relationships, as shown in Figure 2.6.

Thus, the actual implementation or assessment of control systems needs to take this added complex dimension into account. The generic objects that are subjects of control include the following:

■ Data—external and internal, structured and nonstructured, graphics, sound, and other
■ Application systems—the sum of manual and programmed procedures

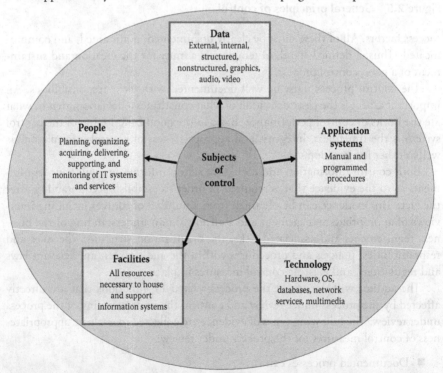

Figure 2.6   Subjects of control.

- Technology—hardware, operating systems, database management systems, networking, multimedia, and other
- Facilities—are all the resources necessary to house and support information systems
- People—include the staff skills, awareness, and productivity resources required to plan, organize, acquire, deliver, support, and monitor information systems and services

Control frameworks commonly consist of high-level control objectives and an overall structure for their classification. The underlying logic for the classification of these control objectives embodies three generic levels of IT work. Starting from the bottom, there are the operational level activities, which are composed of the day-to-day tasks that the business carries out to produce measurable outcomes. Activities within this domain have a life-cycle orientation while tasks are more discrete. The life-cycle orientation that is part of this has control requirements different from discrete activities.

Management level processes are then defined one layer up. These can be viewed as a series of logically related functions with natural divisions in responsibility and control. In essence, this provides the functional definition of IT work from which information requirements can be derived.

At the organization level, processes are naturally grouped together into generic domains. That natural grouping is often defined as the things that an organization has to do in order to be effective. It is the presence or absence of these generic features at any level of functioning that dictate the relative performance of the organization or organizational unit. Thus, control can be dictated from three vantage points:

- Operational—with discrete information requirements/criteria
- Managerial—functions deployed to perform IT work
- Organizational—logically related IT processes

Four generic policy and procedure realms are part of traditional organizational level control:

- Strategy and organization—where the organization creates a policy and procedure framework
- Development and application—where the organization implements policy and procedure
- Enterprise sustainment—where the organization operates and maintains itself
- Assessment and management—where the organization makes day-to-day decisions based on data

Strategy and organization is the domain of tactics and long-term planning. It centers on decisions about the way IT can best contribute to the achievement of business objectives. Furthermore, it assures that the realization of the company's strategic vision is planned, communicated, and managed for different perspectives. Finally, it assures that a proper organization as well as technological infrastructure has been established.

Design and implementation is the domain where strategy is turned into systematic action. Logically, in order to realize a given IT strategy, IT solutions must be identified, developed, or acquired, as well as implemented and integrated into the business process. In addition, this domain covers planned changes in and maintenance to existing systems.

Enterprise sustainment is concerned with the actual delivery of organizational services, which range all the way from traditional security operations to training. The assumption is that persistent sustainment processes have to be set up in order to underwrite the business purpose. This domain also includes the actual information and communications technology infrastructure and operations that require day-to-day control.

Assessment and management is concerned with operational monitoring and review of processes and tactical decision making based on the situational awareness provided by data over time. The focus of the data gathering is on the assessment of the capability of and compliance of organizational operations with control requirements as specified in the other three domains. Thus this domain satisfies the management responsibility to rationally assure the organization's control process requirements as they evolve.

The actual monitoring is facilitated by required behaviors that are embedded in the routine functioning of the organization and which provide management control. The assumption is that these control behaviors define specific logical groupings of management activities that characterize proper practice within that domain. These high-level controls represent discrete areas of management responsibility rather than the information asset itself.

The control framework evolves directly from a strategic information and communication technology plan for the organization. The plan is built around the definition of a comprehensive information and communications technology architecture. Decisions have to be made about the technological direction in order to create such an architecture. Once the architecture is decided on the IT organization and its relationships should be implicit. However, it is necessary to make an explicit statement of the organization structure in order to ensure proper execution in the management of the IT investment.

The explicit structure and interrelationships of the IT function as well as its management aims and direction need to be communicated to all aspects of the organization, top to bottom, and the management of the human resources has to be geared to that direction. Thus, all management requirements have to be incorporated into a management plan that will ensure compliance with all internal and external requirements for the purpose of proper project management, quality assurance, and risk mitigation.

From a practical design and implementation standpoint, the aim is to identify all requisite system solutions and acquire and maintain the necessary system hardware and software. All of the elements of the system have to exist as a complete and comprehensive technology infrastructure, which is overseen by an explicit set of management procedures. The elements of the system have to be installed and validated and all changes to the infrastructure have to be rationally managed.

Then, the enterprise information system structure has to be operated and maintained as a persistent entity over time. That requires explicit negotiation and definition of service-level requirements for all stakeholders. In a modern IT shop, it will also require the explicit management of third-party services. The performance and capacity requirements of the information and communication technology infrastructure of the enterprise have to be intentionally maintained over time in order to ensure capable, appropriate service levels.

Routine sustainment manages data, facilities, and day-to-day operations. Thus, the enterprise sustainment activity is a cost center in most organizations. Consequently, as part of the sustainment process, all resource expenditures have to be identified and accounted for in terms of business outcomes. Sustainment also requires that attention is paid to routine customer and user relations management. In addition, the trustworthiness and security of systems also has to be ensured. This final element requires that all system users are properly educated and trained in system operation. Finally, the integrity of the system itself has to be ensured. This is done through classic configuration management as well as a formal problem identification and incident response process.

Rational management is built around assessment and data gathering. The data are acquired from many points in the process. The aim is to assess the effectiveness of internal controls. Since this is a review activity the aim is to ensure adequate independent assurance of control functioning and correctness. This is often supported by independent audits of explicitly designed and implemented organizational best-practice control objectives.

As we said earlier, best-practice control objective requirements are too intricate to simply cook-up on the spot, so standard control frameworks are utilized. The most common of these standard frameworks are probably the ISO 27000, COBIT, and NIST 800-53 models. All of these models reflect a common body of knowledge in best practice–based information system management control and all of them are supported by some form of audit process. The recommendations of these models are expressed in the form of a set of discrete behavioral controls that are specified for each process. Each of these specific control functions is associated with an individual element of IT work.

These large strategic frameworks can be utilized by IT managers and staff, as well as auditors to ensure proper internal and external operations of the IT function. More importantly, they also communicate best practice to the business process owners. The framework itself is based around the specification of a set of behavioral requirements known as control objectives. Control objectives offer a precise and clear definition of discrete actions to ensure effectiveness, efficiency, and economy of resource utilization in IT work. Thus, the control objectives allow the control framework concepts to be translated into specific actions applicable for each IT process.

Detailed control objectives are identified for each process defined by the framework. These are by definition the minimum controls required. The approach is to utilize a small set of high-level control objectives as a classification and focusing method and then enact the intent of those high-level areas by a set of control statements. Each of these control statements requires a set of potentially applicable control behaviors. Each control statement is related to a corresponding process/activity within the framework.

Each control objective specifies the desired results or purposes to be achieved by implementing specific control procedures within an IT activity. And as such, the complete set dictates a clear policy and best-practice direction for IT control for any enterprise worldwide. The control objectives are defined in a technology-independent fashion. Nonetheless, some special technology environments may require separate coverage for control objectives. That is allowable if the unique additions are tailored to the intent of the overall model.

Each generic control objective within the model is implemented by explicit work instructions that are generated by the organization's tailoring process. The general rule is that each specified control requirement must be accompanied by an explicit set of work instructions. The work instructions specifically designate how each control objective will be formally carried out. Generally, these work instructions are captured and displayed in an organization-wide control plan. The control plan outlines all of the specific behaviors that must be carried out in order to achieve the management aims of the IT function.

The control plan explicitly itemizes each task, the skills required, and the organizational resources needed to accomplish this. In addition to detailing how the procedure will be executed, the control plan details the activities necessary to audit that item. The control plan is developed at the point where the implementation of the control process is formally undertaken. Since the plan is subject to change, it has to be managed itself, which means that it has to be associated with an organizational stakeholder. And it is updated on a regular basis. In addition to the routine behavior requirements, the plan must provide a complete set of procedures for review, approval, change, distribution, withdrawal, and tracking. And because unknowns are given in IT, this plan must be a "living" document.

Auditing and Validating a Control Infrastructure for a Business

The specifications of a formal model such as ISO 27000 or COBIT can be translated into actions that can ensure the processes of any organization where the recommended control process is implemented. That implementation has to consider a range of factors including known weaknesses, risks to the organization, a record of incidents, new developments, and strategic choices. Although the general framework and its control objectives provide direction, guidance for a substantive control process the actual implementation is outside the scope of any of the common control frameworks.

Thus, the effectiveness of the implementation has to be validated through some form of rigorous process. That process is overwhelmingly audit based. Information system control auditing is not part of the general body of knowledge of financial auditing even though they incorporate the generally accepted basics of the generic audit process. Instead of the assurance of financial integrity, information system auditing is based on assurance of the detailed specifications of the chosen model's control objectives.

The aim is to help assure management that its formal controls are sufficient, or to advise management where processes need to be improved. From a management perspective the obvious question is: "Am I doing all right? And if not, how do I fix it?" The auditing process helps to answer these questions (Figure 2.7).

The auditing process enables the auditor to review specific IT processes against a given frameworks recommended control objective requirements. At the highest level, the general audit approach revolves around the following:

■ The specification of a framework, especially its IT process classification
■ Requirements for the audit process itself
■ Requirements for IT process auditing
■ General principles of control

The most common model for assessing control is the standard auditing model. However, another increasingly adopted approach is the risk analysis model. It is important to note that best-practice control objectives are not necessarily applicable always and everywhere. Therefore, proper audit procedure suggest that a comprehensive risk assessment be conducted to determine which of the control objectives has to be specifically focused on and which may be ignored. Anybody involved in assessing control can adopt either model.

Overview of the Auditing Process

Audit is a formally planned and executed activity that is the other side of the coin from controls formulation. It is the active part of the process in that the audit function maintains the correctness and integrity of the controls. Thus, it is a necessary function in the governance-based control formulation process. We will discuss it here as a form of introduction. However, it should be noted that the audit process is distinct from the control formulation process and audit is much more widely performed in all aspects of IT, specifically in the software development process where audit is an indispensable part of the lifecycle.

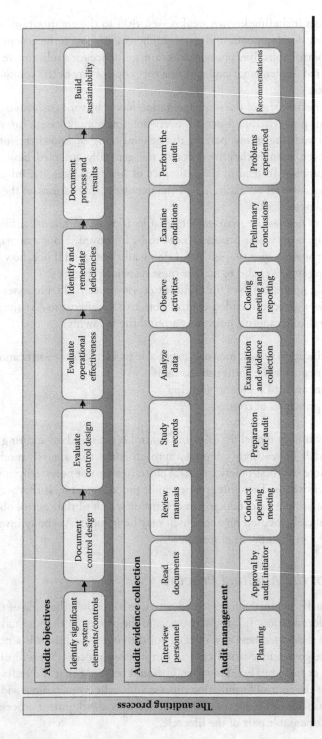

Figure 2.7 The auditing process.

The function of audit processes is to establish the precise status of some aspect of business operation. This is accomplished by identifying a set of management purposes that are operationalized by detailed control objectives and by assessing/auditing the status of the target function with respect to those objectives. The resultant practical process should address a particular area of functioning.

Classic audit establishes and enforces organizational accountability and control, which requires the explicit description and regular assessment of an identified resource. As such, the mission of audit is to know the precise status of an asset under control at all times. In principle, audit is accountable to

- Identify significant system elements/controls
- Document control design
- Evaluate control design
- Evaluate operational effectiveness
- Identify and remediate deficiencies
- Document process and results build sustainability

The audit begins with a review of all aspects of the audit target. That includes all of the current system documentation. If the preliminary review indicates that the system is inadequately controlled, the audit process should go no further. This early exit point is important because every audit is expensive and time consuming.

However, if there is reason to assume that the system's controls are in a condition to be audited, an audit plan should be prepared. This is normally executed by the lead auditor and approved by the client before the audit begins. The audit is initiated by means of an opening meeting with the auditee's senior management. The auditors prepare their working documents from this meeting, including all necessary checklists and forms. The checklists are used to evaluate system elements, while the forms are used to document observations and evidence. Then, the auditors collect the evidence using these documentation tools. Audit evidence is collected by

- Interviewing personnel
- Reading documents
- Reviewing manuals
- Studying records
- Analyzing data
- Observing activities
- Examining conditions
- Performing the audit

Following the collection phase, any evidence that is obtained through interviews must be authenticated from other sources. In essence, interview evidence should, whenever possible, be confirmed by more objective means since it is subjective in nature. Any clues from this evidence that point to possible control system nonconformities must be thoroughly investigated. Then, the system auditors document their observations using all evidence gathered.

Following the analysis and documentation work, the members of the audit team make a list of key nonconformities. This list is based on the evidence obtained and it is appropriately prioritized. The auditors draw conclusions about how well the control system complies with requisite policies and how effectively it achieves its stated objectives. Finally, the auditors discuss their evidence, observations, conclusions, and nonconformities with the auditee's senior managers before they prepare a final audit report.

The lead auditor is responsible for preparing the report. The lead auditor sends the audit report to the client, and the client sends it to the auditee. The auditee is expected to take whatever actions are necessary to correct or prevent control system nonconformities. Follow-up audits might be scheduled in order to verify that corrective and preventive actions were taken.

Audit Management

It is generally recommended that the audit process should be conducted separately and entirely independent of the system to be audited. This is normally overseen by an audit manager who has practical system audit experience. The control standard that will serve as the basis for the audit must be designated prior to the initiation of the process. The nine standard elements of the conventional audit process are

1. Planning
2. Approval of audit plan by initiator
3. Conduct of an opening meeting
4. Preparation for audit by auditors
5. The examination and evidence collection
6. Closing meeting and reporting
7. Preliminary conclusions
8. Problems experienced
9. Recommendations

In addition, there is the general necessity to ensure that audit teams are capable of performing the audit work including the responsibility to select competent auditors and lead auditors. This selection should be officially approved by a separate auditor evaluation panel. The audit manager should select auditors who

■ Understand the system standards that will be applied
■ Are generally familiar with the auditee's products and services
■ Have studied the regulations that govern the auditee's activities

- Have the technical qualifications needed to carry out a proper audit
- Have the professional qualifications needed to carry out an audit
- Are suitably trained

In addition to ensuring auditor competency, audit managers should

- Develop and enforce a code of ethics to govern the audit process
- Monitor and evaluate the performance of the audit teams
- Guarantee consistency—for example, ensure that all auditors make the same observations and draw the same conclusions when confronted with the same evidence
- Plan and schedule audit activities
- Perform the audit reporting process
- Control the audit follow-up process
- Protect the confidentiality of audit information
- Ensure that auditors have the resources they need

Reporting Problems with Controls: Deficiencies and Weaknesses

The identification and remediation of control deficiencies are an essential part of the practical control process. The items of noncompliance are normally reported in the auditor's final report. Where a material control deficiency is identified it is the responsibility of the auditor to report its status to the audit customer.

There are two types of deficiencies—design deficiencies and operating deficiencies. A design deficiency exists when a necessary control is missing or an existing control is not properly designed. That would be a case where even though the control is operating as designed, the control objective is not always met. A significant deficiency is a control deficiency in a significant area of control or an aggregation of such deficiencies that could result in a breakdown of intended functionality that is more than inconsequential. A material weakness is a significant deficiency or an aggregation of significant deficiencies that preclude internal control from providing reasonable assurance that the control object has been secured sufficiently to ensure against exploitation.

Finally, every audit will produce some form of recommendations for corrective action. Those recommendations normally follow their own process independent from the conclusion of the audit. The audit follow-up process should be officially planned and organized as part of audit planning. It is composed of formal steps to assure that rework has been performed and to submit the final report close-out report detailing that particular audit's purpose and scope and the results for the audited organization.

The objectives of control system auditing are to provide management with reasonable assurance that control objectives are being met, and then where there are significant control weaknesses, to substantiate the resulting risks and advise management on corrective actions. Therefore, the auditing process is built around evaluating the appropriateness of stated controls and obtaining an explicit understanding of the relevant business requirements and their related risks, and the control measures that have been deployed to address those risks and requirements. The generally accepted structure of the auditing process is to identify and document explicit control behaviors, evaluate their effectiveness, assess their compliance with their intended purpose, and substantively test for correctness and effectiveness. Compliance is evaluated by testing whether the stated controls are working as prescribed, consistently and continuously. The risk of control objectives not being met is substantiated by using analytical techniques and/or consulting alternative sources.

Auditing Process Steps

The auditing process is built around a number of logical sequential steps. The first step is to determine the correct scope of the audit. This requires investigation, analysis, and definition of the business processes concerned. Platforms and information systems, which are supporting the business process, are audit targets as well as connections with other systems. The IT roles and responsibilities that might be investigated include in- or outsourced organizational objects and functions and the associated business risks and strategic choices.

The next step is to identify the information requirements which are of particular relevance with respect to the business processes. Along with that identification comes the need to identify the inherent IT risks as well as overall level of control that can be associated with the business process. To carry this out properly, there is a need to identify the following:

- Recent changes in the business environment having an IT impact
- Recent changes to the IT environment, new developments, and so on
- Recent incidents relevant to the controls and business environment
- IT monitoring controls applied by management
- Recent audit and/or certification reports
- Recent results of self-assessments

Depending on the information that is obtained, it is possible to target the relevant processes for investigation as well as the resources that apply to them. This could require that certain key processes might be audited several times, each time for a different platform or system. The audit strategy should be determined on the basis of how the detailed audit plan should be further elaborated. Finally, all the steps, tasks, and decision points to perform the audit need to be considered. That includes the following 16 considerations:

1. Definition of audit scope
2. Identification of the business process concerned

3. Identification of platforms, systems and their interconnectivity, supporting the process
4. Identification of roles, responsibilities, and organizational structure
5. Identification of information requirements relevant for the business process
6. Identification of relevance to the business process
7. Identification of inherent IT risks and overall level of control
8. Identification of recent changes and incidents in business and technology environment
9. Identification of the results of prior audits, self-assessments, and certification
10. Identification of monitoring controls applied by management
11. Selection of relevant processes and platforms to audit
12. Identification of the overall process architecture
13. Itemization of resources
14. Establishment of audit strategy
15. Itemization of controls, by risk
16. Identification of decision points

The first 10 items are primarily oriented toward process understanding and determining ownership. This should be a foundation and reference framework for any detailed auditing activity to follow (Figure 2.8).

The general principles of control can also supply additional insight on how to conduct a pepper audit. These principles are primarily focused on process and control responsibilities, control standards, and control information flows. Control, from a management point-of-view, is defined as determining what is being accomplished. That is, evaluating the performance and if necessary applying corrective measures so that the performance takes place according to plan.

The control process consists of four steps. First, a standard of desired performance is specified for a process. Second, a means of sensing what is happening in the process is developed. Third, the entity responsible for ensuring management control compares the process information with the requirements of the standard. Fourth, if what is actually happening does not conform to the standard, the entity responsible for ensuring management control directs that corrective action be taken. This is also conveyed as information back to the control formulation process.

For this process to work, the responsibility for the business or IT process must be clear and that accountability must be unambiguous. If not, control information will not flow and corrective action will not be acted upon. The evaluation can be based on a very wide variety of criteria, from high-level plans and strategies to detailed measurable key performance indicators and critical success factors. Clearly documented, maintained, and communicated control objectives are a must for a good control process.

Clear responsibility for custodianship of these standards also is a requirement for good control. In essence, the control process must be well documented with clear responsibilities. An important aspect in this is the explicit definition of what

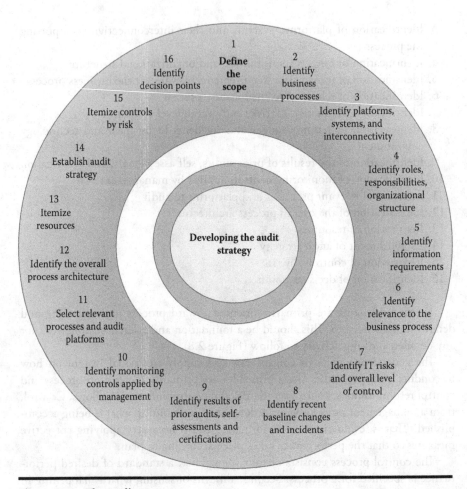

Figure 2.8   The audit strategy.

constitutes a nonconformity, that is, what are the limits of deviation. Finally, the timeliness, integrity, and appropriateness of control information, as well as other information, are basic to the good functioning of the control system and are something the auditor must address.

Both control information and corrective action information will have requirements as to evidence in order to establish accountability after the fact. The following audit steps are performed to document the activities underlying the control objectives as well as to identify the stated control measures/procedures in place. Interview appropriate management and staff to gain an understanding of

- Business requirements and associated risks
- Organization structure
- Roles and responsibilities

- Policies and procedures
- Laws and regulations
- Control measures in place
- Management reporting (status, performance, action items)

Auditors will document the process-related IT resources particularly affected by the process under review in order to obtain the requisite information. The aim is to confirm the understanding of the process under review as well as the key indicators of the adequate performance of the process and the control implications. Effectiveness and appropriateness of control measures for the process under review, or the degree to which the control objective is achieved, can be evaluated using the following criteria:

- Documented processes exist
- Appropriate deliverables exist
- Responsibility and accountability are clear and effective
- Compensating controls exist, where necessary
- The degree to which the control objective is met

A different set of audit steps are necessary in order to ensure that the control measures established are working as prescribed. These require the auditor to obtain direct or indirect evidence to ensure that the audit procedures themselves have been complied properly for the period under review. Therefore, using both direct and indirect evidence the auditor will perform a limited review of the adequacy of the process deliverables. In addition, the auditor will determine the level of substantive testing and additional work needed to provide assurance that the IT process is adequate.

Finally, there are audit steps that need to be performed to substantiate the risk of the control objective not being met. The objective of these steps is to support the audit report and to "shock" management into action where necessary. Needless to say, auditors have to be creative in finding and presenting this often sensitive and confidential information:

- Document the control weaknesses, and resulting threats and vulnerabilities.
- Identify and document the actual and potential impact; for example, through root-cause analysis.
- Provide comparative information, for example, through benchmarks.

When assessing control mechanisms, reviewers should be aware that controls operate at different levels in the operation and also in the lifecycle and that they have intricate relationships. The control framework that is selected will provide some indication as to different control processes, levels, and interrelationships, but actual implementation or assessment of control systems needs to take this added complex dimension into account.

Chapter Summary

Coordination of complex work requires a common and coherent control structure that allows managers to benchmark actions against the policies and procedures of the organization. These policies are dictated by the governance framework (model). The aim is to build a governance framework that will effectively control the activities of all members of the organization.

The purpose of adopting that stance is to avoid a typical piecemeal management system. That is, whether they are universally standard or documented, every enterprise is managed by its commonly accepted practices. These are usually based on some individual unit or manager's appreciation of the proper way to carry out a specific task. And they tend to embed themselves in the organization over time, without any particular logic.

As with any complex deployment, this can only be substantiated through a rational and explicit IT governance planning process. The most straightforward way to overcome that resistance is to initiate the governance from the top. Top-down effectively describes the strategic approach and purposes of information governance. Moreover, it is this strategic concept that drives the deployment of the type of control systems we are discussing in this book. As such, we need to spend some time explaining what the general principles embodied in information governance are and how they work.

The term information governance was coined to describe the strategic function that underwrites due professional care in the management of the organization's information resources. Information governance accomplishes its aims by building a comprehensive structure of rational procedures and relationships, which can be employed to direct and control information assets. As a result, information governance establishes a tangible link between the company's IT resources and its information and business strategy. Ideally, it does this in such a way that it adds value to the enterprise's purposes.

The aim of overall organizational governance is to build a tangible control and accounting structure in order to maintain accountability for specific organizational functions. While information governance is enabled by specification of policies, organizational structures, practices, and procedures required to achieve particular ends. That includes the definition of explicit control elements for any given requirement. Properly stated this insures that due professional care is exercised in the management, use, design, development, maintenance, or operation of information systems and information assets. This is comprehensive and coherent for the aspect being controlled. It is based on explicit control objectives the outcome of which is observable.

This control can be standalone for a given purpose or integrated with other controls to achieve a general accountability. Information governance involves a number of related processes. But, they all serve the same purpose which is to create and enforce ongoing organizational accountability within some sort of control framework. For IT in particular, this represents a different orientation from the usual assessments done for the purpose of process development. The purpose of information governance is to explicitly account for and manage an identified resource on a systematic and ongoing basis, for example, money, parts, and so on. Assessment is exploratory and often one-shot. It is done for the purpose of finding out something specific about an organizational function, for example its level of definition. Thus, the role of information governance is to know the precise status of an asset at all times. In the case of process assessment, this is usually a snapshot rather than an ongoing commitment.

The question is how do we manage risks and secure the information and IT asset. Since both of these goals are tied directly to best practice, the aim is to utilize a common standard that is generally accepted to define the complete set of controls for effective IT governance. That standard would provide them a generally applicable and accepted basis for judging good IT security and control practice. It would also support the determination and monitoring of the appropriate level of IT security and control for a given organization.

The practices should be presented in a logical structure within a domain and process framework. In that respect, there are several reference models that can be selected. However, COBIT, ISO 27000, and NIST 800-53 are arguably the most frequent models used to judge whether management activities are complete and correct. Whatever the reference, the reference framework that utilized it should be built around a well-defined and detailed organizational structure, control policies practices and procedures. COBIT and ISO 27000 are primarily oriented toward conventional business IT in their practical use. NIST 800-53 satisfies the requirements of the FISMA, and is used in the government and more recently in the healthcare industry to conform to HIPAA requirements.

Security and Control

Any responsible corporate or public entity needs to establish measures to ensure the control and security of their information infrastructure. The primary purpose for any of the large-scale control models discussed in this book is to provide a set of these basic recommendations for information managers. Every organization has a basic need to understand the status of its own IT systems and to decide the level of security and control they should provide. The control process formulation must be both direct action oriented as well as generic enough to provide the necessary direction to get the enterprise's information and related processes under control and monitor the achievement of organizational goals. This is done by monitoring the performance within each IT process and benchmarking organizational achievement of those goals over time. Specifically, there must be a means to ensure organizational capability maturity for establishing control over processes in the security and control areas. Ideally, management will be able to map where the organization is today, in relation to the best-in-class ideal.

There is also the need to assess whether the organization is meeting its goals. That assessment needs to be substantiated by explicit measures that will tell management whether an IT process has achieved its security objectives. That requires a set of guidelines that are generic in their application and which prescribe a practical set of actions that can be taken to achieve security goals. In order to do this, the manager needs to know what the indicators of good performance are and what is central to control and the attendant success factors as well as the risks and the generalized best practices for addressing them.

The obvious first requirement in that process is to define the desired outcomes. In essence, companies need to define an explicit link between outcome and strategy at the highest levels of the organization. Then, they define and monitor the internal assessment processes that have been put in place to achieve that outcome. Critical success factors are also required in order to determine whether the IT process has achieved its goals. These factors can be either, strategic, technical, organizational, process, or procedural. The classic assessment process is based on the presence of defined and documented processes, defined and documented policies, and clear accountabilities. Intangibles such as s strong support/commitment of management, appropriate and effective lines of communication, and consistent measurement practices are also involved.

The Role of Audit

It is probably reasonable to assume that managers should be accountable for all aspects of the business process that they direct. This implies that managers must be able to exercise control over their processes. Any audit and control framework is intended to facilitate the execution of those duties. Practically, in order for the organization to achieve its objectives the manager can ensure that an adequate control system is in place if the right set of control behaviors is available to structure the IT governance activity.

The control framework provides the recommendations for the high-level control objectives which will be used to direct the audit and control process. Thus, the foundation for this activity obviously rests on the detailed control objectives. The basic principle involved here is that that control originates from the information that is generated to support business objectives.

The classic purpose of controls is to account for and ensure resources. In fact, from the business perspective this is the only correct application of that term. But it is hard to do that effectively in IT because those resources are both diverse and dispersed. Potential targets for control include any resource that might be considered an organizational asset.

Every organization can tailor an IT control approach suitable to its size and complexity using the explicit controls contained in any one of these popular models. In doing so, though, it is expected that the generic controls in these models will be tailored, or adapted, to reflect the specific circumstances of each organization.

Specifically the business will tailor out controls to ensure the development process, how changes will be made to programs (patch management), operate and maintain a secure computer environment, as well as to ensure access to programs and data. In that respect, controls will be necessary to ensure the process by which the organization will

- Acquire or develop application software
- Acquire technology infrastructure
- Develop and maintain policies and procedures
- Install and test application software and technology infrastructure
- Manage changes
- Define and manage service levels
- Manage third-party services

The aim is to install a comprehensive set of controls that will ensure effective corporate governance and security. These standard measures ought to strengthen internal checks and balances and, ultimately, strengthen corporate accountability. However, it is important to emphasize that it is not sufficient to merely establish and maintain an adequate internal control structure. Companies also have to assess its effectiveness on a regular basis. This distinction is significant. It is not sufficient to simply establish a control framework. Its effectiveness has to be routinely validated for the purposes of security. That is the case because the situation is always changing in the security universe as new threats emerge. And it is not enough to be partially protected from them.

Thus, it is necessary to conduct a routine formal assessment of the effectiveness of the company's internal security on a regular basis. That assessment must include an explicit evaluation of whether internal control over all priority information assets remains effective. Ideally, this is done on an annual or a semiannual basis. In its most rigorous form, this is a responsibility of the company's internal audit function. If that is the case, the auditors will issue an attestation as to the adequacy of the company's internal control over its IT systems and services.

Audits are normally demanded by external organizations such as regulatory bodies to verify compliance with requirements. Audits might also be conducted by the organization itself in order to verify compliance with internal plans, regulations, and guidelines, or to do a third-party verification of compliance with external standards or regulations. The auditor is by definition a disinterested third party, even if the actual audit is conducted internally. Because they are more expensive than reviews and assessments, audits are always carefully planned and resourced. Since they are formal they require careful scheduling, resourcing, and funding assurance. The selection of the auditor and the assignment of roles and responsibilities is also a formal process. The aim is to assure audit integrity. Information system assurance audits always operate within an explicit asset accounting and control framework that is comprehensive and coherent for the aspect being controlled. They must be based on explicit objectives the outcome of which is observable. Information system security audits are normally based around an accounting and control model such as COBIT or ISO 27000 in the private sector and NIST 800-53 in the public sector.

At the highest level the general audit approach is supported by the selected control model, especially the process classification and the definition of the requirements for the audit process itself. That includes the guidelines for the conduct of the IT process auditing and the general principles of control, which are normally specified in the model. The detailed audit guidelines for each IT process are typically specified in the main body of the publication.

Conducting an Audit Process

The first step is to determine the correct scope of the audit. This requires investigation, analysis, and definition of the business processes concerned. Platforms and information systems, which are supporting the business process as well as connections with other systems. The IT roles and responsibilities also need to be defined, including what has been in- or outsourced. That connects the audit to all associated business risks and strategic choices.

The next step is to identify the information requirements that are of particular relevance with respect to the business processes. Then, there is a need to identify the inherent IT risks as well as overall level of control that can be associated with the business process. To achieve this there is a need to identify all recent changes in the business environment having an IT impact and any recent changes to the IT environment such as new developments. Finally, there is the need to identify all recent incidents relevant to the controls and business environment.

On the basis of the information obtained, it is possible to select and tailor out the relevant control processes from the overall audit template selected as well as to target the business resources that apply to them. This could require certain parts of the business operation to be audited several times, each time for a different platform or system. Finally, all the steps, tasks, and decision points to perform the audit need to be considered. That requires the business to define the explicit audit scope and the business processes concerned. It requires the business to identify all platforms, systems and their interconnectivity, supporting the process as well as the roles, responsibilities, and organizational structure of the personnel resources. Finally, the business must identify the information requirements relevant to the execration of the process.

The control process consists of four steps. First, a standard of desired performance is specified for a process. Second, a means of evaluating what is happening in the process is developed. Third, the auditor compares information obtained with standard requirements. Fourth, if what is actually happening does not conform to the standard, the auditor directs that corrective action be taken. This is conveyed as information back to the process.

Both control information and corrective action information will have requirements as to the evidence that is required in order to establish accountability after the fact. This evidence can be obtained from a number of sources including interviews of appropriate management and staff to gain an understanding of the business requirements and associated risks, the organization structure, the roles and responsibilities, policies and procedures within the audit target, any relevant laws and regulations, and existing control measures in place.

Direct or indirect evidence for the selected items is obtained in order to ensure that the audit requirements have been complied with for the period under review using both direct and indirect evidence. That might include a limited review of the adequacy of the process deliverables. The level of substantive testing and additional work needed to provide assurance that the control weaknesses, and resulting threats and vulnerabilities have been addressed and that the actual and potential impact has been identified and documented.

As we said earlier, best-practice control objective requirements are too intricate to simply cook-up on the spot, so standard control frameworks are utilized. The most common of these standard frameworks are probably the ISO 27000, COBIT, and NIST 800-53 models. All of these models reflect a common body of knowledge in best practice-based information system management control and all of them are supported by some form of audit process. The recommendations of these models are expressed in the form of a set of discrete behavioral controls that are specified for each process. Each of these specific control functions is associated with an individual element of IT work.

These large strategic frameworks can be utilized by IT managers and staff, as well as auditors to ensure proper internal and external operation of the IT function. More importantly, they also communicate best practice to the business process owners. The framework itself is based around the specification of a set of behavioral requirements known as control objectives. Control objectives offer a precise and clear definition of discrete actions to ensure effectiveness, efficiency, and economy of resource utilization in IT work. Thus, the control objectives allow the control framework concepts to be translated into specific actions applicable for each IT process.

Detailed control objectives are identified for each process defined by the framework. These are by definition the minimum controls required. The approach is to utilize a small set of high-level control objectives as a classification and focusing method and then enact the intent of those high-level areas by a set of control statements. Each of these control statements requires a set of potentially applicable control behaviors. Each control statement relates to a corresponding process/activity within the framework.

Each control objective specifies the desired results or purposes to be achieved by implementing specific control procedures within an IT activity. And as such, the complete set dictates a clear policy and best-practice direction for IT control for any enterprise worldwide. The control objectives are defined in a technology-independent fashion. Nonetheless, some special technology environments may require separate coverage for control objectives. That is allowable if the unique additions are tailored to the intent of the overall model.

Each generic control objective within the model is implemented by explicit work instructions that are generated by the organization's tailoring process. The general rule is that each specified control requirement must be accompanied by an explicit set of work instructions. The work instructions specifically designate how each control objective will be formally carried out. Generally, these work instructions are captured and displayed in an organization-wide control plan. The control plan outlines all of the specific behaviors that must be carried out in order to achieve the management aims of the IT function.

The control plan explicitly itemizes each task, the skills required and the organizational resources needed to accomplish this. In addition to detailing how the procedure will be executed, the control plan details the activities necessary to audit that item.

The control plan is developed at the point where the implementation of the control process is formally undertaken. Since the plan is subject to change it has to be managed itself, which means that it has to be associated with an organizational stakeholder. And it is updated on a regular basis. In addition to the routine behavior requirements, the plan has to provide a complete set of procedures for review, approval, change, distribution, withdrawal, and tracking. And because unknowns are given in IT, this plan must be a "living" document.

Key Concepts

- Coordination of complex work requires formal controls.
- Controls are substantiated by a standard control structure.
- Controls secure organizational infrastructures.
- Strategic governance is a different process from information governance.
- Information governance secures the ICT assets and function.
- Every organization can tailor a governance process from standard models.
- The aim of practical tailoring is to create a control framework from the model.
- Controls are implemented top-down in a hierarchy.
- Audit is the other side of the coin from control formulation.
- Control is implemented and assessed by audit.
- Audits assess compliance with stated criteria usually framework based.
- Audits address both process effectiveness and control efficiency.
- The aim of audit is to produce objective reports based on evidence.

Key Terms

Audit—formal evidence-based examination of a process or product for the purpose of control.

Auditee—the entity being audited, can be from internal or external sources.

Auditor—the entity performing the audit work.

Audit customer—the entity requesting the audit work, normally for the purposes of ensuring compliance.

Audit framework—the specific standard used to conduct the audit. All criteria within the framework must be confirmed as correct.

Audit management—standard activities planned and implemented to achieve audit goals.

Compliance—a state of agreement or alignment with formally expressed criteria.

Corrective action—recommendations ensuing from an audit for additional action to modify an existing activity or product in order to bring it within given audit criteria.

Governance—planned organization-wide control over all activities meant to achieve goals.

Governance control—a strategic state where organizational actions are stated as explicitly auditable behavior.

Information governance—planned organization-wide control over all information and communication technology operations and functions.

NIST—the body responsible for developing and promulgating standards for federal programs and federal government agencies.

Strategic governance—actions taken to ensure complete and comprehensive long-term planning and deployment of a management operation or functions.

References

Information Systems Audit and Control Association (ISACA). (2013). *Control Objectives for Information and Related Technology (COBIT) v5*. Arlington Heights, IL: ISACA.

International Organization for Standardization. (2012). *ISO 27000, Information Technology—Security Techniques—Information Security Management Systems—Overview and Vocabulary*. Geneva, Switzerland: ISO.

National Institute of Standards and Technology. (2006). *NIST Special Publication 800-53 Revision 4: Security and Privacy Controls for Federal Information Systems and Organizations*. Gaithersburg, MD: Computer Security Division, Information Technology Laboratory, NIST. Accessed July 2015. http://csrc.nist.gov/publications/fips/fips200/FIPS-200-final-march.pdf.

Ponemon Institute Research Report. (2013). *Cost of Cyber Crime Study: United States*. Sponsored by HP Enterprise Security.

Privacy Rights Clearinghouse. (2014). *Chronology of Data Breaches Security Breaches 2005–Present*. San Diego, CA.

Chapter 3

A Survey of Control Frameworks, General Structure, and Application

At the conclusion of this chapter, the reader will understand:

- What is information security governance
- The top security control frameworks and their components
- What security controls are and the variety of security control families
- Examples of individual security controls written for a business

Cybersecurity is a global issue—you might be working at an organization in the United States, however, cyber-attacks come from all over the world. The Internet knows no boundaries. Organizations are reporting that cyber-attacks are increasing in both frequency and impact. In 60% of cases, attackers are able to compromise an organization within minutes (Verizon, 2015). Many organizations do not even know whether they have been exploited by a large-scale threat such as stolen user credentials or corporate assets hijacked for botnet use. And if organizations do not know of their security vulnerabilities, they are unlikely to have created a mitigation strategy for them. In a 2014 cyber-crime survey, 32% of respondents reported that damage caused by insider attacks were more damaging than outsider attacks (US State of Cybercrime Survey, 2014). In another study, the top action comprised of 55% of incidents, was from *privilege abuse*—employees/end users abusing the access they have been given by their organization (Verizon, 2015). In more than 1,300 data breaches and 63,400 security incidents in 95 countries, a 2014 Data Breach Investigations Report found basic lapses at the heart of many of them such as employee mistakes, the use of weak and default passwords, system configuration issues, and inadequate system monitoring (Verizon Enterprise Solutions, 2014). Although corporate espionage is on the rise, employee negligence and posting nonpublic information to a public resource are the second most frequently occurring computer security incidents behind virus and malware infections. And, although the internal employees cited in the report were end-users, sysadmins, and developers, a significant number of incidents were caused by partner errors.

Even the most technically savvy organizations cannot stop hackers and the risk of poorly implemented information technology (IT) security controls can be devastating. Organizations are experiencing an array of security issues from denial of service (DOS) attacks to web application attacks and from cyber-espionage to insider threats (Verizon Enterprise Solutions, 2014). Any part of a computing system whether it be hardware, software, storage media, data, and people can be the target of a crime and any system is most vulnerable at its weakest point.

Surprisingly, many organizations do not have insider-threat programs in place to prevent, detect, and respond to internal threats. Establishing and running an IT security program can be challenging as there are numerous areas to address—from application security, to encryption, to disaster recovery. Additionally, there are regulatory requirements such as Payment Card Industry Data Security Standard (PCI DSS), Sarbanes–Oxley, and the Health Insurance Portability and Accountability Act (HIPAA) that add a layer of complexity. For an IT security system to be effective and add value, a well-defined organization-wide security framework needs to be incorporated that involves all levels of the organizational structure and fine-tuned over time. Although no security framework can prevent all security breaches, adopting an appropriate security framework can demonstrate to regulators that the organization has implemented best practice controls.

There are a variety of IT security frameworks that have been widely adopted. In some cases, the industry or regulatory requirements may drive which security framework to use. Figure 3.1 shows the most widely adopted IT security frameworks and their focus. This chapter provides an overview of these frameworks along with their corresponding security families and controls.

What Is Information Security Governance?

It is the responsibility of the board and the executive management to develop and practice corporate governance. The aim of corporate governance is to provide strategic direction, ensure that business objectives are achieved, manage risk appropriately,

Framework	Focus	Sponsoring organization
COSO	Financial operations and risk management.	Committee of Sponsoring Organizations (COSO)
ITIL	Best practices for managing and delivering IT services.	Information technology Infrastructure Library (ITIL)
ISO	International member organization focusing on IT service management, information security management, corporate governance of IT security, IT risk management, and quality management.	International Organization for Standardization (ISO)
COBIT	International governance, assessment, and management of IT security and risk management process.	Information Systems Audit and Control Association (ISACA)
NIST	IT security standards for federal agencies mandated by the Federal Information Security Management Act (FISMA).	National Institute of Standards and Technology (NIST)
CSF	Voluntary risk-based framework that focuses on IT security and risk management processes.	Presidential Executive Order 13636, Improving Critical Infrastructure Cybersecurity, dated 12 Feb 2013
ISF	International member organization focusing on IT security, governance, and managing information risk.	Information Security Forum (ISF)
PCI DSS	IT security standard for the protection of credit card account data security. Card companies include Visa, MasterCard, American Express, Discover, and Japan Credit Bureau.	Payment Card Industry (PCI) Security Standards Council
SANS Institute	Although not a framework, the widely adopted top 20 critical security controls are based on the NIST SP 800-53 control standards.	SANS Institute

Figure 3.1   IT Security control frameworks overview.

and ensure the organization's resources are used responsibly. Information security governance is a subset of corporate governance and the most fundamental purpose of an information security program is to help ensure the preservation of the organization and its ability to operate. In a properly governed organization, information assurance activities support the organizational goals and objectives while identifying and reducing risk to definable and acceptable levels. Increasing predictability, improving trust in customer relationships, and protecting the organization's reputation are significant benefits of good governance. As senior managers are considered ultimately responsible and legally liable for losses due to cybersecurity breaches, it is vital that they understand the significance of and implement effective information security governance.

To exercise effective IT governance, boards of directors and executive management must have a clear understanding of what to expect from their enterprise's information security program.

Effective information security governance should result in six outcomes to include (Information Systems Audit and Control Association [ISACA], 2012) the following:

1. Strategic alignment—security activities must be aligned with the business strategy to support the organization objectives. Security solutions take into account the governance style, organizational culture, technology deployed, and the structure of the organization.
2. Risk management—risk mitigation should be based on the organization's risk profile, acceptable levels of risk, understanding of risk exposure, and the potential impact/consequences of residual risk.
3. Business process management/value delivery—this includes the integration of all relevant information assurance processes and practices to maximize the effectiveness and efficiency of security activities.
4. Resource management—efficient and effective use of information security knowledge and infrastructure to ensure knowledge is captured and available to develop and document security processes and practices.
5. Performance management—develops a measurement process, aligned with strategic objectives, to aid in effective decision making. This includes continuous monitoring and reporting of information security processes and independent external assessments and audits.
6. Integration—ensures that processes function as intended from end to end.

Information security governance requires strategic direction and commitment, and as such, members of the board need to be involved in setting and approving policy, appropriate resource allocation, and assigning responsibility for information security management. The organization's executive management team is then responsible for ensuring the needed infrastructure, resources, and organizational functions are made available to carry out the directives of the board and any governmental regulatory agency that is required. Many organizations have created the position of chief information security officer (CISO) and have given it the responsibility and authority over the full scope and breadth of information security activities. The CISO develops, oversees, and manages the information security program and initiatives to include strategic, personnel, infrastructure, policy enforcement, emergency planning, security training, and awareness. The CISO also leads the evaluation and assessment of the security program to ensure that all aspects are in compliance with security requirements.

Security affects all aspects of the organization and to be effective it must be pervasive throughout the organization. Ideally, information security will be managed in such a way as to create an organizational security culture.

IT Governance Frameworks—An Overview

With the exponential growth of security breaches and the increasing dependency on external business partners to achieve organizational success, the effective use of enterprise-wide frameworks and implementation of integrated security controls are critical in order to mitigate data theft (Berson and Dubov, 2011; Davis and Schiller, 2011; ISACA, 2012). An enterprise security framework is an overarching structure that identifies interlinked key elements, which collectively contribute to a consistent approach to managing risk. The interlinked key elements or principles often include processes to identify the current state of the organization, levels of risk the organization is willing to accept, security requirements, priorities, strategic goals and mission, resource availability and competencies, compliance, security controls, implementation of security controls, best practices, authorization levels, assessment, financial budgets and costs, governance, disaster recovery, and ongoing monitoring. From a holistic perspective, the absence of a planned approach can result in a rather piecemeal approach or a series of reactionary implementations to satisfy those in the organization who have the loudest voice.

The following is an overview of the most widely used enterprise security frameworks.

COSO Framework

The Foreign Corrupt Practices Act of 1977 (FCPA) made bribery illegal in foreign countries and was the first regulation requiring organizations to implement internal control initiatives and keep extensive records of transactions for disclosure purposes. With the collapse of the savings and loan industry in the mid-1980s, the demand for governmental oversight of accounting standards and the auditing profession paved the way for the creation of formal standards and frameworks. In an attempt to avoid governmental intervention, five private accounting organizations created the Committee of Sponsoring Organizations (COSO) and funded the National Commission on Fraudulent Financial Reporting (also known as the Treadway Commission, named after the chairman) in 1985. COSO is credited with formalizing the concepts of *internal control* and *framework*. Their aim was to improve the quality of financial reporting and issued a comprehensive guideline called *Internal Control-Integrated Framework* in 1992. By establishing a common definition for *internal control* and a framework, the intention was that public companies could self-regulate and apply the voluntary industry guidelines and thus avoid the need for governmental regulation. They viewed internal control as a *process* designed to provide effectiveness and efficiency of operations, reliability of financial reporting, and compliance with applicable laws and regulations (COSO, 2004). Figure 3.2 shows the updated COSO Enterprise Risk Management—Integrated Framework (2004).

The COSO framework has been updated from the original cube to emphasize the importance of identifying and managing risks across the enterprise (COSO, 2004). The framework considers risk management activities at all levels of the

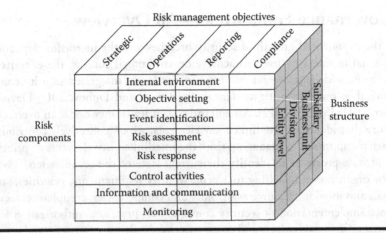

Figure 3.2 The COSO Enterprise Risk Management—Integrated Framework. (From Committee of Sponsoring Organizations, *Enterprise Risk Management Framework Reference Copy, 2004*. https://www.coso.org. With permission.)

organization as shown on the right side (business structure) of the cube: enterprise level or the entire entity; division or subsidiary level; or the at business unit level. The eight risk components are geared toward achieving an organization's risk management objectives (depicted along the top of the cube). Entity objectives can be viewed in the context of four categories:

1. Strategic—objectives should be aligned with and support the entity's mission.
2. Operations—risk management activities should provide assurance of the effective and efficient use of resources.
3. Reporting—reliable reporting to ensure internal control.
4. Compliance—with laws and regulatory agencies.

The new COSO framework consists of eight interrelated risk components:

1. Internal control environment—sets the tone of an organization providing discipline and structure on how risk is viewed and addressed.
2. Objective setting—the chosen objectives must support and align with the organization's mission and are consistent with its risk appetite.
3. Event identification—all events that impact the achievement of an organization's objectives must be identified and distinguished between risks and opportunities.
4. Risk assessment—risks are analyzed as a basis for determining how they should be managed.
5. Risk response—management defines risk responses and develops a set of actions to align risks with the organization's risk tolerances.

6. Control activities—policies and procedures are established and implemented to help ensure the risk responses are effectively carried out.
7. Information and communication—relevant information is communicated in a form and timeframe that enable people to carry out their responsibilities.
8. Monitoring—the enterprise risk management is monitored and modified as necessary and accomplished through ongoing management activities and/or separate evaluations.

Due to widespread reliance on information systems, COSO introduced controls for IT and classified them into to two broad groupings: (1) *General computer controls* to include controls over IT management, infrastructure, security management, software acquisition, development, and maintenance and (2) *Application controls*. A more detailed overview of controls will be discussed later in the chapter.

IT Infrastructure Library Framework

Also in the mid-1980s, the UK Government's Central Computer and Telecommunications Agency developed its own set of recommendations to address the growing dependence on IT. The UK government recognized that "utilizing consistent practices for all aspects of an IT service life cycle could assist in driving organizational effectiveness and efficiency, as well as achieving predictable service levels" (Arraj, 2013, p. 3). Originally called the *IT Infrastructure Library*, the ITIL as it is now called, originated as a collection of 31 books, each covering a specific practice within IT management. ITIL V3 was published in 2007 and consolidate the library into five core publications with updates made in 2011 (Iden and Eikebrokk, 2014). Although a substantial amount of content has been added to ITIL 2011, no entirely new concepts were added. Figure 3.3 shows the ITIL 2011 life cycle and its components:

ITIL 2011 is organized around a *service life cycle* and comprises five distinct volumes that include: *ITIL Service Strategy* and *ITIL Service Design* that outlines the initial project definition and analysis of business requirements; the *ITIL Service Transition* which covers the migration into the live environment; the *ITIL Service Operation* which covers the management of a live operation; and *ITIL Continual Service Improvement*. The *ITIL Service Strategy* is the first volume and considered the hub or core of the ITIL framework to ensure alignment of the business objectives and IT. The service strategy is designed to guide users in the building of a clear strategy and understand what services and to whom they should be offered; how internal and external marketplaces should be developed; differentiate value from the competition; create value for customers; managing service providers; financial management control; asset management; optimal allocation of resources; and how service performance will be measured (Marrone et al., 2014).

The *ITIL Service Design* phase of the life cycle provides guidance for the design and development of new or changed services that adapt to the changing business

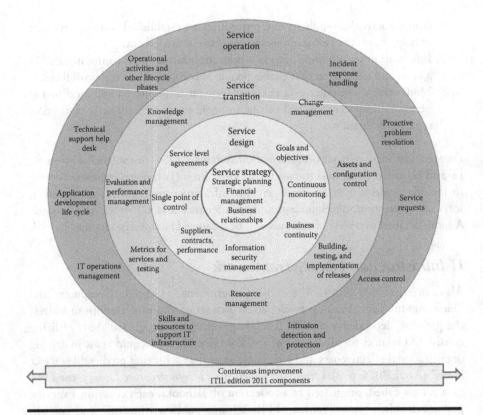

Figure 3.3   ITIL edition 2011 components.

requirements. The key activities include the planning and coordination of design activities; ensure that the design of services is consistent; service management of information systems, architectures, and technology; the production of service design packages; the management of interfaces; and continuous improvement of service design activities and processes (Cartlidge et al., 2012).

The *ITIL Service Transition* phase of the life cycle focuses on the implementation of all services with consideration given to ensure customer expectations are met and managed by the service provider. This phase includes supporting knowledge transfer and decision support processes involving all relevant parties to ensure that knowledge is available and that work is reusable for similar events that may happen in the future (Cartlidge et al., 2012).

The *ITIL Service Operation* phase of the life cycle deals almost exclusively with the user to ensure that services actually deliver value to the organization. The four functions defined in this phase: service desk, technical management, application management, and IT operations management work in conjunction with each other to actively support all phases of the ITIL life cycle. ITIL 2011 can be adapted and used in conjunction with other frameworks such as Control Objectives for Information and Related Technology (COBIT) and International Organization for Standardization (ISO) 27000 (Cartlidge et al., 2012).

ISO 27001

The ISO officially began in 1947 and is an independent, nongovernmental membership organization. The ISO 27001 is the international standard that describes best practices for an information security management system (ISMS). First published in mid-1990 as a code of practice, the British Standard 7799-2, as it was called, morphed into ISO Standard 17799 by December 2000. The standard was updated in 2005 (ISO 27001:2005) and emphasized a model to structure the processes called *plan-do-check-act* (PDCA). The latest version was jointly published in 2013 with the International Electrotechnical Commission (IEC) for the primary purpose for use as a standard to develop an information security program. The three standards that are of interest to information security are ISO 27001, ISO 27002, and ISO 27005. The ISO/IEC 27001:2013 standard provides the specifications and focuses on how well the organization's overall IT security plan is protecting the organization's information assets. This standard also includes guidance on stakeholder requirements, leadership and commitment, organizational roles and responsibilities, actions to address risks and opportunities, support of resources and security awareness, operational planning and control, performance monitoring, and continual improvement (ISO/IEC, 2013).

The updated ISO/IEC 27002 standard no longer emphasizes the PDCA cycle that was part of the 27002:2005 and includes 14 security control clauses that contain a total of 35 main security categories and 114 individual security controls. The previous standard, ISO 27002:2005, had 11 security control areas with 133 controls (ISO/IEC, 2013). As a member organization, the details of ISO/IEC 2700X standards are only available to those who purchase the standard. Additionally, organizations who wish to become certified must conform to the ISO 27001 standard. Figure 3.4 outlines the ISO/IEC 27002:2013 security control area components.

As the specification, ISO/IEC 27001 states what is expected to be included in an effective IT security plan and ISO/IEC 27002 can be considered the second part of ISO/IEC 27001 in that it provides guidance on the implementation of the specification. ISO/IEC 27002 provides recommended best practices for the selection of security controls best suited for the organization that can then be used to implement the ISO/IEC 27001 standard.

A third standard that works in conjunction with the two previously mentioned standards, ISO/IEC 27005 is a security risk management framework that includes guidance on the identification, assessment, treatment, acceptance, communication, monitoring, and review of risk. Since risk management is an integral part of all information security management activities and has a series of interrelated processes, ISO/IEC has created a separate framework for risk management activities. The outcomes of the risk management processes will inform the overall IT security plan.

	ISO/IEC 27002 Information technology—security techniques—code of practice for information security management	
		Framework components
1.	Information security policy	Management is responsible to define, develop, and implement an IT security program for the organization that details security policies in a library.
2.	Organization of information security	IT governance is critical for the success of an IT security program. IT governance should be structured to support both internal and external business partners.
3.	Human resources security	All employees, vendors, contractors, etc., who require access to information assets need to be trained on the security awareness aspects of access prior to, during, and after termination or change of employment.
4.	Asset management	Information assets must be identified and inventoried and a classification scheme should be developed to ensure that assets are managed and secured.
5.	Access control	Security requirements are developed to establish an access control policy that restricts access rights to information assets.
6.	Cryptography	The use of cryptography to protect the confidentiality, authenticity, and integrity of information using cryptographic authentication, key management, digital signatures, and message authentication.
7.	Physical and environmental security	The prevention of unauthorized access to physical assets include securing areas, implementing physical access controls, and protection of critical IT equipment.
8.	Operations security	Ensuring security operation of information processing facilities includes documenting operating procedures, change management, continuous monitoring, backups, and IT audit considerations.
9.	Communications security	The security of network services, controlling access to information by third parties, confidentiality or non-disclosure agreements, and electronic messaging should be appropriately protected.
10.	System acquisition, development, and maintenance	Information security should be built into all applications by the use of a Systems Development Life Cycle (SDLC), which outlines processes for specifying, acquiring, testing, implementing, and maintaining IT systems.
11.	Supplier relationships	Policies and procedures are necessary to monitor suppliers' information security controls to ensure that access to company information, network services, access rights, and service level agreements are developed and implemented.
12.	Information security incident management	An Incident Response Plan is critical to the appropriate handling of any security breach. Risk assessments and security controls must be evaluated and reporting of security events to external entities must be handled properly.
13.	Information security aspects of business continuity management	In the event of a disaster or crisis, continuity of information security management plans must be previously tested and in place to ensure the organization can survive an adverse situation. Controls are designed to minimize the impact of a security breach.
14.	Compliance	Compliance with legal, regulatory, and contractual obligations and controls to meet these requirements should be defined and documented.

Figure 3.4   The ISO/IEC 27002 framework components.

COBIT 5

In 1998, the IT Governance Institute (ITGI) was formed by the ISACA as a nonprofit, independent research entity to advance international thinking on governance and management of enterprise IT. ITGI developed COBIT and is also an internationally recognized framework for IT governance and security control. COBIT 5, released in 2012, provides a comprehensive framework to "help enterprises create optimal value from IT by maintaining a balance between realizing benefits and optimizing risk levels and resources use" (ISACA, 2012, p. 13). Figure 3.5 shows the five key principles for governance and management of enterprise IT.

The COBIT 5 framework consists of the following five key principles (ISACA, 2012):

1. Meeting stakeholder needs—the governance system should consider all stakeholders and the enterprise goals for IT are used to formalize and structure the stakeholder needs.
2. Covering the enterprise end-to-end—covers all functions and processes within the enterprise and is inclusive of everything and everyone that is relevant to governance and management of IT.
3. Applying a single, integrated framework—aligns with other latest relevant standards and frameworks.

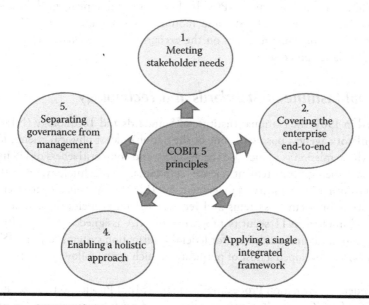

Figure 3.5   COBIT 5 framework for governance and management of enterprise IT. (From Information Systems Audit and Control Association, *COBIT 5: A Business Framework for the Governance and Management of Enterprise IT*, ISACA, Rolling Meadows, IL, 2012. With permission.)

4. Enabling a holistic approach—identifies seven categories of enablers to include principles, policies, and frameworks; processes; organizational structures; culture, ethics, and behavior; information; services, infrastructure, and applications; and people, skills, and competencies.
5. Separating governance from management—provides a clear distinction between these two disciplines.

The COBIT 5 includes a process reference model, representing all of the IT processes generally found in an enterprise such as governance; planning and organizing an IT security plan; building and implementing the plan; delivering service and support; and monitoring and evaluating processes to ensure an effective IT security program. This model can be adapted for use in smaller organizations which may use fewer processes to larger organizations which may use more to cover the same objectives (ISACA, 2012). Figure 3.6 shows the 37 governance and management processes within COBIT 5.

The COBIT 5 model divides the governance and management processes of enterprise IT into the following two main process domains:

1. Governance—five processes include evaluate, direct, and monitor in order to provide direction for the overall IT security program.
2. Management—four domains comprised of thirty-two processes include align, plan, and organize (APO); build acquire and implement (BAI); deliver, service, and support (DSS); and monitor, evaluate, and assess (MEA). The management domains focus on the execution of decisions developed in the governance processes.

National Institute of Standards and Technology

Founded in 1901, the National Institute of Standards and Technology (NIST) is a nonregulatory agency, possessing one of the nation's oldest physical science laboratories, whose mission is to increase the visibility and competitiveness of US innovation by advancing measurement science, standards, and technology. In 2002, the Federal Information Security Management Act (FISMA) was enacted to strengthen the information security systems and requires federal agencies to develop, document, and implement IT security programs. FISMA assigned the responsibility to develop standards and guidelines for federal information systems to the NIST and as such NIST developed a host of publications such as the following:

■ Federal Information Processing Standard (FIPS) Publication 199 established *Standards for Security Categorization of Federal Information and Information Systems*. As part of a risk-based approached, this standard requires the assessment of federal information systems to rate each system as low, moderate, or high impact for the categories of confidentiality, integrity, and availability.

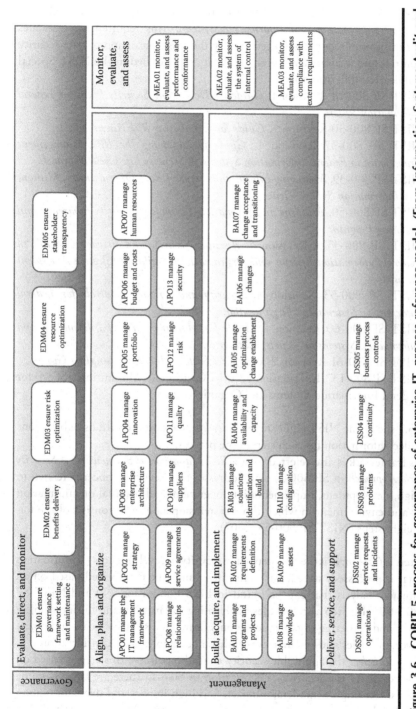

Figure 3.6   COBIT 5 process for governance of enterprise IT, process reference model. (From Information Systems Audit and Control Association, *COBIT 5: A Business Framework for the Governance and Management of Enterprise IT*, ISACA, Rolling Meadows, IL, 2012. With permission.)

- FIPS Publication 200 established *Minimum Security Requirements to Federal Information and Information Systems.* This requirement mandates the minimum security requirements by the selection of appropriate security controls and assurance requirements that are described in the NIST Special Publication (SP) 800-53.
- NIST SP 800-18 Revision 1, *Guide for Developing Security Plans for Federal Information Systems.*
- NIST SP 800-30 Revision 1, *Guide for Conducting Risk Assessments.*
- NIST SP 800-37 Revision 1, *Guide for Applying the Risk Management Framework to Federal Information Systems: A Security Life Cycle Approach.*
- NIST SP 800-39, *Managing Information Security Risk: Organization, Mission, and Information System View.*
- NIST SP 800-50, *Building an Information Technology Security Awareness and Training Program.*
- NIST SP 800-53 A Revision 4, *Assessing Security and Privacy Controls in Federal Information Systems and Organizations: Building Effective Assessment Plans.*
- NIST SP 800-53 Revision 4, *Security and Privacy Controls for Federal Information Systems and Organizations.*
- NIST SP 800-60 Revision 1, *Guide for Mapping Types of Information and Information Systems to Security Categories.*
- NIST SP 800-61 Revision 2, *Computer Security Incident Handling Guide.*
- NIST SP 800-137, Information Security Continuous Monitoring (ISCM) for Federal Information Systems and Organizations.

Figure 3.7 shows the NIST eight step *security life cycle* and the various publications for detailed information for each step in the process.

This framework is also referred to as a *Risk Management Framework: A Security Life Cycle Approach* in SP 800-37 and addresses the "security concerns related to the design, development, implementation, operation, and disposal of information systems and environment in which those systems operate" and consists of the following eight steps (NIST SP 800-53, 2007):

- Step 1: *Categorize* is the first step in the security life cycle process—information that is processed, stored, and transmitted must be categorized based on an impact analysis that can be found in FIPS Publication 199 and NIST SP 800-60. This step also includes establishing the mission and business objectives and gathering organization inputs from laws, strategic goals and objectives, priorities and resource availability, and supply chain considerations.
- Step 2: *Select* the applicable security control baseline—this step is based on the results of the security categorization in Step 1. There are three baseline levels: low-impact, moderate-impact, and high-impact and depending upon the baseline chosen, a set of recommended security controls are provided in

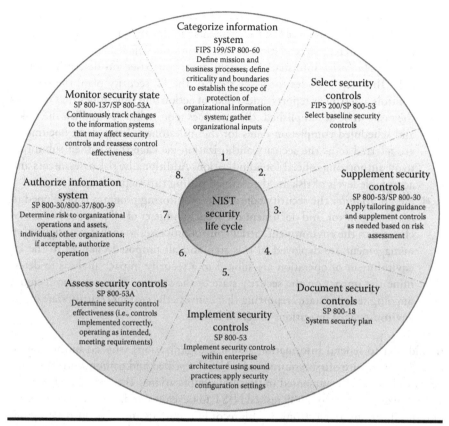

Figure 3.7   NIST security life cycle.

SP 800-53. The controls are organized into three categories: management, operational, and technical.

■ Step 3: *Supplement* the security controls—organizations can tailor and supplement the security control baseline as needed based on the outcomes of their risk assessment and local conditions.

■ Step 4: *Document* the security controls—formal documentation is developed that provides an overview of the security requirements for all information systems and describes the security controls that are in place and planned for meeting those requirements.

■ Step 5: *Implement* the selected security controls and document the functional description and implementation details for each of the controls in the IT security plan. The functional description should include the planned inputs, expected behavior, and expected outputs.

■ Step 6: *Assess* the security controls. This step involves developing, reviewing, and approving a security assessment plan that includes objectives, a detailed road map, and procedures of how the assessment will be conducted. The results of the security control assessments are documented to include issues, findings, and recommendations for correcting any deficiencies in the controls.

■ Step 7: *Authorize* information system operation based on determination of risk. This step includes the assessment of the IT security plan, the security controls assessment reports, and a plan of action and milestones that outlines the tasks to be accomplished, the resources required to accomplish the tasks, and scheduled completion dates for the milestones. These three documents are referred to as the security authorization package that is then submitted to an authorizing official for adjudication. Additionally, risk assessments and acceptable levels of risk are determined during this step.

■ Step 8: *Monitor* the security controls. A monitoring program is developed to manage, control, and document the security impact of all proposed or actual changes to the environment. Strict control processes to include configuration management are deployed in this step and all proposed changes to the IT environment of operation are subject to a security impact analysis to determine the impact on the security state of the system. This step also includes ongoing security status reporting that conveys the current security state of the environment of operations to senior leaders.

In addition to federal information systems, organizations who do business with federal agencies are often required to be NIST certified and comply with the standards and policies documented in the above publications. The American Recovery and Reinvestment Act of 2009 tasked NIST to develop standards and implementation specifications for electronic health record IT systems and developed a program for the certification of health IT. Health care organizations who accept Medicare and Medicaid must conform to the NIST standards and policies defined in the meaningful use of electronic health records requirements in order to continue to be reimbursed by those federal agencies.

Cybersecurity Framework—Improving Critical Infrastructure Cybersecurity

In February 2013, the president issued Executive Order 13636 titled the *Framework for Improving Critical Infrastructure Cybersecurity* for the creation of a voluntary framework based on existing standards, guidelines, and practices for reducing cyber-risks to critical infrastructure. The *Cybersecurity Framework* (CSF) enables organizations to apply the principles and best practices of risk management to improving the structure and resilience of critical infrastructure regardless of size, degree of cybersecurity risk, or the level of cybersecurity sophistication that exists within the organization (NIST, 2014). The framework is a risk-based approach and is composed of three parts: the Framework Core, the Framework Implementation Tiers, and the Framework Profiles. Each component is designed to consider the business drivers and connect them to cybersecurity activities (NIST, 2014). The components are as follows:

1. Framework Core—is a set of cybersecurity activities, desired outcomes, and applicable references that are common across critical infrastructure. Consists of five concurrent and continuous functions (identify, protect, detect, respond, recover). When considered together, these functions provide a high-level strategic view of the life cycle of an organization's management of cyber-risk (NIST, 2014). It is not a checklist of actions, but presents key cybersecurity outcomes that are identified by industry. Figure 3.8 shows the four elements of the framework: functions, categories, subcategories, and informative references. The category column can include logical groupings of controls such as *access control*, detection processes, and so on. The subcategory column can include information relevant to each category such as the activities performed to ensure each task within a category is addressed. The informative references column can include the specific standards, guidelines, procedures, and/or controls that were created to address each subcategory.

Cybersecurity Framework core			
Functions	Categories	Subcategories	Informative references
Identify			
Protect			
Detect			
Respond			
Recover			

Figure 3.8 Cybersecurity framework core structure.

2. Framework Implementation Tiers—provide the context on how the organization views risk and the processes in place to manage that risk (NIST, 2014). Figure 3.9 shows the four tiers that are characterized by a range of increasing degree of rigor (partial, risk informed, repeatable, and adaptive). When selecting the tier, organizations should consider their risk management practices, threat environment, legal and regulatory requirements, the business and mission objectives, and any organizational constraints. To reduce cybersecurity risk and increase cost effectiveness, organizations are encouraged to implement Tier 2 or greater.
3. Framework Profiles—represent the outcomes based on business needs and alignment of standards, guidelines, and practices to the Framework Core. Current profiles that represent "as is" states can be helpful in identifying opportunities to improve rigor and possibly increase to a higher tier (NIST, 2014).

The goal of the framework is to provide a common language to increase understanding and assist in the management of both internal and external cybersecurity risks. It can be used to help prioritize cybersecurity risk activities, and to align policy, business, and technological approaches to managing that risk.

Information Security Forum Standard of Good Practice for Information Security

Founded in 1989 originally as the European Security Forum, the Information Security Forum (ISF) is an independent, not-for-profit paid membership organization that has developed best practice methodologies, processes, and tools in information security. The ISF conducts research on cyber, information security, and risk management and has developed the *Standard of Good Practice for Information Security*. The standard has four main categories (ISF, 2014):

1. Security governance—this category includes recommendations on a security governance approach and outlines the components of effective security governance.
2. Security requirements—this category provides best practices on managing information risk assessment and methodologies; confidentiality, integrity, availability requirements; information risk treatment; as well as legal, regulatory compliance; and information privacy.
3. Control framework—this category includes 20 high-level areas that detail 97 business activities and provide specific best practice recommendations to achieve the area objective.
4. Security monitoring and improvement—this category provides best practices on security audit management; a four step security audit process that includes planning, fieldwork, reporting, and monitoring; security monitoring; information risk reporting, and monitoring information security compliance.

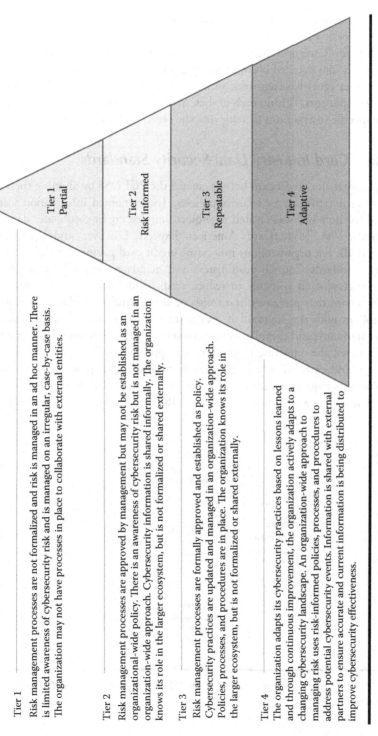

Figure 3.9 Cybersecurity framework implementation tiers.

Cybersecurity Framework implementation tiers

Tier 1
Partial

Tier 2
Risk informed

Tier 3
Repeatable

Tier 4
Adaptive

Tier 1
Risk management processes are not formalized and risk is managed in an ad hoc manner. There is limited awareness of cybersecurity risk and is managed on an irregular, case-by-case basis. The organization may not have processes in place to collaborate with external entities.

Tier 2
Risk management processes are approved by management but may not be established as an organizational-wide policy. There is an awareness of cybersecurity risk but is not managed in an organization-wide approach. Cybersecurity information is shared informally. The organization knows its role in the larger ecosystem, but is not formalized or shared externally.

Tier 3
Risk management processes are formally approved and established as policy. Cybersecurity practices are updated and managed in an organization-wide approach. Policies, processes, and procedures are in place. The organization knows its role in the larger ecosystem, but is not formalized or shared externally.

Tier 4
The organization adapts its cybersecurity practices based on lessons learned and through continuous improvement, the organization actively adapts to a changing cybersecurity landscape. An organization-wide approach to managing risk uses risk-informed policies, processes, and procedures to address potential cybersecurity events. Information is shared with external partners to ensure accurate and current information is being distributed to improve cybersecurity effectiveness.

Figure 3.10 shows the overall structure of the ISF *Standard of Good Practice for Information Security.*

Each main "category" includes a group of high-level subject "areas" that are broken down into detailed business activities or "topics." For example, the security governance category has two areas: security governance approach and security governance components. Within each of these areas are detailed business activities that provide specific instructions in achieving the objective for each area.

Payment Card Industry Data Security Standards

In 2004, five major credit card brands created the PCI DSS by aligning their individual information systems security policies. The combined information security standard (version 1.0) was created to protect branded credit cardholder data from five brands: Visa, MasterCard, American Express, Discover, and Japan Credit Bureau (JCB). For organizations processing credit card payment transactions, the Security Standards Council administers and mandates that validation of compliance be conducted annually to reduce credit card fraud. Any organization in the value chain that processes, transmits, or stores cardholder data is required to be compliant with the standard if they want to process any of these cards. The auditing standards and compliance requirements are the same for all size organizations, however, the reporting requirements to prove compliance vary. In addition to internal and external security scans, organizations that process large volumes of transactions require annual validation by an external qualified security assessor (QSA) that creates a report on compliance (ROC). For organizations that handle

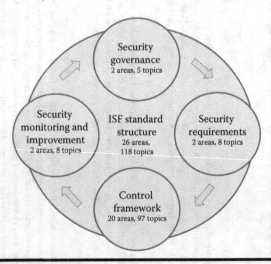

Figure 3.10 Overall structure of the ISF *Standard of Good Practice for Information Security.*

smaller volumes of transactions, a self-assessment questionnaire (SAQ) is required annually. The security standard is not a framework per se, however, it is a popular standard used among IT security professionals and worth mentioning. The security standard is organized into 6 control objectives that have 12 corresponding security requirements. The 12 security requirements are (PCI DSS, 2015) as follows:

1. **Build and maintain a secure network**—this includes installing and maintaining a firewall configuration to protect cardholder data. There are 5 requirements with 18 additional subrequirements detailed for this requirement.
2. **Do not use vendor-supplied defaults for system passwords and other security parameters**—this includes developing configuration standards, implementing security features on required services, protocols, or daemons, encryption procedures and policy, and system component inventory policy. There are six requirements with six additional subrequirements detailed for this requirement.
3. **Protect stored cardholder data**—this includes data retention, disposal policies, storage policies and procedures, and cryptographic key management processes and procedures. There are 7 requirements with 15 subrequirements for this requirement.
4. **Encrypt transmission of cardholder data across open, public networks**—this area includes managing cryptography and security protocols, wireless and cellular technologies. There are three requirements with one subrequirement for this requirement.
5. **Use and regularly update antivirus software or programs.** There are four requirements and two subrequirements detailed for this area.
6. **Develop and maintain secure systems and applications**—this includes a risk assessment process and policy, a change control process and procedures, software development best practices to address coding vulnerabilities, security policies, and operational procedures for developing secure systems. There are 7 requirements and 17 additional subrequirements detailed for this area.
7. **Restrict access to cardholder data by business need to know**—this includes an access control procedures and policy, separation of duties policy, and least privileges policy. There are three requirements with seven additional subrequirements detailed for this area.
8. **Assign a unique ID to each person with computer access**—this includes a user identification policy, authentication policy, and password policy. There are 8 requirements for this area with 15 additional subrequirements detailed for this area.
9. **Restrict physical access to cardholder data**—this includes developing a physical access policy, visitor access policy, media destruction policy, inventory control policy, and a security training policy. There are 10 requirements and 17 additional subrequirements detailed for this area.

10. **Track and monitor all access to network resources and cardholder data**—this is the development of audit trail procedures and policy, time synchronization policy, and a log review and security event policy. There are 8 requirements and 24 additional subrequirements detailed for this area.

11. **Regularly test security systems and processes**—this includes testing wireless access points, network vulnerability scans, penetration testing, intrusion detection and prevention policy, deployment of change-detection tools, and continuous monitoring policy. There are 6 requirements and 10 additional subrequirements detailed for this area.

12. **Maintain a policy that addresses information security for all personnel**—this includes a security policy, risk-assessment process, remote-access policy, security training policy to include a security awareness program, background check policy for new hires, policy and procedures to manage service providers with whom cardholder data is shared, and an incident response plan. There are 12 requirements and 29 additional subrequirements detailed for this area.

Figure 3.11 shows the six control objectives and their corresponding security requirements.

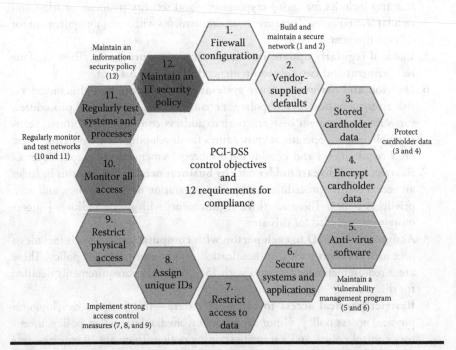

Figure 3.11 The PCI-DSS control objectives and 12 security requirements.

SANS Institute

In 1989, the SANS Institute was founded as a private research and education organization that specializes in training information security professionals on a variety of topics to include cyber and network defenses, incident response, digital forensics, penetration testing, and audit. In 2006, SANS established the SANS Technology Institute which is a graduate school focusing exclusively on cybersecurity. The SANS Institute readily makes available numerous CIS security configuration benchmarks, assessment tools, and security metrics definitions. Although SANS is also not a framework, they are well known and regarded for their top 20 list of critical security controls, which are updated and derived from the most common attack patterns and vetted across a broad community of government and industry (SANS, 2013). Originally the critical security controls were recommendations created to provide a prioritized list of controls that would have the greatest impact in improving risk posture against real-world threats as opposed to a requirement framework that risked becoming an exercise in reporting on compliance. The controls work in conjunction with NIST SP 800-53 and the NIST CSF with the objective of focusing on a smaller number of immediate actionable controls with a high-payoff. Figure 3.12a and b shows the SANS Top 20 critical security controls with mappings to the CSF, NIST 800-53, ISO/IEC 27002, and PCI DSS standards.

It is strongly recommended to carefully select and use a framework to guide the organization through the complex process of protecting information assets. Effective security requires the active engagement at all levels of the organization. The use of a comprehensive framework to assess and manage risk, classify information assets, assign roles and responsibilities, integrate organizational processes, implement effective security controls, train all users, develop incident handling plans, continuously monitor, and implement meaningful metrics will allow management to organize teams with the right skill sets to create a strong cybersecurity program.

IT Security Controls

Cybersecurity must be addressed as a significant concern since it mitigates business risks and allows for the smooth functioning of daily activities in order for organizations to achieve their strategic goals and carry out their mission. For every organization, senior managers must make the critical decisions as to how much risk they are willing to tolerate and to decide the appropriate security levels. Additionally, they must understand the financial implications of cybersecurity implementation efforts and weigh the risks in relation to the value of assets. With the numerous IT security standards and guidelines that currently exist, they must also determine the ideal approach that addresses regulation and compliance issues, boost performance results, and represent a high level of security for the investment.

	Critical security control (SANS)	Description	CSF	NIST 800-53 Rev 4	ISO 27002: 2013	PCI DSS 3.0
1	Inventory of authorized and unauthorized devices	Actively manage all hardware, giving access to only authorized devices	ID.AM-1 ID.AM-3 PR.DS-3	CA-7, CM-8, IA-3, SA-4, SC-17, SI-4, PM-5	A.8.1.1 A.9.1.2 A.13.1.1	2.4
2	Inventory of authorized and unauthorized software	Actively manage all software so that only authorized software is installed and can execute	ID.AM-2 PR.DS-6	CA-7, CM-2, CM-8, CM-10, CM-11, SA-4, SC-18, SC-34, SI-4, PM-5	A.12.5.1 A.12.6.2	
3	Secure configurations for hardware and software	Establish, implement, and actively manage the security configuration of laptops, servers, and workstations	PR.IP-1	CA-7,CM-2, CM-3, CM-5-9, CM-11, MA-4, RA-5, SA-4, SC-14,34, SI-2, SI-4	A.14.2.4 A.14.2.8 A.18.2.3	2.2, 2.3, 6.2, 11.5
4	Continuous vulnerability assessment and remediation	Continuously acquire, assess, and take action on new information in order to identify vulnerabilities, remediate, and minimize	ID.RA-1,2 PR.IP-12 DE.CM-8 RS.MI-3	CA-2, CA-7, RA-5, SC-34, SI-4, SI-7	A.12.6.1 A.14.2.8	6.1, 6.2, 11.2
5	Malware defenses	Control the installation, spread, and execution of malicious code at multiple points in the enterprise	PR.PT-2 DE.CM-4 DE.CM-5	CA-7, SC-39, SC-44, SI-3, SI-4, SI-8	A.8.3.1 A.12.2.1 A.13.2.3	5.1–5.4
6	Application software security	Manage the security lifecycle of all in-house developed and acquired software	PR.DS-7	SA-13, 15, 16, 17, 20, 21, SC-39, SI-10,11, 15, 16	A.9.4.5 A.12.1.4 A.14.2.1 A.14.2.6-8	6.3, 6.5-6.7
7	Wireless access control	The processes and tools used to track, control, prevent, and correct the security use of wireless devices		AC-18, 19, CA-3, 7, CM-2, IA-3,SC-8, SC-17, SC-40, SI-4	A.10.1.1 A.12.4.1 A.12.7.1	4.3, 11.1
8	Data recovery capability	The processes and tools used to properly back up critical information with a proven methodology for timely recovery	PR.IP-4	CP-9, CP-10, MP-4	A.10.1.1 A.12.3.1	4.3, 9.5-9.7
9	Security skills assessment and appropriate training to fill gaps	Identify the specific knowledge, skills, and abilities needed to support defense for all functional roles in the enterprise	PR.AT-1-5	AT-1-4, SA-11, 16, PM-13, 14, 16	A.7.2.2	12.6
10	Secure configurations for network devices	Establish, implement, and actively manage the security configuration of network infrastructure devices	PR.AC-5 PR.IP-1 PR.PT-4	AC-4, CA-3, 7, 9, CM-2, 3, 5, 6, 8, MA-4, SC-24, SI-4	A.9.1.2 A.13.1.1 A.13.1.3	1.1, 1.2, 2.2, 6.2

Figure 3.12 SANS top 20 critical security controls with mapping. (Adapted from SANS Institute, *Critical Security Controls for Effective Cyber Defense—Version 5, 2014.* https://www.sans.org/media/critical-security-controls/fall-2014-poster.pdf)

(Continued)

	Critical security control (SANS)	Description	CSF	NIST 800-53 Rev 4	ISO 27002: 2013	PCI DSS 3.0
11	Limitation and control of network ports	Manage the ongoing operational use of ports, protocols, and services on networked devices	PR.AC-5 DE.AE-1	AC-4, CA-7,9, CM-2,6, 8, SC-20-22, SC-24, SI-4	A.9.1.2 A.13.1.1, .2 A.14.1.2	1.4
12	Controlled use of administrative privileges	The processes and tools used to track, control, prevent, and correct the use, assignment, and configuration of administrative privileges	PR.AC-4 PR.AT-2 PR.MA-2 PR.PT-3	AC-2, 6, 17, 19, CA-7. IA-2, 4, 5, SI-4	A.9.1.1 A.9.2.2-6 A.9.3.1 A.9.4.1-4	2.1, 7.1-3, 8.1-3, 8.7
13	Boundary defense	Detect, protect, and correct the flow of information transferring networks of different trust levels	PR.AC-3 PR.AC-5 PR.MA-2 DE.AE-1	AC-4, 17, 20, CA-7, 9, CM-2, SA-9, SC-7, 8, SI-4	A.9.1.2,A.12.4.1 A.12.7.1 A.13.1.1, 3 A.13.2.3	1.1-3, 8.3, 10.8, 11.4
14	Maintenance, monitoring, and analysis of audit logs	Collect, manage, and analyze audit logs that could help recover from an attack	PR.PT-1 DE.AE-3 DE.DP-1-5	AC-23, AU-2-14, CA-7, IA.10, SI-4	A.12.4.1-4 A.12.7.1	10.1-7
15	Controlled access based on the need to know	The processes and tools used to track, control, prevent, correct secure access to critical assets	PR.AC-4,5 PR.DS-1,2 PR.PT-2,3	AC-24, CA-7, MP-3, RA-2, SC-16, SI-4	A.8.3.1 A.9.1.1 A.10.1.1	1.3, 4 4.3, 7.1-3, 8.7
16	Account monitoring and control	Actively manage the life-cycle of system and application accounts	PR.AC-1 PR.AC-4 PR.PT-3	AC-2, 3, 7, 11,12 CA-7, IA-5, 10 SC-17, 23, SI-4	A.9.1.1 A.9.2.1-6 A.9.3.1 A.9.4.1-3 A.112.8	7.1-3, 8.7,8
17	Data protection	The processes and tools used to prevent data exfiltration	PR.AC-5 PR.DS-2, 5 PR.PT-2	AC-3, 4, 23, CA-7,9,IR-9, MP-5, SA-18, SC-8, 28, 31, 41, SI-4	A.8.3.1 A.10.1.1-2 A.13.2.3 A.18.1.5	3.6 4.1-3
18	Incident response and management	Protect the organization's information and reputation by developing and implementing an incident response infrastructure	PR.IP-10,DE.AE-2,4, 5, DE.CM-1-7, RS.RP-1, RS.CO-1-5,RS.AN-1-4, RS.MI-1-2, RS.IM-1-2, RC.RP-1, RC.IM-1-2, RC.CO-1-3	IR-1-8, 10	A.6.1.3 A.7.2.1 A.16.1.2 A.16.1.4-7	12.10
19	Secure network engineering	Make security an inherent attribute of the enterprise	PR.AC-5	AC-4, CA-3,9, SA-8, SC-20-22, 32,37	A.13.1.3 A.14.2.5	
20	Penetration tests and red team exercises	Test the overall strength of an organization's defenses		CA-2, 5, 6, 8 RA-6, SI-6, PM-6, 14	A.14.2.8 A.18.2.1, 3	11.3

Figure 3.12 (Continued) SANS top 20 critical security controls with mapping. (Adapted from SANS Institute, *Critical Security Controls for Effective Cyber Defense—Version 5, 2014.* https://www.sans.org/media/criticalsecurity-controls/fall-2014-poster.pdf)

It is critical for any organization to have a governance structure with an IT security program that is periodically evaluated and updated. Every system that is in production and every business process that is implemented should be assessed for the existence of risk. Once an organization has identified and documented their security requirements and a thorough risk assessment has been conducted, appropriate security controls should be selected. Internal security controls are the safeguards or countermeasures that are deployed to protect the confidentiality, integrity, and availability of the IT environment.

There are generally three types of controls: preventive, detective, and reactive. Preventive controls are designed to stop or prevent an attack from happening. Requiring badge access to enter a secured data center (physical access control) or requiring passwords (password policy) are examples of preventive controls. Detective controls identify that an intrusion event has already occurred. Controls such as continuous monitoring, an antivirus software policy, motion detectors are examples of detective controls. Reactive controls are also referred to as corrective controls in that they do not prevent an attack but they provide a way to detect when an attack has happened and possibly corrected the situation. Operating system upgrades, a patch management policy, and a backup data restoration policy are examples of corrective controls that can mitigate or lessen the impact of a manifested threat.

Another facet of controls is that they can have technical, administrative, and physical implementations. An example of a technical control is the deployment of an intrusion detection tool to support near-real-time analysis of events in support of detecting system-level attacks. An example of an administrative control is security awareness training whereas the organization ensures that all users are exposed to basic information system security awareness before gaining authorized access to the network. An example of a physical control is a visitor control policy that controls physical access to information systems by authenticating visitors before authorizing access to facilities or other area designated as publicly accessible.

Frameworks such as NIST 800-53, ISO/IEC 27002, and COBIT have clear sets of processes and controls to provide an IT governance structure and control within an organization. Many organizations find that they need to use a blend of security standards and controls to accomplish their business objectives and satisfy auditing requirements.

Security Control Organization

NIST has created standards and controls for numerous disciplines most notably the 800-53 Security and Privacy Controls (NIST SP 800-53A, 2014). The NIST SP 800-53 provides a catalogue of security and privacy controls and a process for selecting controls to protect organizational operations, assets, and individuals from hostile cyber-attacks, natural disasters, structural failures, and human errors (NIST SP 800-53A, 2014). The security controls are designed to be technology-neutral;

focus on the fundamental safeguards and countermeasures necessary to protect information during processing, at rest, and during transmission; and are complimentary with other security standards. The security controls are step 2 within the bigger picture of the *security life cycle* shown in Figure 3.7.

NIST has a well-defined structure in which their security controls are organized and are ordered into *classes* and *families*. There are three classes of security controls: management, operational, and technical. Within all three classes, the NIST standard includes a total of 17 security control families and are shown in Figure 3.13.

Each control family contains individual security controls related to the security functionality of that family with the objective of satisfying the breadth and depth of security requirements. For example, in the security control family of *access control*, there are 20 individual controls. Figure 3.14 shows the list of the 20 individual controls for the access control family.

The individual controls are then documented with specific requirements that must be met. For example, the individual NIST access control, AC-1, access control policy and procedures objective is to "determine if the organization develops and documents an access control policy that addresses the purpose, scope, roles, responsibilities, management commitment, coordination among organizational entities, and compliance" (NIST SP 800-53A, 2014). Additionally, this control must also

- Define personnel or roles to whom the access control *policy* are to be disseminated.
- Disseminate the access control *policy* to organization-defined personnel or roles.
- Develop and document *procedures* to facilitate the implementation of the access control policy and associated access control controls.

	Security control class	Security control family	Identifier
1	Management	Certification, accreditation, and security assessments	CA
2	Management	planning	PL
3	Management	Risk assessment	RA
4	Management	System and services acquisition	SA
5	Operational	Awareness and training	AT
6	Operational	Configuration management	CM
7	Operational	Contingency planning	CP
8	Operational	Incident response	IR
9	Operational	Maintenance	MA
10	Operational	Media protection	MP
11	Operational	Physical and environmental protection	PE
12	Operational	Personnel security	PS
13	Operational	System and information integrity	SI
14	Technical	Access control	AC
15	Technical	Audit and accountability	AU
16	Technical	Identification and authentication	IA
17	Technical	System and communications protection	SC

Figure 3.13   NIST security control families.

Security Control Number	Access Control 20 individual controls	
1	AC-1	Access control policy and procedures	The organization develops, disseminates, and periodically reviews/updates: (1) a formal, documented, control policy; and (2) formal, documented procedures to facilitate the implementation of the access control policy and associated controls.
2	AC-2	Account management	The organization manages information system accounts, employs automated mechanisms, terminates temporary, emergency, and inactive accounts after organization-defined time; ensures actions are audited; and reviews information system accounts.
3	AC-3	Access enforcement	The organization enforces assigned authorizations for controlling access to the system; ensures that access to security functions and information is restricted to authorized personnel in accordance with applicable policy.
4	AC-4	Information flow enforcement	The information system enforces assigned authorizations for controlling the flow of information within the system and between interconnected systems in accordance with applicable policy.
5	AC-5	Separation of duties	The information system enforces separation of duties through assigned access authorizations.
6	AC-6	Least privilege	The information system enforces the most restrictive set of rights/privileges or accesses needed by users.
7	AC-7	Unsuccessful login attempts	The information system enforces a limit of consecutive invalid access attempts by a user during a time period.
8	AC-8	System use notification	The information system displays and approved, system use notification message before granting system access.
9	AC-9	Previous logon notification	The information system notifies the user, upon successful logon, of the date and time of the last logon, and the number of unsuccessful logon attempts since the last successful logon.
10	AC-10	Concurrent session control	The information system limits the number of concurrent sessions for any user.
11	AC-11	Session lock	The information system prevents further access to the system by initiating a session lock that remains in effect until the user reestablishes access using appropriate identification and authentication procedures.
12	AC-12	Session termination	The information system automatically terminates a session after an organization-defined time of inactivity.
13	AC-13	Supervision and review—access control	The organization supervises and reviews the activities of users with respect to the enforcement and usage of information system access controls.
14	AC-14	Permitted actions without identification or authentication	The organization identifies specific user actions that can be performed on the information system without identification or authentication.
15	AC-15	Automated marking	The information system marks output using standard naming conventions to identify and special dissemination, handling, or distribution instructions.
16	AC-16	Automated labeling	The information system appropriately labels information in storage, in process, and in transmission.
17	AC-17	Remote access	The organization employs automated mechanisms to facilitate the monitoring and control of remote access methods.
18	AC-18	Wireless access restrictions	The organization establishes usage restrictions and implementation guidance for wireless technologies and documents, monitors, and controls wireless access.
19	AC-19	Access control for portable and mobile devices	The organization uses authentication and encryption to protect wireless access to the information system.
20	AC-20	Use of external information systems	The organization establishes usage restrictions and guidance for portable and mobile devices and employs removable hard drives or cryptography to protect information residing on portable and mobile devices.

Figure 3.14   Individual controls within the access control family.

- Define personnel or roles to whom the *procedures* are to be disseminated
- Disseminate the *procedures* to organization-defined personnel or roles
- Define the frequency to review and update the current access control policy
- Review and update the current access control policy with the organization-defined frequency
- Define the frequency to review and update the current access control procedures
- Review and update the current access control procedures with the organization-defined frequency

Figure 3.15 shows the *access control policy and procedures* control graphically.

Another example of an individual control is the AC-17, *remote access* control in the NIST access control family. Figure 3.16 shows the remote access control from NIST SP 800-53A Revision 4.

To operationalize or apply the AC-17 remote access control in an organization, a policy document is written and disseminated to all employees. Figure 3.17a and b shows a sample of what a remote access control policy document looks like or can be fashioned for an organization.

For a full listing of all control families and their respective individual controls, see NIST SP 800-53A Revision 4.

ISO/IEC structures their security control families a little differently; however, they have the same common goal of establishing best practices around IT control. The ISO/IEC 27002 standard refers to their control families as security control clauses. There are 14 security control clauses that contain a total of 35 main security categories and 114 individual controls. Figure 3.18 shows the 14 major security control clauses that comprise the ISO/IEC 27002:2013 security standard (ISO/IEC, 2013).

To compare the NIST access control family (AC-17) with ISO/IEC's access control security control clause (A.9). Figure 3.19 shows the ISO/IEC access control security control clause with the respective security categories and individual controls.

There are 14 individual security controls under the four main categories of the ISO/IEC 27002:2013 access control security clause. Security controls are the basic countermeasures and tools that security professionals implement and monitor in order to ensure the confidentiality, integrity, and availability of the information assets in the organization.

Every IT environment is unique in that the organizational culture, strategic goals, and mission; and knowledge, wisdom, and availability of resources all impact the ultimate decisions that managers must make to manage risk and select the appropriate security controls. With the rise in cybersecurity breaches and increase in corporate espionage, organizations cannot afford to take a piecemeal or reactionary approach to protecting their critical systems and information.

Family: Access control

AC-1	Access control policy and procedure	
	Assessment objective: Determine whether the organization:	
AC-1(a)(1)	AC-1(a)(1)[1]	Develops and documents an access control policy that addresses:
	AC-1(a)(1)[1][a]	Purpose
	AC-1(a)(1)[1][b]	Scope
	AC-1(a)(1)[1][c]	Roles
	AC-1(a)(1)[1][d]	Responsibilities
	AC-1(a)(1)[1][e]	Management commitment
	AC-1(a)(1)[1][f]	Coordination among organizational entities
	AC-1(a)(1)[1][g]	Compliance
	AC-1(a)(1)[2]	Defines personnel or roles to whom the access control policy are to be disseminated.
	AC-1(a)(1)[3]	Disseminates the access control policy to organization-defined personnel or roles.
AC1(a)(2)	AC-1(a)(2)[1]	Develops and documents procedures to facilitate the implementation of the access control policy and associated access control controls.
	AC-1(a)(2)[2]	Defines personnel or roles to whom the procedures are to be disseminated.
	AC-1(a)(2)[3]	Disseminates the procedures to organization-defined personnel or roles.
AC1(b)(1)	AC1(b)(1)[1]	Defines the frequency to review and update the current access control policy.
	AC-1(b)(1)[2]	Reviews and updates the current access control policy with the organization-defined frequency.
AC1(b)(2)	AC-1(b)(2)[1]	Defines the frequency to review and update the current access control procedures.
	AC-1(b)(2)[2]	Reviews and updates the current access control procedures with the organization-defined frequency.
	Potential assessment methods and objects: Examine: [SELECT FROM: Access control policy and procedures; other relevant documents or records]. Interview: [SELECT FROM: Organizational personnel with access control responsibilities; organizational personnel with information security responsibilities].	

Figure 3.15 NIST access control policy and procedures control.

Family: Access control

AC-17	Remote access		
	Assessment objective: Determine whether the organization:		
	AC-17(a)	AC-17(a)(1)	Identifies the types of remote access allowed to the information system.
		AC-17(a)(2)	Establishes for each type of remote access allowed:
		AC-17(a)(2)[a]	Usage restrictions
		AC-17(a)(2)[b]	Configuration/connection requirements
		AC-17(a)(2)[c]	Implementation guidance
		AC-17(a)(3)	Documents for each type of remote access allowed:
		AC-17(a)(3)[a]	Usage restrictions
		AC-17(a)(3)[b]	Configuration/connection requirements
		AC-17(a)(3)[c]	Implementation guidance
	AC-17(b)		Authorizes remote access to the information system prior to allowing such connections.

Potential assessment methods and objects:
Examine: [SELECT FROM: Access control policy; procedures addressing remote access implementation an usage (including restrictions); configuration management plan; security plan; information system configuration settings and associated documentation; remote access authorizations; information system audit records; other relevant documents or records].
Interview: [SELECT FROM: Organizational personnel with responsibilities for managing remote access connections; system/network administrators; organizational personnel with information security responsibilities].

Figure 3.16 NIST Remote access control.

ABC		**ABC Company Standard Operating Procedure**	

Subject:	Remote Access Policy	**Created Date:**	2/28/2015
Policy ID:	T-1017	**Effective Date:**	03/23/2015
Department:	ALL	**Revision Date:**	2/28/2015
Author:	Anne Kohnke	**Revision No.:**	1.0

PURPOSE

The purpose of this policy is to state the requirements for remote access to computing resources hosted at ABC Company using remote access technologies.

MOTIVATION

In order to access computing resources at ABC Company from remote locations, use of ABC remote access services is required. A remote access connection is a secured private network connection built on top of a public network. Remote access provides a secure, encrypted connection or tunnel over the Internet between an individual computer and a private network. Use of remote access allows authorized members of the ABC Company community to securely access ABC network resources as if they were at corporate headquarters.

ROLES AND RESPONSIBILITIES

This policy applies to all ABC Company employees, contractors, vendors and agents with a ABC Company-owned or personally-owned computer used to connect to the ABC Company network. This policy applies to remote access connections used to perform work on behalf of ABC Company including reading or sending email and viewing intranet web resources

Department of Information Technology
  • Responsible for implementing and maintaining ABC Company's remote access services. Therefore, IT is also responsible for activities related to this policy and will manage the configuration of ABC Company's remote access Service.

Department Managers:
  • Enforce this policy

All Employees:
  • Understand and comply with this policy.

POLICY FOR REMOTE ACCESS

ABC Company employees and authorized third parties (customers, vendors, suppliers, etc.) may under some circumstances, utilize remote access to access the ABC Company computing resources for which they have been granted access. Regular, full-time employees that have a valid ABC Domain User Account may request remote access to the ABC network by completing a Remote Access Request Form. A letter of justification must accompany the request. The letter should address, in sufficient detail, what resources will be accessed and how they cannot be accessed by conventional means. Requests omitting a letter of justification will be returned to the requestor as incomplete. A copy of the Remote Access Request Form may be found in the forms section of the ABC Company website.

Figure 3.17 Sample remote access control policy document.

(Continued)

ABC Company Standard Operating Procedure

Remote access is valid for a set period of time. Request or should indicate the data remote access should take effect and the date access should expire. Remote access may be granted for a period of up to twelve months, after which remote access for the account will expire. Requesters will be notified via tele or email approximately thirty (30) days before remote access expires. Account holders may resubmit a Remote Access Request Form up to thirty (30) days before the remote access expiration date to continue remote access without disruption.

General

1. Storage of confidential information on any non-state owned device is prohibited. Confidential information may not be stored on any portable device without prior written approval from agency Secretary (or delegated authority). Approved storage on any portable device must be encrypted.

2. It is the responsibility of ABC Company employees and contractors with remote access privileges to ABC Company's corporate network to ensure that their remote access connection is given the same consideration as the user's on-site connection to ABC Company.

3. All remote access users are expected comply with ABC Company policies, may not perform illegal activities, and may not use the access for outside business interests.

Requirements

1. Remote access must be strictly controlled by the use of unique user credentials. For information on creating a strong password please review ABC Company's *Password Policy & Guidelines*.

2. Remote access passwords are to be used only by the individual to whom they were assigned and may not to be shared.

3. All remote access connections that utilize a shared infrastructure, such as the Internet, must utilize some form of encryption. For information on acceptable encryption technologies please review ABC Company's Acceptable Encryption Policy.

4. Reconfiguration of a home user's equipment for the purpose of split-tunneling or dual homing is not permitted at any time.

5. All hosts that are connected to ABC Company internal networks via remote access technologies must have up-to-date anti-virus software implemented.

6. All hosts that are connected to ABC Company internal networks via remote access technologies must have current operating system security patches installed.

7. Personal equipment that is used to connect to ABC Company's networks must meet the requirements of ABC Company-owned equipment for remote access.

8. Organizations or individuals who wish to implement non-standard Remote Access solutions to the ABC Company production network must obtain prior approval from ABC Company.

Enforcement

Any employee found to have violated this policy may be subject to disciplinary action, up to and including termination of employment. Deliberate, unauthorized disclosure of confidential information may result in civil and/or criminal penalties.

Figure 3.17 (*Continued*)   Sample remote access control policy document.

Identifier		ISO/IEC 27002 security control clauses
1	A.5	Information security policies
2	A.6	Organization of information security
3	A.7	Human resource security
4	A.8	Asset management
5	A.9	Access control
6	A.10	Cryptography
7	A.11	Physical and environmental security
8	A.12	Operations security
9	A.13	Communications security
10	A.14	System acquisition, development, and maintenance
11	A.15	Supplier relationships
12	A.16	Information security incident management
13	A.17	Information security aspects of business continuity management
14	A.18	Compliance

Figure 3.18   ISO/IEC security control clauses.

Chapter Summary

Organizations are experiencing an array of security issues from DOS attacks to web application attacks and from cyber-espionage to insider threats (Verizon Enterprise Solutions, 2014). Any part of a computing system whether it be hardware, software, storage media, data, and people can be the target of a crime and any system is most vulnerable at its weakest point. Surprisingly, many organizations do not have insider-threat programs in place to prevent, detect, and respond to internal threats.

It is the responsibility of the board and the executive management to develop and practice corporate governance. The aim of corporate governance is to provide strategic direction, ensure that business objectives are achieved, manage risk appropriately, and ensure the organization's resources are used responsibility. Information security governance is a subset of corporate governance and the most fundamental purpose of an information security program is to help ensure the preservation of the organization and its ability to operate. To exercise effective IT governance, boards of directors and executive management must have a clear understanding of what to expect from their enterprise's information security program. Ideally, information security will be managed in such a way as to create an organizational security culture.

An enterprise security framework is an overarching structure that identifies interlinked key elements, which collectively contribute to a consistent approach to managing risk. The interlinked key elements or principles often include processes to identify the current state of the organization, levels of risk the organization is willing to accept, security requirements, priorities, strategic goals and mission, resource availability and competencies, compliance, security controls, implementation of security controls, best practices, authorization levels, assessment, financial

	Main security category	Control objective	Individual controls
		ISO/IEC 27002:2013, Security control clause: access control	
9.1	Business requirements of access control	To limit access to information and information processing facilities.	9.1.1 Access control policy 9.1.2 Access to networks and network services
9.2	User access management	To ensure authorized user access and to prevent unauthorized access to systems and services.	9.2.1 User registration and de-registration 9.2.2 User access provisioning 9.2.3 Management of privileged access rights 9.2.4 Management of secret authentication information of users 9.2.5 Review of user access rights 9.2.6 Removal or adjustment of access rights
9.3	User responsibilities	To make users accountable for safeguarding their authentication information.	9.3.1 Use of secret authentication information
9.4	System and application access control	To prevent unauthorized access to systems and applications.	9.4.1 Information access restriction 9.4.2 Secure log-on procedures 9.4.3 Password management system 9.4.4 Use of privileged utility programs 9.4.5 Access control to program source code

Figure 3.19   ISO/IEC access control security control clause.

budgets and costs, governance, disaster recovery, and ongoing monitoring. From a holistic perspective, the absence of a planned approach can result in a rather piece-meal approach or a series of reactionary implementations to satisfy those in the organization who have the loudest voice.

For an IT security system to be effective and add value, a well-defined organization-wide security framework needs to be incorporated that involves all levels of the organizational structure and fine-tuned over time. There are a variety of IT security frameworks that have been widely adopted and some cases, the industry or regulatory requirements may drive which security framework to use. This chapter provided an overview of nine widely used IT security frameworks: COSO, ITIL, ISO/IEC, COBIT, NIST, CSF, ISF, PCI DSS, and SANS.

Once an organization has identified and documented their security requirements and a thorough risk assessment has been conducted, appropriate security controls should be selected. Internal security controls are the safeguards or countermeasures that are deployed to protect the confidentiality, integrity, and availability of the IT environment. There are generally three types of IT security controls: preventive, detective, and reactive. Another facet of controls is that they can have technical, administrative, and physical implementations.

Frameworks such as NIST SP 800-53 and ISO/IEC 27002 have clear sets of processes and controls to provide an IT governance structure and control within an organization. Many organizations find that they need to use a blend of security standards and controls to accomplish their business objectives and satisfy auditing requirements. This chapter showed a comparison of the access control set of controls from NIST and ISO/IEC and provided an example of how to apply or operationalize a remote access policy that can be used in an organization.

Key Terms

COBIT—formed in 1998 by the ISACA, the COBIT were created to advance international thinking on governance and the management of enterprise IT system.

COSO—it is also known as the Treadway Commission, named after the Chairman.

CSF—it was created in 2013 by executive order and formally titled the *Framework for Improving Critical Infrastructure Cybersecurity*.

ISF—founded in 1989, it is a global membership organization that developed the *Standard of Good Practice for Information Security*.

ISO/IEC—the ISO is a global membership organization that jointly published the current documents with the IEC for use as a standard to develop an information security program.

IT Security Governance—is the system by which an organization directs and controls IT security.

ITIL—it was developed in the mid-1980s by the UK Government, originated as a collection of 31 books each covering a specific practice within IT management.

NIST—it is a nonregulatory agency whose mission is to increase the visibility and competitiveness of US innovation.

PCI DSS—the Payment Card Industry, formed in 2004, combined five major credit card information system security policies and developed the Data Security Standard.

SANS Institute—founded in 1989, the SANS institute is a private research and education organization that publishes a top 20 critical security controls that are widely used recommendations.

Security control framework—is a structure that organizes and categorizes security controls or countermeasures that are processes and procedures established to minimize risk and create business value.

Security controls—are safeguards to prevent, detect, counteract, or minimize security risks to information assets and physical property.

References

Arraj, V. (2013). *ITIL: The Basics*. A Compliance Process Partners White paper. https://www.axelos.com.

Berson, A. and Dubov, L. (2011). *Master Data Management and Data Governance, 2nd ed.* New York, NY: McGraw-Hill.

Cartlidge, A., Rudd, C., Smith, M., Wigzel, P., Rance, S., Shaw, S., and Wright, T. (2012). *An Introductory Overview of ITIL 2011.* itSMF UK. London, UK: TSO.

Committee of Sponsoring Organizations. (2004). *Enterprise Risk Management Framework Reference Copy.* https://www.coso.org.

Davis, C. and Schiller, M. (2011). *IT Auditing: Using Controls to Protect Information Assets, 2nd ed.* New York, NY: McGraw-Hill.

Iden, J. and Eikebrokk, T. R. (2014). Using the ITIL process reference model for realizing IT governance: An empirical investigation. *Information Systems Management*, 31: 37–58.

Information Security Forum. (2014). *The Standard of Good Practice for Information Security.* ISF.

Information Systems Audit and Control Association. (2012). *COBIT 5: A Business Framework for the Governance and Management of Enterprise IT.* Rolling Meadows, IL: ISACA.

International Organization for Standardization/International Electrotechnical Commission. (2013). *Information Technology Security Techniques Code of Practice for Information Security Controls.* ISO/IEC.

Marrone, M., Gacenga, F., Cater-Steel, A., and Kolbe, L. (2014). IT service management: A cross-national study of ITIL adoption. *Communications of the Association for Information Systems*, 34(49): 865–892.

National Institute of Standards and Technology. (2014). *NICE Cybersecurity Workforce Framework 2.0.* Gaithersburg, MD: NIST.

National Institute of Standards and Technology Special Publication 800-53. (2007). *Recommended Security Controls for Federal Information Systems Revision 2.* Gaithersburg, MD: NIST.

National Institute of Standards and Technology Special Publication 800-53A Revision 4. (2014). *Assessing Security and Privacy Controls for Federal Information Systems and Organizations.* Gaithersburg, MD: NIST.

PCI DSS. (2015). *The Prioritized Approach to Pursue PCI DSS Compliance.* Payment Card Industry Security Standards Council.

SANS. (2014). *Critical Security Controls for Effective Cyber Defense.* SANS Institute. https://www.sans.org/critical-security-controls.

US State of Cybercrime Survey. (2014). CERT Division of the Software Engineering Institute at Carnegie Mellon University.

Verizon. (2015). *2015 Data Breach Investigations Report.* Verizon Enterprise Solutions.

Verizon Enterprise Solutions. (2014). *Verizon Data Breach Investigations Report.* Retrieved from https://www.verizonenterprise.com/DBIR/2014/.

Chapter 4

What Are Controls and Why Are They Important?

After reading this chapter and completing the case project, the reader will:

- Understand the definition of controls and their importance in protecting information and communications technology (ICT) systems from security threats and vulnerabilities
- Be able to distinguish between goal-based and implementation controls while understanding each broad control type within each of the two groups
- Understand common approaches toward security control formulation and development

No matter how large or small an organization, there needs to be a plan to ensure the security of critical ICT assets. Such a plan is called a security program by information security professionals and is facilitated through the selection and implementation of appropriate control mechanisms designed to act as countermeasures for preserving confidentiality, availability, and integrity of all components that make up the organizations ICT infrastructure. Whether the plan is five or two hundred pages long, the process of creating a control-based security program will make organizations think holistically about their security. A security program provides the framework for keeping an organization at a desired security level by assessing the risks they face, deciding how they will mitigate them, and planning for how to keep the program and security practices up to date.

In this chapter, the focus will be on the controls that security programs are built on. Through a complete discussion of management and behavioral controls you will come away knowing what they are and how they are formulated. In understanding the underlying principles associated with controls, you will also understand how they are aggregated into an everyday system of integrated security activities.

Picking Up Where Chapter 1 Left Off

In Chapter 1, you learned about three fundamental pillars for ICT security: confidentiality, integrity, and availability. However, as the security discipline has evolved, it has become apparent that a fourth core requirement is missing: accountability. Accountability addresses the need for the ability to trace the activities to the responsible source. For example, audit logs and digital signing of emails would both be controls that ensure accountability. Although you would not see the combined concept of the security objectives—confidentiality, integrity, availability, and accountability (which we will now reference with the acronym CIAA)—on a Certified Information Systems Security Professional (CISSP) exam, other certification exams, or security publications, many security professionals have been using this expanded view of cybersecurity for many years. Given the increased impact of supply chain concerns within the scope of ICT risk management, accountability requirements have come to the forefront of an organization's security priority list.

Another introductory level security concept is that there are three underlying principles that influence cybersecurity standards, guidelines, and control decisions: least privilege, separation of duties, and defensive in depth. The CIAA pillars discussed above and these three cybersecurity principles are effectively managed through the development, implementation, and audit of security controls. In cybersecurity, there are five functions of controls: identify, protective, detective, responsive, and recovery. The Framework for Improving Critical Infrastructure Cybersecurity (CSF) describes each of these five functions as indicated in the following list:

- *Identify*—develop the organizational understanding to manage cybersecurity risk to systems, assets, data, and capabilities
- *Protect*—develop and implement the appropriate safeguards to ensure delivery of critical infrastructure services
- *Detect*—develop and implement the appropriate activities to identify the occurrence of a cybersecurity event
- *Respond*—develop and implement the appropriate activities to take action regarding a detected cybersecurity event
- *Recover*—develop and implement the appropriate activities to maintain plans for resilience and to restore any capabilities or services that were impaired due to a cybersecurity event (National Institute of Standards and Technology, 2014b)

Each of those functions is supported by one or more administrative, technical, and operational control categories. By definition, controls are a security mechanism, policy, or procedure that can successfully counter attacks, reduce risk, resolve vulnerabilities, and otherwise improve security within an organization. The National Institute of Standards and Technology (NIST) (2014a) Special Publication 800-53 *Security and Privacy Controls for Federal Information Systems and Organizations* more formally defines controls as stated below.

> ... the safeguards/countermeasures prescribed for information systems or organizations that are designed to: (i) protect the confidentiality, integrity, and availability of information that is processed, stored, and transmitted by those systems/organizationsthe; and (ii) satisfy a set of defined security requirements.

Whether an organization is considering a technical or operational control to mitigate risk, or an administrative solution such as training and new procedures or policies, the control needs to focus on the hardware, telecommunications, and software that protect sensitive information in one of the following three states:

- Data at rest
- Data in transit
- Data in process

These information-centric states define what the control needs to affect. The threats and vulnerabilities that must be considered change dramatically based on the state of the data, although the sensitivity factor does not. These criteria need to be given consideration as appropriate controls are selected. Together, the underlying principles related to information states, and the information security fundamentals introduced in Chapter 1 provide the basis for security control selection, development, and audit.

Goal-Based Security Controls

Security controls help reduce risks in an organization and to be efficient, cybersecurity professionals are expected to understand them from five perspectives: their goals, and how they are classified and selected, how they are implemented, how they are tested for effectiveness, and finally how they are audited.

As stated in the previous section, it is normal to see controls referred to as countermeasures or safeguards, referencing their ability to counter threats and provide safeguards to reduce vulnerabilities, but they are all the same. More specifically, security controls attempt to prevent or limit the impact of a security incident. A security incident is an adverse event or series of events that can negatively affect the confidentiality, integrity, or availability of an organization's IT systems and data. This includes intentional attacks, malicious software (malware) infections, accidental data loss, and much more (Figure 4.1).

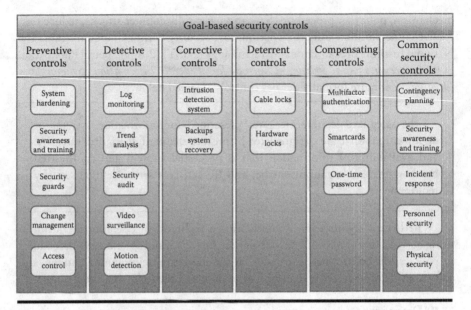

Figure 4.1 Goal-based security controls.

In this and other chapters of this book, we used the Federal Information Processing Standard Publication 199 (FIPS 199) as a means for classifying security controls supporting the five functions of the CSF throughout the risk management life cycle. Another common way of classifying controls is based on their goals in relationship to security incidents (NIST, 2004). Though we have already seen reference to one of these goal-based controls through the description of the CSF functional breakdown, some common classifications are prevention, detective, corrective, deterrent, and compensating.

- *Preventive controls:* attempt to prevent an incident from occurring.
- *Detective controls:* attempt to detect incidents after they have occurred.
- *Corrective controls:* attempt to reverse the impact of an incident.
- *Deterrent controls:* attempt to discourage individuals from causing an incident.
- *Compensating controls:* are alternative controls used when a primary control is not feasible.
- *Common controls:* are implemented across multiple ICT systems.

Preventive Controls

In a perfect world, an organization would not have any security incidents and that is the primary goal of preventive controls. Some examples include the following:

- *Hardening:* Is the process in which an ICT system or application is provided a greater level of security than its default configuration. This may include disabling unneeded services and protocols, protecting management interfaces and applications, protecting passwords, and disabling unnecessary accounts.

■ *Security awareness and training:* These involve making users aware of security vulnerabilities and threats thereby preventing incidents. When users understand how social engineers operate, for example, they are less likely to be tricked. Typically, uneducated users can be easily deceived into giving a social engineer their passwords, but educated users will see through the tactics and keep passwords secure.

■ *Security guards:* These prevent and deter many physical attacks. For example, guards can prevent unauthorized access into secure areas of a building by first verifying user identities.

■ *Change management:* Ensures that changes do not result in unintended outages. For example, as an alternative to managers making ad hoc changes, they could be expected to submit the change to a change management process where further review of the change takes place. Note that change management is an operational control, which attempts to prevent incidents. In other words, it is both an operational control and a preventive control.

■ *Account disablement policy:* Ensures that ICT system access accounts are disabled when employment with the organization is terminated. This prevents anyone, including ex-employees, from continuing to use these accounts.

Detective Controls

While preventive controls attempt to prevent security incidents, it is inevitable that an organization will be victim to a security event at some point. Detective controls attempt to sense when vulnerabilities have been exploited, resulting in a security incident. An important point is that detective controls discover the event after it is occurred. Some examples of detective controls include the following:

■ *Log monitoring:* There are many different log records that detail the activity on ICT systems and networks. For example, firewall logs record details of all traffic that the firewall blocked. By monitoring such logs, it becomes possible to detect incidents. Some automated methods of log monitoring automatically detect potential incidents and report them to the appropriate organizational personnel immediately after they have occurred.

■ *Trend analysis:* In addition to monitoring logs to detect any single incident, organizations can also monitor logs to detect trends that occur in system and network activity. For example, an intrusion detection system (IDS) attempts to detect attacks and raise alerts or alarms. By analyzing past alerts, the Cybersecurity Incident Response Team (CSIRT) can identify trends such as an increase of attacks on a specific system.

■ *Security audit:* As you read in Chapter 2, security audits can examine the security posture of an organization. For example, a password audit can determine if the password policy is ensuring the use of strong passwords. Similarly, a periodic review of user rights can detect if users have more permissions than necessary, given their system access responsibilities.

■ *Video surveillance:* A closed-circuit television (CCTV) system can record activity and detect what occurred. It is worth noting that video surveillance can also be used as a deterrent control.

■ *Motion detection:* Many alarm systems are able to detect motion from potential intruders, and initiate alarms when the potential for physical security attack is imminent.

Comparing Detection and Prevention Controls

Before continuing, it is worth underscoring the differences between detection and prevention controls. A detection control cannot predict when an incident will occur and it cannot prevent it from taking place. Prevention security controls stop the incident from occurring at all. For example, recall our previous discussion of video cameras and guards. A simple camera that is in plain view and has no recording capabilities can prevent incidents from taking place because it acts as a deterrent. Now, compare that to a CCTV system with recording abilities. Such a device would include cameras, which can deter and prevent incidents, but the full system is also a detection control because of its recording capabilities. Cybersecurity professionals can take advantage of those capabilities by review the recordings to detect incidents after they have occurred. Likewise, guards are primarily prevention security controls. They will deter many incidents just by their presence. If attackers try to circumvent a security system, such as trying to sneak into a secured area, guards can intervene and stop the attack before it ever takes place.

Corrective Controls

Corrective controls are designed to reverse the impact of an incident or problem after it has occurred. Recall the discussion provided of the five CSF functions. Corrective controls are typically implemented in order to achieve the outcomes of response and recovery. Some examples of corrective controls are as follows:

■ *Active IDS:* Active IDSs are a form of detection system that detects an attack and then makes necessary configuration changes to the environment in order to block the attack from continuing.

■ *Backups and system recovery:* Backups ensure that operations personnel can recover data if it is lost or corrupted. Similarly, system recovery procedures ensure the CSIRT and oversight managers can recover a system after a failure.

Deterrent Controls

Deterrent controls are designed to discourage a threat. Some deterrent controls attempt to discourage potential attackers from initiating the event, while others focus on internal security by discouraging employees from violating established organizational security policy.

Many deterrent controls can be effectively described as preventive controls. For example, we have stated that a security guard is charged with the responsibility of controlling access to a restricted area of a building. That guard will deter most unsanctioned entry into the restricted area. This deterrence prevents security incidents related to unauthorized access. Moreover, a social engineer might try to hoax a building receptionist but if organizational security policy requires visitors to go through the security guard first, it will deter many social engineers and prevent unauthorized entry.

While deterrent controls can be implemented using physical artifacts or through software configuration, the following list identifies some physical security controls used to deter threats:

■ *Cable locks:* Securing computer equipment to furniture with a cable lock deters thieves from stealing that equipment. Thieves cannot easily steal computer equipment secured this way. If they try to remove the lock, they destroy the equipment being secured. On the other hand, a thief could cut the cable with a large cable cutter. However, someone walking through a secured area with a four-foot cable cutter would certainly look suspicious.

■ *Hardware locks:* Other locks such as locked doors securing a wiring closet or a server room also deter attacks. Many server bay cabinets also include locking cabinet doors.

Compensating Security Controls

Compensating controls are alternative controls used instead of a primary control. As an example, an organization might require smart cards as part of a multifactor authentication solution. However, it might take time for new employees to receive their smart card. To allow new employees to access the network and still maintain a high level of security, the organization might choose to implement a time-based one-time password (TOTP) as a compensating control. The compensating control still provides multifactor authentication.

Common Security Controls

An organization level view of an ICT security program requires the identification of common security controls that can be applied to one or more ICT systems within an organization or across an entire supply chain.

Common security controls can apply to

- All organizational ICT systems
- A group of information systems at a specific site
- Common information systems, subsystems, or applications (i.e., common hardware, software, and/or firmware embedded within ICT components) installed at multiple operational sites

While many controls are unique in their implementation, assessment, and audit procedures, common security controls have the following characteristics:

- The development, implementation, and audit of common security controls can be assigned to a centralized ICT function within the organization (other than the functional area whose systems will implement or use those common security controls).
- The results from the audit of the common security controls can be used to support the security certification and accreditation processes in the case the controls are implemented in ICT systems within federal agencies. Likewise, the results can be used for affirmation of regulatory compliance in the case the controls are implemented in ICT systems of organizations within the private sector.

Many management and operational controls (e.g., contingency planning controls, incident response controls, security awareness and training controls, personnel security controls, and physical security controls) are excellent candidates for common security control status. The underlying objective is to reduce security costs by centrally managing the development, implementation, and audit of the common security controls designated by the organization, and in turn, sharing audit results with the users of information systems where those common security controls are applied. Security controls not designated as common controls are considered system-specific controls and are the responsibility of the individual groups providing oversight of each ICT system.

A control is considered hybrid when one part of the control is common to multiple systems, while another part of the control is considered to be system specific. For example, an organization may view a security control related to incident response policy and procedures as a hybrid control with the policy portion of the control considered to be common and the procedures portion of the control, system specific.

The process of grouping security controls into either common security controls or system-specific security controls can save the organization a significant amount of money in casts associated with control development and implementation. Moreover, this grouping mechanism provides a greater degree of consistency of control application across the entire organization and its supply chain. Likewise, significant savings can also be realized in the audit process. Rather than auditing common security controls in every information system, the audit process draws upon any applicable results from the most current assessment of the common security controls performed at the organizational level.

Implementation-Based Security Controls

Another method of classifying security controls is based on how they are implemented. The three common implementation classifications are technical, management, and operational (Figure 4.2).

- Technical controls use technology.
- Management controls use administrative or management methods.
- Operational controls are implemented by people in day-to-day operations.

Technical Controls

A technical control can be characterized as one that uses technology to reduce vulnerabilities. The security team installs and configures a technical control, and the

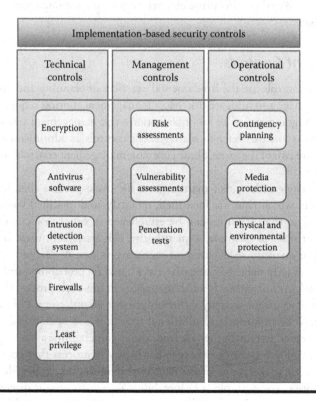

Figure 4.2   Implementation-based security goals.

technical control in turn provides the appropriate level of protection automatically. The following list provides a few examples.

- *Encryption:* Encryption is a strong technical control used to protect the confidentiality of data. This includes data transferred over a network, and data stored on devices such as servers, desktop computers, and mobile devices. Cryptography uses the combination of algorithms and public key infrastructures to convert data into an undecipherable format during transfer.
- *Antivirus software:* Once installed, the antivirus software provides protection against malware and spyware infection.
- *IDSs:* An IDS is installed and configured by an organization in order to monitor a network or host for intrusions and provide ongoing protection against identified threats.
- *Firewalls:* Network firewalls restrict network traffic going in and out of a network.
- *Least privilege:* The principle of least privilege stipulates that an individual or process is granted only the privileges needed to perform an intended task or function. Based on this principle, privileges are a combination of rights and permissions.

Management Controls

Management controls use the fundamental practices of planning and assessment to reduce and manage and mitigate risk. Most management controls require implementation of an ongoing review of an organization's risk management strategies. Some guidelines and standards refer to management controls as administrative controls, though they are two of the same. Some common management controls are as follows:

- *Risk assessment:* Is a risk management life-cycle process that serves as the means in which risks are identified, quantify, and qualified within an organization so that priorities can be established in order to focus on the most serious risks. For example, a quantitative risk assessment uses cost and asset values to quantify risks based on monetary values. A qualitative risk assessment uses judgments to categorize risks based on probability and impact.
- *Vulnerability assessment:* Is a risk management life-cycle process that attempts to identify current security vulnerabilities or weaknesses within the organization. When appropriate, additional technical and operational controls are implemented to reduce the risk from those vulnerabilities.
- *Penetration test:* Is a risk management life-cycle process that goes a step further than a vulnerability assessment by attempting to exploit identified vulnerabilities. For example, a vulnerability assessment might discover a server is not kept up-to-date with current patches making it vulnerable to security

attack. A penetration test would attempt to compromise the server by exploiting one or more of the unpatched vulnerabilities.

Operational Controls

Operational controls help ensure that day-to-day operations of an organization comply with their underlying risk management plan. The big distinction between operational and technical controls is that people (not technology) implement operational controls. Examples of operational controls include the following:

- *Contingency planning:* Business continuity includes several activities that help an organization plan and prepare for potential ICT security events. The goal is to reduce the overall impact on the organization if an event occurs.
- *Media protection:* Media includes physical media such as USB flash drives, external and internal drives, and backup tapes. The protection controls can range from protocols established for keeping media in a secure area within an organizations data center, to the secure transfer and storage of archive data at an undisclosed off-site location.
- *Physical and environmental protection:* Includes physical controls such as cameras, door locks, and environmental controls such as heating and ventilation systems. These are similar to the detective and deterrent goal-based controls discussed earlier.

Combining Implementation with Goals

It is important to note that the control types (technical, management, and operational) and control goals (preventive, detective, corrective, deterrent, and compensating) are not mutually exclusive. In other words, you can describe most controls with both terms. We just saw evidence of that in the discussion of physical and environmental protection operational controls.

As another relevant example, encryption is a preventive technical control. It prevents the loss of data confidentiality and thus classified as a preventive control and is implemented with technology so it is also classified as a technical control.

Tying Security Controls to Architecture

It is common practice for the organization to allocate security controls to an ICT system consistent with the organization's enterprise architecture and information security architecture. Enterprise architecture is a management practice employed by organizations to maximize the effectiveness of mission/business processes and information resources in helping to achieve mission/business success. "Enterprise architecture establishes a clear and unambiguous connection from investments (including information security investments) to measurable performance improvements whether for an entire organization or portion of an organization. Enterprise architecture also provides an opportunity to standardize, consolidate, and optimize information technology assets" (Loche and Gallagher, 2011). Within the scope of standardized system life cycles, "both product and process standards contain generic advice because it has to be appropriate to all situations that the standard is written to address. For that reason, the recommendations of both product and process standards have to be customized for their advice to apply correctly. In its applied, real-world form, this customization is typically called process engineering or enterprise architecture" (Shoemaker and Sigler, 2015). Moreover, security professionals no longer view security as a product or a solution. Rather, it is commonly viewed as an in-depth system that must be incorporated throughout the business. The best way to manage security risk and compliance requirements is through a systematic approach that addresses the entire security life cycle and is built on a standards-based security infrastructure. That infrastructure is widely known as the organization's information security architecture (sometimes called enterprise information security architecture). If organizations do not implement effective security controls they place data integrity, information confidentiality, and the availability of business-critical applications at a much greater risk.

"The information security architecture is an integral part of the organization's enterprise architecture. It represents that portion of the enterprise architecture specifically addressing information system resilience and providing architectural information for the implementation of security capabilities. The primary purpose of the information security architecture is to ensure that mission/business process-driven information security requirements are consistently and cost effectively achieved in organizational information systems and the environments in which those systems operate consistent with the organizational risk management strategy" (Loche and Gallagher, 2011). As an information security architecture evolves, organizations should identify and implement common security controls supporting multiple ICT systems to the greatest extent possible. In addition to individual functional components, such ICT systems include existing and newly developed supply chain management (SCM), customer relationship management (CRM), enterprise resource planning (ERP), and electronic commerce systems. As mentioned in a previous section, when common controls are used to support a specific ICT system, they are referred to by each individual system as inherited controls. Common controls provide a cost effective and consistent information security across the organization and can, in turn, use to simplify risk management activities. Regardless of the organization's ICT infrastructure, the main point to be made is that by applying security controls to an ICT system as either system specific, hybrid, or common, it becomes a necessity for the organization to assign responsibility and accountability to each individual organizational entity to ensure the proper development, implementation, assessment, authorization, and monitoring of each of the individual controls.

The former point is not to down play the high degree of flexibility an organization has in deciding which families of security controls are appropriate to satisfy the intended identify, protect, detect, respond, and recover functional outcomes throughout the organization and its supply chain. Since the security control formulation and development process includes the assignment and establishment of security capabilities provided by the selected security controls, the organization must open the lines of effective communication among all affected individuals that are either receiving or providing the security capabilities. To that extent, the communication must include but not be limited to making certain that common control effectiveness, continuous monitoring, and audit results are readily available to the individuals within the organization and supply chain that are directly affected by the inheriting common controls, and that any configuration management applied to the common controls are effectively communicated to those affected by such changes.

Figure 4.3 illustrates how security controls are tied to enterprise IT governance and information security infrastructures within an organization using risk management to produce information for senior management, informing them on the ongoing state of organizational ICT systems security, and the missions and business processes supported by those systems.

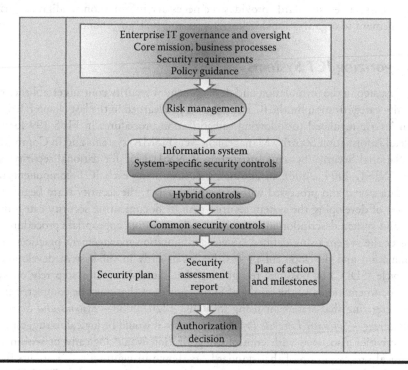

Figure 4.3   Enterprise IT governance through authorization.

The Security Control Formulation and Development Process

Any information resource with value to an organization requires some degree of security protection. For example, in the case of federal systems, the appropriate level of security is proportionate to the value of the system including the value of the system components as much as the value of the information that the system stores and processes, the degree of harm that could result from a loss of confidentiality, integrity, or availability, and the risk that such loss could occur. These factors are the focus of the risk assessment process for ICT systems and provide a starting point for formulation and development of security controls. The wide variety of ICT system components within an organization's supply chain result in significantly different security requirements, with the potential for equally different corresponding protective mechanisms to satisfy the requirements. The activities explained in this section, which make up the underlying Risk Management Framework, are intended to assist organizations in approaching cybersecurity in a consistent manner regardless of how varied or unique the ICT system components may be. The use of standard methods for categorizing, selecting, implementing authorizing, assessing, and monitoring helps to provide a consistent basis from which to make control decisions. From an organizational perspective, such a framework as associated standards provides the necessary information to align ICT risk management to organizational risk strategies and ICT governance.

Categorizing ICT Systems

The first step in the formulation and development of security controls establishes the security categorization for the ICT system. As you learned in the last chapter, federal agencies are regulated to following categorization procedures in FIPS 199 for the Federal Information Security Management Act (FISMA) systems and in Committee on National Security Systems Instruction (CNSSI) 1253 for national security systems (NIST, 2004; 2008). In addition to categorizing each ICT component and the data stored and processed within them, in step 1, the security team begins the process of developing the system security plan by documenting security categorization and system description information, while executing appropriate procedures to register the system using defined system configuration management practices. The formulation and development process begins as early in the system development life cycle (SDLC) as possible, recognizing that the tasks in this step rely on system documentation and the results of SDLC processes that must be completed first. Characterizing that statement using ISO/IEC 12207:2008—*Systems and Software Engineering—Software Lifecycle Processes* as a basis, it would be logical to suggest that the activities associated with control categorization would logically fit within the technical process group of that standard. As shown in Figure 4.4, key inputs from the early stages of the SDLC include a system concept of operations (CONOPS) or

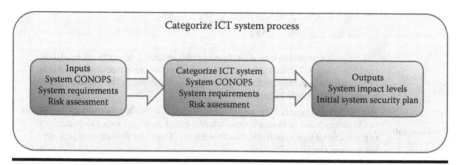

Figure 4.4   Categorize ICT system process.

other pertinent documentation, none of which are more important than the system functional and technical requirements specified within the system requirements specification. Some security and privacy documentation produced outside the control formulation process are also useful for security categorization, including privacy impact assessments and initial system risk assessments, particularly to help identify anticipated impacts from threat events and comparing those impacts to predefined levels. The impact level determined through the security categorization process is the key output of step 1, documented in the draft system security plan along with the system description.

Without discounting the importance of the planning processes that should occur before the categorization activities of the control formulation process, the ability to adequately execute subsequent steps depends largely on the results of the security categorization. Moreover, the consequence stemming from systems with higher impact level designations requiring a greater number of security controls and control enhancements, security control implementation, and assessment activities for those systems tend to take longer and require a substantially higher amount of effort and organizational resources. The tasks within the security categorization process identify the potential impact to the organization caused by the loss of confidentiality, integrity, or availability of any of the information in an ICT system. Although private sector organizations and federal agencies follow different guidelines for security categorization and security control selection, a common understanding exists on the definitions of confidentiality, integrity, and availability and of the low-, moderate-, and high-impact levels assigned to information types and information systems. Using the categorization definitions provided in CNSSI 1253 and FIPS 199 as a means to explain, Figure 4.5 shows a definition summary of each categorization level (NIST, 2004; 2008).

The process of security control categorization stipulates that organizations first identify each type of information stored or processed by an ICT system and then consider the potential impact corresponding to confidentiality, integrity, and availability. After assigning impact levels to the information types, the categorization of all data types relevant for an ICT system dictates the security categorization of the entire ICT system.

FIPS 199 security control categories and definitions	
Low	The potential impact is Low if the loss of confidentiality, integrity, or availability could be expected to have a limited adverse effect on organizational operations, organizational assets, or individuals, other organizations, or the national security interests of the United States.
Moderate	The potential impact is Moderate if the loss of confidentiality, integrity, or availability could be expected to have a serious adverse effect on organizational operations, organizational assets, individuals, other organizations, or the national security interests of the United States.
High	The potential impact is High if the loss of confidentiality, integrity, or availability could be expected to have a severe or catastrophic adverse effect on organizational operations, organizational assets, individuals, other organizations, or the national security interests of the United States.

Figure 4.5   FIPS 199 security control categories and definitions.

Identifying Information Types

The first task in the security categorization process is to identify the types of information the system will receive as input, store, process, or provide as output. This step requires a thorough understanding of the system's purpose and intended use. Pertinent information resources necessary to accomplish this task are typically obtained either by reviewing the CONOPS or other system description documentation developed during the SDLC initiation phase or by discussing the system and its underlying data with the users and management from within the functional areas supported by the system. Depending on organizational policies and procedures for security categorization, organizations may group information types into categories defined by guidelines such as FIPS 199 or CNSSI 1253. Organizations need to establish and are encouraged to use catalog of information types to establish consistent information type identification and consistent security categorization determinations for information types across all the information systems an organization operates. Many federal agencies, for example, use NIST SP 800-60—*Guide to Mapping Types of Information and Information Systems to Security Categories*, as a guideline for their categorization activity (NIST, 2008). However, organizations have the flexibility to define or identify their own information types and to select their own impact levels.

Categorization of Information Types

Each information type associated with ICT systems must be evaluated to determine the potential impact to the organization stemming from the loss of the three security objectives: confidentiality, integrity, or availability. In this task, the organization considers the impact level for each security objective independently. The end result is a three-part categorization for each information type. Syntactically, each categorization can be represented as

Information type = [confidentiality, level; integrity, level; availability, level]

Organizations need to consider many different types of possible adverse effects to accurately determine the appropriate impact level, since the impact level assigned represents the worst-case scenario, regardless of the nature of the security event. Moreover, to ensuring that system-specific impact level determinations are consistent with predetermined standards and guidelines, organizations can use impact and risk information provided in risk assessment documentation to validate their information type categorizations.

Categorization of Information Systems

Once impact levels for all information types have been assigned, the next task is to determine the security categorization for the information system by analyzing the underlying information types and adjusting the system-level categorization as necessary to reflect system-specific factors. The minimum information system security categorization for each security objective is the highest impact level assigned among any of the system's information types. This activity can be extended a step further by assigning a single security categorization value for the entire system equal to the highest impact level among the three security objectives, and using that value to determine the minimum security control baseline. In short, this means that a high-impact system is one in which at least one security objective is assigned a high-impact level, and a low-impact system would be one in which no security objectives are assigned an impact level other than low. Syntactically, each information system categorization can be represented as

Information system = [confidentiality, level; integrity, level; availability, level] = resulting level

The resulting level, as described above, is subsequently used to determine overall system security categorization and serve as the basis for selecting a security control baseline to satisfy minimum security requirements. It should be noted, that the possibility exists in which the appropriate impact level for an information system may be higher than the level produced through examination of the information types alone. Organizations may decide to raise the impact level for the system due, in part, by the following:

■ The aggregate or combination of multiple information types may increase the sensitivity level, in turn increasing the risk, and as a consequence increasing the impact level.
■ A connected system may have a higher impact level. Considering the interdependencies of the two systems, the impact level of the system being categorized is subsequently increased.

■ Factors beyond the boundaries of the information a system may influence the potential impact to the organization if loss, damage, or compromise. In such cases, the impact level may be higher.

To that extent, organizations should categorize their systems and underlying information types based not only on the systems' intrinsic value and sensitivity of their information types but also on the impact to other systems or operational functions indirectly supported by the system.

Description of the Information Systems

The next task of the classification step of the control formulation process gathers functional and technical details about the system and documents the information in the system security plan. Because the system security plan is a vital document within the scope of the organization's overall security strategy, and also serves as the source of security requirements and corresponding controls for all organizational ICT systems, the system description should be accurate, current, and provide a significant amount of criteria that is intended to identify the characteristics of the system pertinent to the specific security measures designed to mitigate risk associated with operating the system. Each organization determines the appropriate amount of information and level of detail needed in its information system descriptions based in part by the system's security categorization, the scope or type of system, and the extent to which accompanying system documentation produced through the SDLC is available. Through this process of incorporating information system descriptions from existing security plans and other documents developed throughout the SDLC, the organization should use this as an opportunity to employ configuration management processes in order to ensure existing documents remain accurate and up-to-date.

Selection of Security Controls

The second step in the security control formulation and development process identifies the security controls necessary to satisfy an ICT system's security requirements and contains tasks associated with documenting those controls in the system security plan. From an input → processing → output perspective, the results of the system security categorization completed in the last section serve as input to the selection of security controls, considering the impact level assigned to the information system corresponds to a baseline set of security controls that, in combination, provide the minimum security necessary to protect systems categorized at each impact level. In this part of the process, organizations use security requirements and risk assessment documentation developed for the system in combination with the system security categorization to identify the appropriate security control baseline and modify that baseline to address the needs of the system. The outputs of the security control selection process, as indicated in Figure 4.6, are a tailored security control baseline, system monitoring strategy,

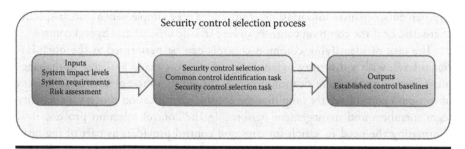

Figure 4.6 Security control selection process.

and an approved initial version of the system security plan. Security control selection identifies all the controls relevant to each ICT system regardless of which functional until or supply chain organization is responsible for providing them. Most ICT systems include a mix of system specific, common, and hybrid security controls. Security control baselines defined in system security plans indicate the type for each control and, in the case of common or hybrid controls, may incorporate control information in other system security plans. At the conclusion of this step, organizations have the information needed to finalize the resource allocation and timeline for the entire security control formulation and development process. The security control baseline defined during this step serves as the basis for security control implementation and assessment activities conducted in the next two subsequent steps. Therefore, the effectiveness of the remaining parts of the process depends on the accuracy and thoroughness of security control selection. Organizations first identify relevant controls using published standards and guidelines, as well as including system-specific considerations. Based on their knowledge of relevant controls, they are able to determine how those controls will be provided and monitored once the system is operational.

Identification of Common Controls

The entire set of security controls selected to support an ICT system typically includes both system-specific controls provided by the system or the operational and management functions dedicated to the system and common controls provided by other systems or parts of the organization (or external organizations) that protect multiple systems. As we discussed earlier in the chapter, few ICT systems have sufficient scope or resources to provide all of the necessary security controls at a system-specific level. Instead, organizations specify common controls that their ICT systems inherit, either exactly as implemented by common control providers or with some system-specific modifications, thus creating hybrid controls. Prior to selecting security controls, system owners need to identify common control providers and the security controls available for their ICT systems to use, and understand common controls in sufficient detail to determine if they meet the system's security requirements. When available common controls do not fully satisfy ICT system security requirements, organizations must determine whether to implement a system-specific alternative or if the common control can be partially utilized as a hybrid control.

The task of identifying common controls can be performed at the organizational level, with a directory or inventory of controls made available to management overseeing the identification process. The ability to use preidentified sources of common controls vastly simplifies the control identification process for security team members and management performing the control selection process, thus eliminating the need to search for common control providers as part of the task, and allowing attention to be focused on assessing the suitability of available controls. The security team members and management performing common control identification should also be aware of the potential that more than one provider exists for the same control, as is often the case when more than one operating environment is available for information system deployment, thus adding the additional activity of evaluating the provider based on characteristics such as credibility, reliability, and their own security posture.

Based on the scope and complexity of an ICT system, many security controls are generally considered to be good candidates for inheritance from common control providers. Organizations with existing ICT security programs and well-defined management structures often take advantage of common management controls such as risk management strategies, contingency plans, and continuous monitoring strategies. Security controls that represent security requirements that many systems share can also be provided as common controls, such as those associated with security awareness and training, personnel security, and incident response. ICT systems housed within data centers or hosted by external organizations, that could extend from members of an organization's supply chain to systems that take advantage of as-a-service technologies, typically identify common controls that provide physical and environmental protection, maintenance, media protection, and configuration management, although high-impact systems or those processing other sensitive information may require system-specific controls or service-level agreements to satisfy security requirements.

We must not neglect the importance that there are also some controls for which a certain amount of system-specific implementation is expected or required, including management controls such as the system security plan, security assessments, plan of action and milestones, and privacy impact assessment. If the organization's risk management policy states that system-specific requirements be identified as part of their control implementation then hybrid controls are likely the most appropriate.

Formal Security Control Selection

While following federal standards and guidelines is not a requirement within private industries, as it is in the public sector, organizations following such standards and guidelines begin security control selection by identifying the baseline security controls corresponding to the impact level assigned to the information system during security categorization. As discussed in Chapter 3, one such guideline is NIST

Special Publication 800-53 (NIST, 2014c). Excerpts of that guide present controls based on three criteria, one each for low-impact, moderate-impact, and high-impact systems—that identify the subset of controls and control enhancements applicable to systems in each security category. The established baselines represent a starting point for the selection of security controls, serving as the basis for the reduction, or supplementation of security controls in ICT systems.

In some instances, an organization may find that a baseline security control applies for a system, but implementing the control specified in the baseline is beyond the organization's resource capacity from triple constraint (scope, time, and cost) perspective. Prior to deciding to accept, avoid, or otherwise respond to the threats and vulnerabilities affecting the organization by failing to implement a required control, management should consider the selection of compensating controls as an alternative that satisfies the same security objectives. These controls are designed to satisfy the requirement of a security measure that is determined to be too difficult or impractical to implement. For example, segregation of duties (SoD) is an internal control designed to prevent error and fraud by ensuring that at least two individuals are responsible for the separate parts of any task. However, SoD can be difficult for businesses with small staffs. Other types of compensating controls may include maintaining and reviewing logs and audit trails. Nevertheless, compensating controls should only be used when they can be picked from a guideline such as NIST SP 800-53 or some other appropriate resource *and* the organization accepts the repercussions associated with substituting the compensating controls for those specified in the security control baseline. As with the selection of common or hybrid controls, organizations must document the selection of compensating controls and explain the rationale for choosing alternative controls instead of the ones in the baseline.

In still other cases, considering system-specific controls may also lead organizations to select supplemental security controls beyond the minimum requirements specified in the appropriate baseline for the system. Again, guidelines such as NIST SP 800-53 provide vital information for the implementation of supplemental controls and control enhancements, which organizations may elect to choose from the requirements in a higher level baseline or from among several optional controls and enhancements in the security control catalog that are not assigned a baseline. Each individual organization must determine the necessity for supplemental controls by comparing the security requirements defined for each ICT system with current capabilities and the expected effect of implementing baseline controls. Moreover, any requirements that have not been satisfied by baseline controls may indicate a need for supplemental control considerations. All decisions regarding the addition of supplemental controls or enhancements should be documented to the extent that it provides supporting feasibility analysis in order for management, and other organizations within the supply chain to understand the basis for the control implementation.

The documentation related to security controls must also include criteria related to the reductions or additions made to the security control baselines. This information not only satisfies standardized definitions of the contents of security control documentation in the system security plan, but also provides guidance to management oversight and security team responsible for implementing and configuring the security controls to satisfy the system's defined security requirements. In most instances, management, operational, and technical controls include parameters associated with policy, acceptable use, time periods, frequency of execution, or other attributes that vary among ICT systems. Selection of controls is not complete until values for these parameters have been determined and documented at the level of abstraction necessary to support effective and efficient implementation and configuration of each control.

Milestone: Completion of the Security Plan

The completion of security control selection signifies a pivotal point within the organizations security/risk management process. While performing the tasks of control categorization and selection, organizational management responsible for along with security teams document the results of all the key activities that were performed into the system security plan and submit the plan to senior executives review and approval. This interim approval evaluates the system security plan for completeness, in addition to verifying compliance with industry and regulatory requirements in terms of content, structure, and level of detail. The approval process also aims to assess the extent to which the set of security controls selected for implementation are consistent with the impact level assigned to the system and confirm that they will satisfy the system's security requirements. At a minimum, the version of the plan submitted for approval at this stage should include a statement of the system security categorization, the system description, and also a listing of security controls selected for the system including common, hybrid, and system-specific designations. Acceptance of the system security plan by senior executives is also an important milestone in the SDLC process, as the agreed-upon set of selected security controls is a key input to system development or acquisition. It also serves as a means for verified buy-in by top-level management in terms of the significance of security requirement to the underlying efforts toward achieving the organization's strategic mission, vision, and objectives.

Implementing Security Controls

Chapter 5 will provide a complete presentation of security control activities associated with implementation. In this chapter, however, we will prepare you for that discussion by putting that process into perspective in terms of the underlying security control formulation and development process.

Through the tasks associated with security control implementation, the organization incorporates the controls identified and approved as part of the security plan within the functional and technical requirements identified for the system and its overall design. There are two primary tasks in implementation: security

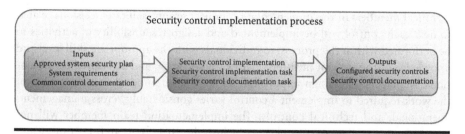

Figure 4.7   Security control implementation process.

control implementation and security control documentation. Both tasks should be completed as part of the overall development (or acquisition) and implementation processes of the SDLC. This is achieved through a series of activities in which the members of the security team responsible for ensuring the completion of the security control formulation and development process collaborate with system architects and system developers working to deliver the system. The best-case scenario would include coordinated interaction between the security team and the functional and technical members of the system development team beginning early in the SDLC so that roles and expected contributions from all team members are understood by the time the system enters the development phase. As you can see in Figure 4.7, existing documentation in the form of system requirements and descriptions of system specific and common controls developed during system categorization and security control selection provides the mechanisms from which security control implementation activities are performed. More specifically, the activities performed as part of the SDLC development phase, include architectural design, system engineering, testing, and preparation of supporting documentation. The details regarding the completion of these activities vary depending on the type of controls to be implemented and their source. That becomes important because different controls could have been custom developed, and enabled through deployment or configuration characteristics already designed into the system. Likewise, they could have been delivered using commercially available or open-source tools, or inherited from common control providers. The outputs of the implementation process include a set of implemented, correctly configured controls documented at a level of detail sufficient to support security control assessment and to allow functional and technical verification and validation against the requirements specified for the ICT system.

Setting the Stage for Control Implementation through Security Architecture Design

Coming out of the security control selection process, the security plan will provide criteria relative to what controls and control enhancements will be implemented for the ICT system. Prior to engaging in control implementation, functional and technical members of the implementation project group facilitate decisions related to how each control will be implemented and assign responsibility of activities to be performed within the process, to individuals with the appropriate skill level and knowledge of the system; including hardware, software, and associated configurations. Managers that assign responsibilities need to be mindful that the nature of the work required to implement a control varies considerably across management, operational, and technical controls. The implementation team member will not have expertise in all three control types inclusively. Therefore, careful planning and consideration must be made relative to the individuals performing each activity and the control type being implemented.

Part of the process of designing the security architecture for the ICT system is distinguishing among the different types of controls and identifying the resources available within the organization to provide adequate support. The activities performed during architectural design consider the system as a whole, the functions, and services it will perform in the context of the organization's enterprise architecture. By approaching design from this perspective, it is easier to identify existing business processes, services, technologies, and capabilities the system may be able to reuse and ensures that the system does not conflict with or duplicate functions or services already deployed in the organization. The architecture design process also produces detailed diagrams, at varying levels of abstraction, showing the different components making up the system and its operating environment, points at which it connects to other systems or environments (internally and externally), and the placement or integration of security controls.

The underlying outcome of security architecture is to specify which security controls apply to the various components of the ICT system and clearly establish the context by which common or hybrid controls are allocated to the system. In the case of common controls, the security architecture design process must analyze the descriptions in common control documentation to understand and fulfill specified requirements for the ICT system or to determine if any of the controls are better suited for hybrid or system-specific implementation.

Control Implementation through Security Engineering

It may be appropriate to begin by understanding the definition of security engineering. Unfortunately, a generally accepted definition does not exist. There are, however, activities that are generally included in security engineering. The Systems Security Engineering Capability Maturity Model suggests the following list of activities to be generally accepted (International Organization for Standardization, 2008a):

1. Identify the organizational security risks
2. Define the security needs to counter identified risks
3. Transform the security needs into activities

4. Establish confidence and trustworthiness in correctness and effectiveness in a system
5. Determine that operational impacts due to residual security vulnerabilities in a system or its operation are tolerable (acceptable risks)
6. Integrate the efforts of all engineering disciplines and specialties into a combined understanding of the trustworthiness of a system

Current international and federal guidelines on effective information resources management stipulate the integration of security in all phases of the SDLC, a notion that is often easier to accept in principle than to put into practice. Security engineering activities are generally performed throughout the design, development, and implementation of technical controls, although published guidelines emphasize the importance of considering management and operational controls such as policies and procedures when designing and implementing system security. Important to note: security engineering within the software development life cycle consists of security-focused design, software development, coding, and configuration, some or all of which may be relevant for a given ICT system and thus considered as part of the overarching SDLC.

The advantage of applying security engineering principles to control implementation is that they provide a plethora of general guidance and protocols that establish a basis for security control design and development. However, developers and other ICT personnel charged with implementing ICT system security controls often require more explicit development and implementation instruction. While many of the popular industry standards address secure coding and associated security-related development techniques applicable to ICT systems using custom-developed software, missing from those are prescribed development practices at a level of abstraction that would provide guidance toward custom development using specific technologies or programming languages. Rather, the standards and guidelines that are currently available focus on implementing and validating secure configuration for different types of system components and ICT products. To that end, the potential for a single ICT system to implement controls subject to different standard configuration specifications, development and implementation practices, and other published sources of secure engineering, makes it essential for professionals involved in security control implementation to provide detailed documentation describing the implementation and configuration of each security control.

Security Control Documentation

In the second of two major activities in the security control implementation process, organizations should update the system security plan to describe the details of the implementation activities already having taken place. The plan should be updated with details for system specific, hybrid, and common controls (taking into consideration the details related to working with common control providers where appropriate), and to provide criteria to emphasize the intention of engaging in security control assessment.

In addition to updated control descriptions provided in the system security plan, the implementation of management and operational controls also results in the development of several other documents that either directly represent required security controls or describe security controls as implemented. Such documents typically include plans for configuration management, contingency operations, incident response, system maintenance and administration, continuous monitoring, and security awareness and training. Documentation for technical controls not only includes technical implementation details but also functional descriptions of the expected control behavior in addition to the inputs and outputs expected for each component in the ICT system. One of the difficult tasks that managers face is determining the amount of information and level of detail to provide for each required implemented control, considering factors such as the complexity, testing, audit, and impact level of the system while also balancing the effort required to produce adequate documentation other system development processes and security control formulation and development processes potentially competing for the same resources. Organizations should make it a priority to utilize existing sources of technical documentation whenever possible while developing security control documentation; this includes gaining access to functional and technical specifications from vendors responsible for IT products incorporated into the ICT system, policies, procedures, in addition to plans for management and operational controls from the organization functional units that implement them. Likewise, similar documentation should also be sought from common control providers.

Security Control Assessment

Similar to the approach we took in the last section, Chapter 8 will provide a complete presentation of security control activities related to validation and verification. In this chapter, however, we will prepare you for that discussion by putting the process of assessment into perspective in terms of the underlying security control formulation and development process.

The security control assessment process aims to gather and evaluate security control information and evidence produced by the ICT risk management program, common control providers, and individuals responsible for developing and deploying the ICT system. The security assessment process and the security control assessors who execute it normally have no prior responsibility in the development or enhancement of any security controls. The underlying basis from which assessment works on is to consider what has already been implemented or accomplished and produce a series of conclusions as to whether the security controls implemented for the system satisfy intended objectives. Figure 4.8 depicts the security control assessment process. You can see from the figure that the entire process relies on documentation and other critical artifacts developed during prior steps of the formulation

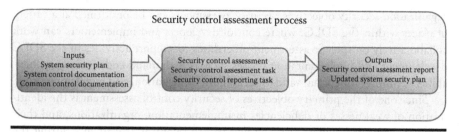

Figure 4.8 **Security control assessment process.**

and development process. Accordingly, it produces a separate set of documentation recording the assessment results, identifying any findings differing from expectations defined at the outset of the process, and makes recommendations for corrective actions to address any weaknesses or deficiencies found in the security posture of the ICT system.

The security control assessment and the security assessment report that gets produced during the assessment process provides vital information that can be used by management to make system-level decisions, but assessments support many other security, risk, and information resources management processes executed at a much higher level of abstraction than the processes associated with control formulation and development. "The information produced during control assessments can be used by an organization to:

- Identify potential problems or shortfalls in the organization's implementation of the Risk Management Framework
- Identify security- and privacy-related weaknesses and deficiencies in the information system and in the environment in which the system operates
- Prioritize risk mitigation decisions and associated risk mitigation activities
- Confirm that identified security- and privacy-related weaknesses and deficiencies in the information system and in the environment of operation have been addressed
- Support monitoring activities and information security and privacy situational awareness
- Facilitate security authorization decisions, privacy authorization decisions, and ongoing authorization decisions
- Inform budgetary decisions and the capital investment process" (National Institute of Standards and Technology, 2014a).

With regard to its role within the security control formulation and development process, it is important to note that security control assessment is both the main focus under discussion in this step of the process and additionally plays a key role in continuous monitoring and other operational security management activities in the subsequent step (which we discuss later in this chapter). Depending on individual organization security objectives, security assessments can be performed at a variety of places within the SDLC, where control developers and implementers can work collaboratively on specific assessment procedures to support activities in the SDLC development and implementation phases such as design and code reviews; vulnerability scanning; functional validation; and unit, integration, and regression testing.

Since one of the primary objectives of security control assessment is the identification of weaknesses or deficiencies in implementation, organizations, and their common control providers also conduct security control assessments during the operations and maintenance phase of the SDLC to confirm the proper function and configuration of controls allocated to each ICT system. For federal agencies, periodic control assessments for operational systems help satisfy requirements specified in FISMA and provide compliancy with agency and system-specific continuous monitoring strategies developed later in the control formulation and development process.

It is not uncommon for organizations to also conduct security assessments during the disposal phase of the SDLC to help ensure that sensitive information or other assets are removed from the information system and its storage media prior to disposal.

Components of Security Control Assessment

Generally, organizations utilize security control assessment guidelines as a means for facilitating the activities of this process. For example, federal agencies are required to use NIST SP 800-53A. Private sector industries are also beginning to see the value of that publication and are beginning to implement regulations for its use. NIST SP 800-53A provides detailed assessment procedures presented in a standard format. Each assessment procedure includes one or more assessment objectives that state specifically what the assessment team is trying to determine in order to evaluate the effectiveness of each control. Every assessment objective is further, associated with assessment methods and assessment objects that define how the assessment team should evaluate the control and what the focus of evaluations using each method should be. According to the NIST SP 800-53A guideline, assessment methods include examine, interview, and test:

■ The examine method is the process of reviewing, inspecting, observing, studying, or analyzing assessment objects that may include specifications, mechanisms, or activities.
■ The interview method is the process of holding discussions with individuals or groups of individuals (the assessment objects) within an organization to facilitate assessor understanding, achieve clarification, or obtain evidence regarding implemented security controls.
■ The test method is the process of exercising one or more assessment (National Institute of Standards and Technology, 2014c).

The assessment team normally works closely with organizational management and other members of the security team during the security control assessment planning process to choose the appropriate methods and objects for each control and to determine the applicable scope of each assessment method. The degree to which each method is applied can vary from basic, focused, to comprehensive; resulting in a set of requirements for performing examination, interviewing, and testing with a scope and level of detail consistent with the minimum assurance requirements for the system. The guidelines that the organization uses to plan and perform the control and assessment process should describe expectations for each level defined for the examinations, interviews, and tests performed. Security control assessment teams and security teams use this guidance to plan the level of effort and amount and nature of evidence needed to perform the assessment of each control and to guide the level of detail needed for assessment information documented during the assessment process, within security assessment reports.

While the NIST SP 800 series of guidelines is quickly becoming the de facto tandard for security control formulation in addition to all other security-related policies and procedures within the public and private sector. Organizations have considerable flexibility to adapt security control assessment procedures to suit their ICT systems and the environments in which those systems operate. Much as the security control selection process allows organization to tailor minimum security baselines to reflect the requirements of each system, security personnel and security control assessment teams can tailor the recommended assessment procedures in Special Publication 800-53A or use industry-specific guidelines. In either case, the degree to which assessment protocols are presented is analogous to test plans within the system or software development life cycles. The motivation for developing such a guide is to have predefined xamination methods, interview topics, and test cases established in order to streamline the assessment process and to provide a presence of process repeatability.

The assessment cases defined in the NIST guidelines or developed proprietarily, explain specific steps the assessment team should follow to gather evidence and evaluate controls and control enhancements using each of the relevant assessment methods. Assessment cases are developed from a government or industry-wide perspective, so for organizations following procedures prescribed in industry guides, assessment cases may still need to be adjusted for organizational or system-specific requirements. Where available assessment cases must align well with organization and system-level needs. Their use can reduce the time and level of effort required to develop security assessment plans.

Conducting Security Control Assessment

Based on the criteria contained within a preapproved security control assessment plan, the process attempts to verify the implementation of security controls documented in the system security plan by examining evidence produced by control implementers, interviewing personnel with knowledge of the system, and testing relevant controls to determine whether they function as expected. The assessment follows defined procedures included for each control in the plan, examining, interviewing, or testing relevant assessment objects and reviewing available evidence to make a determination for each assessment objective. For each determination statement included in selected assessment procedures, the evaluation of evidence by the assessment team results in a conclusion of "satisfied" or "other than satisfied." The assessment team realizes assessment objectives for each control by performing the prescribed assessment methods on appropriate assessment objects and documenting the evidence used to evaluate each determination statement. The assessment team will render a conclusion of satisfied if there is substantive evidence that the control meets the assessment objective. A finding of other than satisfied indicates that the evidence found, is insufficient to meet the assessment objective.

It is important to note that, while the discovery of weaknesses or deficiencies in a control's implementation may result in an other-than-satisfied conclusion, that same conclusion may be acceptable in other circumstances, such as cases where the assessment team cannot obtain enough information to evaluate control to the level of detail necessary. Security control assessment findings should be objective, evidence based, and indicative of the way the organization implements each security control. The assessments must be supported by documentation and observation as sources of evidence for each assessed controls and must be demonstrate completeness, correctness, and a high level of quality of evidence presented.

To justify each other-than-satisfied conclusion, the assessment team documents what aspects of the security control were deemed unsatisfactory or were unable to be assessed and describes how the control, as implemented, differs from what was planned or expected. It is important that the assessment team document security control assessment results at a level of detail appropriate for the type of assessment being performed and consistent with organizational policy and any requirements or expectations specified by the management and senior executives that will review the assessment results.

Authorizing Security Controls

The underlying focus of the authorization process is the process of

- Ensuring that managing risk from the operation and use of ICT systems is consistent with the organization's mission/business objectives and overall risk strategy previously established by senior management.
- Ensure that the information security requirements, including security controls, are properly integrated into the organization's enterprise architecture and SDLC process.

■ Support consistent, well informed, and ongoing security authorization decision making through a process of continuous monitoring, while providing system transparency, and risk-related information.
■ Achieve the desired level of secure information and information systems through the consistent use and reevaluation of risk mitigation strategies.

In general, security authorization is the process of assessing the overall security of an ICT system in order to identify risks and determine which of those risks have been adequately mitigated to the extent that the cost (in terms of schedule allocation, human resources, monetary expense, etc.) of exploiting them is greater than the gain for exploiting them. When risks cannot be sufficiently mitigated, the authorization process provides a vehicle for documenting those risks. Such documentation will, in turn, be used by senior management in determining whether that system can operate within the organization. A new system authorization is required with a system is initially deployed, and should be updated with each successive change to the system or the environment from which it operates. Figure 4.8 depicts the security control authorization process.

Authorization Process

Cloud-based systems have certainly changed the landscape in terms of how security strategies are formulated. However, staying within the scope of physical system, information resources are allocated to the system in order to define its boundary; selecting, implementing, assessing controls, in addition to making vital authorizing decisions. "One of the most challenging problems for information system owners, authorizing officials, chief information officers, senior information security officers, and information security architects is identifying appropriate boundaries for organizational information systems. Well-defined boundaries establish the scope of protection for organizational information systems (i.e., what the organization agrees to protect under its direct management control or within the scope of its responsibilities) and include the people, processes, and information technologies that are part of the systems supporting the organization's missions and business processes. Information system boundaries are established in coordination with the security categorization process and before the development of security plans. Information system boundaries that are too expansive (i.e., too many system components and/or unnecessary architectural complexity) make the risk management process extremely unwieldy and complex. Boundaries that are too limited increase the number of information systems that must be separately managed and as a consequence, unnecessarily inflate the total information security costs for the organization. The following sections provide general guidelines to assist organizations in establishing appropriate system boundaries to achieve cost-effective solutions for managing information security-related risks from the operation and use of information systems" (National Institute of Standards and Technology, 2010).

The point is that even though ICT systems are decomposed into smaller subsystems, that can and should be assessed individually, the components (or subsystems) are defined upfront and authorization is applied to the ICT system as a whole. Each subsystem is composed of hardware, software, an operating system, and data stores. Selected and implemented security controls must be applied to each of these layers of the system. The previous steps of the formulation and development process we have discussed in this chapter can be interpreted as the criteria for security authorization testing, and are based on the view of systems as predefined collections of platforms, software applications, and data stores that are owned and operated by a single organization for the purpose of providing computerized resources to a select group of users.

Monitoring Security Controls

In the final phase of security control formulation and definition, the focus shifts from realizing adequate security to maintaining effective security going forward, by monitoring the system for any changes potentially impacting its security posture and adjusting the implemented security controls as necessary to keep information security risk within an acceptable level as defined in the organization's risk management plan. The objectives that an organization strives to achieve in this phase are analogues to the transition in the system or software development life cycles from the implementation phase to the operations and maintenance phase. Security monitoring is one of several operational and administrative functions implemented for each organization's ICT systems; other related processes include: configuration management, system maintenance, and system, environment, and network performance monitoring. Continuous system security management is motivated, in part, by the activities and timelines in the security plan, but also incorporates routine administrative and maintenance activities in addition to monitoring the system, its operating environment, and the possibility of the occurrence of security events or the emergence of new threats or vulnerabilities that introduce new sources of risk that must be considered as part of the organization's underlying risk management strategy. The security documentation developed during the previous phases of the security control formulation and definition process provide the basis for ongoing security management tasks, in combination with organizational risk management and continuous monitoring strategies and processes or services that help management and security teams identify threats and vulnerabilities or other factors impacting system security.

Throughout the security control monitoring phase, managers and security personnel perform many of the same tasks completed during earlier phases of the process through the activities associated with security testing, training, and the implementation of operational controls, and provide regular security status reports (as specified by the risk management plan) to senior executives. Together, this information represents key outputs of security control monitoring activities that enable

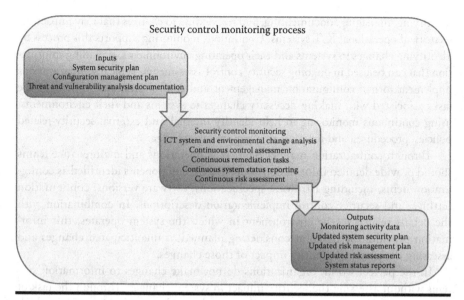

Figure 4.9   Security control monitoring process.

ongoing management of ICT security risk and help determine when more detailed reviews of system security are necessary. Figure 4.9 depicts the inputs, activities, and outputs of the security control monitoring phase.

With the exception of ICT system disposal, which only occurs after the operational and maintenance phase and the system or system component will no longer be used by the organization, the tasks of the security control monitoring phase of the formulation and development process fall within the context of continuous monitoring. These tasks include the following:

- Monitor the ICT system and environmental changes
- Conduct continuous security control assessments
- Conduct continuous remediation activities
- Continuously update security plan and risk management strategy
- Provide adequate security status reporting
- Conduct ongoing risk assessments

Monitor the System and Environmental Change

ICT systems and their associated security risk can and often do change dramatically over time. Such changes take place within system components and operating environments as well as internal or external nontechnical artifacts that pose additional threats and vulnerabilities to those systems. Monitoring for change is a key activity that emphasizes the importance of implementing a consistent, structured approach for identifying, managing, documenting, and responding to changes that may impact the security of operational ICT systems. Continuous monitoring supports this process by identifying changes to systems and their operating environments, providing information that can be used in ongoing security control assessments. Typically, organizations implement formal configuration management and control processes to manage the tasks associated with making necessary changes to systems and their environments, using continuous monitoring to help identify internal **and** external security-related policies, procedures, and practices that require such change.

Through configuration management, ICT operations and maintenance teams should provide detailed information about system components identified as configuration items, including hardware specifications, software versions, configuration settings, and security control implementation descriptions. In combination with the details related to the environment in which the system operates, this information provides the basis for considering planned or unanticipated changes and assessing the potential security impact of those changes.

In the perfect world, organizations do not make changes to information systems without assessing the security impact in system changes. Through the task of performing impact analysis, organizations are able to determine the extent to which planned or already occurred changes to the ICT system or its operating environment affect the security posture of the system or the risk its operation poses to the organization.

Conduct Continuous Security Control Assessment

In an earlier section of this chapter, we stated that security control assessment addresses all security controls implemented for an ICT system. Its purpose is to assess the effectiveness of controls as implemented and identifying weaknesses or deficiencies that can be addressed by correcting control configurations or augmenting the implemented baseline with additional controls or control enhancements. It would be a mistake for an organization to assume that the effectiveness of security controls as assessed in the earlier phases of formulation and development will be consistent over time given the nature of changes that take place to internal and external environments in which their systems operate. New vulnerabilities often develop in operating systems, software applications, infrastructure components, external service providers, and external supply chain ICT systems, all of which may cause new sources of risk to be identified and require reevaluation of the extent to which the set of implement security controls adequately protect operational systems.

Continuous security assessments provide a mechanism for organizations to confirm the continued effectiveness of their security controls or evaluate the achievement of security objectives for changed or newly implemented controls, such as those implemented as corrective actions specified in the plan of action and milestones or in response to information system or environment changes identified through continuous monitoring.

Conduct Continuous Remediation Activities

Organizations must also have in place processes for determining appropriate remedies necessary to correct weaknesses and deficiencies discovered in ongoing assessments and documenting the actions taken. It is common practice that key individuals within the security and risk management function of an organization to receive the results of continuous monitoring activities and ongoing control assessments through routine security status reports, monitoring dashboards or other summary representations, or updated security assessment report documentation. This information is used to review recommendations for correcting weaknesses or deficiencies in their system security controls and to assess the risk, threats, and vulnerabilities that have been identified. When the appropriate course of action is risk mitigation, the organization begins the task of planning and initiating remediation activities. The plan developed for this purpose should include details related to corrective actions and the schedule for their completion to the plan and appropriate milestones.

Important to note, any security controls added, modified, or enhanced during the continuous monitoring process or as a result of ongoing security control assessments should be reassessed on a scheduled basis to ensure that the actions taken satisfactorily continue to rectify the identified weaknesses or deficiencies.

Continuously Update the Security Plan and Risk Management Strategy

In order to effectively achieve the continuous monitoring objectives of maintaining situational awareness of all operational information systems and enabling real-time risk management, organizations must establish the technical and procedural processes associated with the collection and communication of accurate security status information to affected users, senior executives, and affected third parties with established supply chain connections to the ICT system. A popular mechanism for organizations to provide this information is to implement automated monitoring tools and summarize the monitoring data they produce in a format and level of abstraction that provides adequate reporting and support for risk management implications.

Since the system security plan, risk management plan, and security assessment report collectively represent the main source of security information about an ICT system, it is imperative that organizations keep the information in these documents current, updating them as necessary to reflect changes effected as a result of continuous monitoring activities, ongoing assessments, or responses to risk associated with new threats or vulnerabilities.

Provide Adequate Security Status Reporting

The fundamental purpose of security status reporting is to summarize system security information collected through continuous monitoring and other ongoing operational security activities and make that information available in the form of a report to operational management, senior executives, and third party suppliers whose own ICT systems are affected by the security activities performed.

Reporting occurs on an ongoing basis at a frequency and level of abstraction specified in organizational and system-specific monitoring strategies or as needed to comply with applicable regulatory requirements. The results of all ongoing security management and monitoring activities should be documented in the status reports to provide knowledge of changes or lack thereof to operational systems security, establish tracking and individual accountability for the completion of corrective actions and security-related administration and maintenance functions, and to identify trends in the organizational information security program.

Moreover, the information contained within security status reports provide current data related to the security state of each ICT system, including the effectiveness of implemented security controls where this data can be effectively collected through forms of automated monitoring. Security status reports also provide detail about the ongoing monitoring activities employed on each system. Such information contained within the reports helps management identify the types of controls or specific controls implemented, the various types of monitoring used, and indication of monitoring frequency. Another vital ingredient to the reports is that they also provide information related to the weaknesses, deficiencies, or vulnerabilities identified through security control assessments or control monitoring and report progress on resolving those issues.

Conduct Ongoing Risk Assessments

As management charged with oversight of organizational security regularly review the security status reports and updated system security documentation, their focus of attention is not only on the current changes to ICT system security changes, but also determine whether the current risk identified in the reports and documentation is acceptable to the organization. The use of automated continuous monitoring and security reporting tools can aide in the process of reassessing information security risk, although given the subjective nature of risk level assignment and the organization's determination of risk tolerance, the entire scope of risk assessment activities generally cannot be completely automated. Risk is dynamic; the sources and magnitude of risk faced by the organization change over time due to factors identified through continuous monitoring and ongoing security assessments and provided in security status reports. Management must constantly evaluate how changing circumstances affect the information security risk to the organization's underlying mission or business needs in an effort to determine the level of protection required to maintain an adequate level of security.

Chapter Summary

By definition, controls are a security mechanism, policy, or procedure that can successfully counter attacks, reduce risk, resolve vulnerabilities, and otherwise improve security within an organization. The main focus of control formulation and development should be on the security of hardware, telecommunications, and software. Moreover, the level of control implementation chosen should protect sensitive information in one of the following three states: data at rest, data in transit, and data in process.

Security controls can be grouped in one of two categories: goal based and implementation. Goal-based controls are named based on the role they play in achieving adequate system security. These controls include: preventive controls that attempt to prevent an incident from occurring in the first place, detective controls that attempt to detect incidents after they have already occurred, corrective controls attempt to reverse the impact of an incident, deterrent controls that attempt to discourage individuals from causing an incident, compensating controls, which serve as alternatives used when a primary control is not feasible of sufficient, and common controls that are implemented across multiple ICT systems. Implementation-based controls are named based on the groups of individuals that implement the control and the amount of technology that control requires to adequately protect the system. These controls include: technical controls that use technology extensively, management controls use administrative or management methods, and operational controls are implemented by people in day-to-day operations.

Integrating information security into organizational infrastructure requires a carefully coordinated set of activities to ensure that fundamental requirements for information security are addressed and risk to the organization from information systems is managed efficiently and cost effectively. Security control formulation and development is a structured approach that can be used to determine the appropriate level of risk mitigation needed to protect the information systems, information, and infrastructure supporting organizational mission/business processes from security threats. The steps of this process guide organizations in developing good practices for securing its information and information systems by helping organizational leadership understand the current status of their security programs and the security controls planned or in place to protect their information and information systems in order to make informed judgments and investments that appropriately mitigate risk to an acceptable level. The guidelines discussed in this chapter provide a methodology that can be applied in an iterative manner to both new and legacy information systems within the context of the SDLC and the underlying enterprise architecture. The steps included within this methodology include: categorize—which considers the impact level associated with the loss of confidentiality, availability, and integrity of information and ICT system, select—in which an initial baseline of security controls is chosen supplemented as needed based on risk conditions, implementation—which are the activities associated with the implement of security controls in the ICT system, control assessment—involves the assessment of effectiveness of the security controls implemented into the ICT system, control authorization—includes the official management decision to authorize operation of an information system and to explicitly accept the risk to organizational operations, organizational assets, individuals, other organizations based on the implementation of an agreed-upon set of security controls, and monitor—contains the activities associated with continuously monitoring and assessment of the security control implementation within the ICT system.

Key Concepts

■ Regardless of the category of control, the underlying goal is to protect data at rest, data in transit, and data in process.
■ One way of classifying controls is based on their goals in relationship to security incidents (preventive, deterrent, corrective, detective, and common).
■ Implementation-based controls are based on how they are used and implemented within an organization. These controls consist of (technical, operational, and managerial.
■ The driving force behind what and how security controls are chosen for implementation is based on enterprise IT governance and oversight, core missions and values, business processes, security requirements, and policy guidance.
■ The security control formulation and development process that makes up the underlying risk management framework provide organizations a mechanism for approaching cybersecurity in a constant and organized manner.

Key Terms

Control baseline—the minimum set of security controls defined by an organization based on a predetermined level of impact.
Control formulation and development—process by which controls are categorized, selected, developed or implemented, assessed, and monitored.
Control remediation—the activities associated with resolving any issues and applying updates necessitated after discovery through control assessment and monitoring processes.
Enterprise architecture—is a conceptual blueprint that defines the structure and operation of an organization. From the perspective of this chapter and book, the intent is to determine how an organization can most effectively achieve its current and future security objectives.
Hybrid controls—a security control that is part common control and part system-specific control. A broader definition characterizes it as a customized common control.

Security posture—the approach an organization takes regarding security, from planning to implementation. It is comprised of technical and nontechnical policies, procedures and controls that provide protection from both internal and external threats.

System CONOPS—it describes systems characteristics for an ICT system from a user's perspective. Additionally, it provides the organization, mission, and objectives from an integrated systems point of view and is used to communicate quantitative and qualitative ICT system characteristics.

System-specific controls—the controls selected and implemented with the intention to be used by the ICT system for which they are designed.

References

International Organization for Standardization. (2008a). *Information Technology—Security Techniques—Systems Security Engineering—Capability Maturity Model® (SSE-CMM®): ISO/IEC 21827*. Geneva, Switzerland: ISO.

International Organization for Standardization. (2008b). *ISO/IEC 12207:2008 Systems and Software Engineering-Software Lifecycle Processes*. Geneva, Switzerland: ISO.

Loche, G. and Gallagher, P. (2011). *Managing Information Security Risk: Organization, Mission, and Information System View—NIST SP 800-39*. Gaithersburg, MD: National Institute of Standards and Technology.

National Institute of Standards and Technology. (2004). *FIPS PUB 199—Standards for Security Categorization of Federal Information Systems*. Gaithersburg, MD: NIST.

National Institute of Standards and Technology. (2008). *Guide to Mapping Types of Information and Information Systems to Security Categories—SP 800-60*. Gaithersburg, MD: NIST.

National Institute of Standards and Technology. (2010). *Guide for Applying the Risk Management Framework to Federal Information systems: NIST SP 800-37 Rev 1*. Gaithersburg, MD: NIST.

National Institute of Standards and Technology. (2014a). *Assessing Security and Privacy Controls in Federal Information Systems and Organizations—Building Effective Assessment Plans: NIST SP 800-53Ar4*. Gaithersburg, MD: NIST.

National Institute of Standards and Technology. (2014b). *Framework for Improving Critical Infrastructure Cybersecurity*. Gaithersburg, MD: NIST.

National Institute of Standards and Technology. (2014c). *NIST SP 800-53 Rev 4: Security Controls for Federal Information Systems and Organizations*. Gaithersburg, MD: NIST.

Shoemaker, D. and Sigler, K. (2015). *Cybersecurity: Engineering a Secure Information Technology Organization*. Boston, MA: Cengage Learning.

Chapter 5

Implementing a Multitiered Governance and Control Framework in a Business

---

At the conclusion of this chapter, the reader will understand:

- The process for constructing formal control systems
- The practical elements of information governance
- What constitutes a control objective
- The principle domains of practical control
- The elements and steps of the control formulation process
- The general development and management of a control baseline
- The business aspects of control process formulation
- The elements of capability maturity in practical control systems

Constructing Practical Systems of Controls

The goal of this chapter is to demonstrate the practical tailoring of a standard framework into an explicit set of everyday controls. In particular, we see how a comprehensive and fully auditable cybersecurity control system (CCS) can be created and certified for compliance using a framework model. That includes the creation of the process and mechanisms for the decomposition, risk-assessment, policy definition, discrete control creation, and maintenance of formal best-practice cybersecurity protection. In order to substantiate this, a real-world example of the implementation of this process will be provided at the end of this chapter.

In Chapter 2, we learned that a standard framework, such as ISO 27000, Control Objectives for Information and Related Technology (COBIT) or NIST SP 800-53 Rev. 4 can be adapted to serve as the template for defining a practical information governance infrastructure. And, we discovered that auditable proof of conformance to the best-practice recommendations of such a framework is an excellent means of demonstrating that the business is both trustworthy and secure. That trustworthiness can be assumed because the best practices that are embodied within such a standard model span the gamut of expert advice and consensus with respect to the correct way to ensure a given organizational application. Therefore, standard models such as 27000, COBIT, and NIST SP 800-53 can be considered to be authoritative points of reference from which an organization's across-the-board cybersecurity approach can be evaluated for adequacy and capability.

However, because they are intended to be generic, all of these models essentially serve as frameworks rather than the actual implementation of practical controls. So in that respect, they need to be viewed as comprehensive specifications of the functions required for instituting practical cybersecurity controls, rather than the controls themselves.

The creation of a functioning, real-world control system requires the performance of an individually planned and intentionally executed control formulation process within the specific setting where the controls will be operated. That process must be able to help the business deal more effectively with the many demands and requirements of cybersecurity across the organization. And, it should serve as the basis for getting that specific enterprise's information and IT-related assets under direct security control. In addition, in compliance situations, such as those imposed by FISMA, the approach should also embody some form of explicit audit mechanism that will allow the business to demonstrate both the effectiveness and also the compliance of its security controls.

Making Information Governance Tangible

As we saw in Chapter 2, the mandate of information governance is to add value to the business as well as to help it achieve its goals. Consequently, capable information governance will link technology processes, resources, and information to the overall purposes of the enterprise. And as we said earlier, since information is an asset, all organizations have the obligation to assure its uninterrupted confidentiality, integrity, and availability for use just it does for its other more common business elements such as finance.

Therefore, managers have the responsibility to establish a tangible internal control system, which will explicitly protect the everyday functioning of the information processing and retrieval processes of the particular business. In that respect, there are seven universally desirable characteristics, which an information governance infrastructure should embody:

Effectiveness—that is, the organization's information must be ensured relevant and pertinent to the business process that it serves as well as delivered in a timely, correct, consistent, and usable manner.

Efficiency—in the simplest terms information must be made readily available through the most optimal (productive and economical) means possible.

Confidentiality—sensitive information must be protected from unauthorized disclosure or access as well as tampering.

Integrity—the accuracy and completeness of information as well as its validity must be assured in accordance with the values and expectations of the business purpose.

Availability—information must be accessible when required by the business process. This requirement applies to all present and future situations. It also applies to the safeguarding of the necessary resources and associated capabilities to carry this out.

Compliance—all information and information processing must comply with those laws, regulations, and contractual arrangements to which the business process is subject, that is, externally imposed business criteria.

Reliability—relates to the provision of appropriate information for management to operate the entity and for management to exercise its financial and compliance reporting responsibilities.

These generic qualities are operationalized through an explicit set of control behaviors that are executed in a practical, day-to-day systematic fashion. In the light of defined business aims, those behaviors offer the capacity to directly mitigate and control the design, development, maintenance, and operation of the operational information and communications technology (ICT) systems of the business. Moreover, since there are never enough resources to realistically fulfill the mandate for complete trustworthiness, the overall control system formulation process should allow decision makers to perform a sort of triage in prioritizing each of these elements. Decision makers satisfy the requirement for prioritization by explicitly defining the precise level of control required for every one of the ICT functions that they are attempting to secure.

What is required to operationalize the practical intent of the generic model is for the organization to conduct a thorough security risk assessment and control formulation process. And then implement a validated set of real-world control behaviors. These control behaviors should be logically consistent in their interaction with each other. They should be fully auditable and documentable. And finally and most importantly, they should ensure and satisfy the purpose and intent of the business operation.

Control Objectives

Since they are central to the ideas in this text, we need to stop here to define what a practical control objective is. By definition, a practical control objective is a precise account of the desired behavior. That includes the purpose to be achieved by implementing that given set of defined actions. As a consequence, a precise statement of expected behavior must accompany each control objective. The statement must explicitly justify and explain how that behavior will achieve the general requirement for effectiveness, efficiency, confidentially, integrity, availability, compliance, and reliability.

Control objectives establish a clear and distinct link between the anticipated security protection and the business purposes. In that respect, control objectives can be considered to be the specification of the exact set of activities that the ICT function proposes to carry out in order to achieve stated business goals. Control objectives provide a concrete description of the requisite outcome of an explicitly specified action.

Therefore, control objectives must be stated in an action-oriented way and they must directly accomplish some explicit business purpose that has been described by the business strategic planning function. Since the organization's control objectives have been traditionally "businessy" in nature, they have always tended to be focused on supporting the financial accounting aspects of the business. The large organizational control standards that we are discussing here simply adopt conventional security best practice into a specification of the same kind of mechanism for ensuring systematic cybersecurity functioning.

Given that intention, the models discussed in this chapter are all guidelines for the classification of control objectives in order to achieve the security purposes of an organization. They specify an explicit set of high-level control objectives for each of the security domains that make up the model. Then each of the detailed control objectives in the model is tied to a general business requirement for secure information. This applies to the various areas of need within the organization. In addition, each specific control objective behavior has to be directly traceable to the information resource it has been set to control.

Besides the control traceability requirement, the standard areas of organizational functioning addressed by the model should have at least one high-level control objective associated with it. In addition, a rationale must be provided for the inclusion of whatever behavior is specified as part of the actual security system. Besides rationalizing the inclusion of a control behavior, there should also be a specification of the presumed impact of not achieving a business goal. The latter feature will aid the real-world prioritization process.

Finally, there must be some form of tangible specification of the approach that will be employed to evaluate the effectiveness of each control objective. The performance of each control objective has to be capable of being tangibly assessed. Therefore, each specified objective must be stated in terms that will support the precise measurement of operational performance.

That assessment must be driven by assignment of the priority of the information elements that are most critical to the business process. As a consequence, the actual outcome of the specification of control performance assessment is an explicit evaluation based on the real-world measurement and prioritization criteria. That outcome gives the organization the practical means to determine if, or when, a process has been successfully completed. If there is also a compliance requirement, there has to be a specific definition of the approach that will be used to audit the controls.

The Process of Defining and Implementing Security Controls

The security controls that are implemented by an organization are always defined by a risk assessment. This risk evaluation is done first in order to identify the elements of the relevant model that are applicable to a particular business situation. Both ISO 27000 and COBIT touch on every aspect of IT security. They help the organization examine and categorize all of the risks and legal requirements associated with its information assets. Neither of these standards hammers the shape of the organization's security processes into a narrowly defined or rigid mold. Instead, the control objective categories force the organization to examine every aspect of the requisite security system.

The actual deployment of controls is driven by managerial decision making about the degree of security that is required within a particular setting. And the understanding that underlies this approach is that all situations are different. Thus the requirements of all of these standards force companies to undertake a step-by-step assessment of their security needs and appropriate responsibilities with respect to their information assets.

The actual control formulation process centers on defining and deploying a set of rational actions that are designed to ensure that a given aspect of the company's information resources is secured. The process starts with the formulation of explicit policies toward each of the protected artifacts and elements that will fall within the secured space. Then it ranges down to the more detailed implementation issues, which are identified by the risk assessment and managed by the control objectives.

The control models under discussion here are structured on one simple and pragmatic belief. That is, cybersecurity can be best understood and the actual assurance defined using a standard set of common categories of security functioning. The security itself is then implemented by the definition and deployment of specifically designed control objective behaviors. Accordingly, all of these frameworks define an explicit set of high-level areas of control and an appropriate number of control objective requirements are specified within those domains. The complete set of these control objectives is assumed to describe and embody all aspects of security for the operation.

By developing concrete mitigation responses to the specification of control behavior requirements, the organization can ensure that a capable, real-world, control-based ICT security system is in place for any type of organization and at any level of security desired. The risk assessment that guides the implementation process is a necessary requirement for establishing that control. Management then uses the selected risk assessment approach to map where the organization is in relation to the best-practice requirements that are specified in the standard.

However, besides the ability to address identified risk, the practical realization of a security control framework also has to be periodically judged for effectiveness. Therefore, a defined set of critical success factors also has to accompany the security system plan. They are normally subjective rather than concrete. These factors include qualities like "reliable" or "easy to modify." And the terminology is expressed in ways that management can easily grasp and act on.

Since these factors are subjective, objective, or empirical, measures have to be defined to make these factors meaningful to managers. The aim is to let management understand whether a process has achieved its assurance objectives. Also critical success factors force the organization to address such vital management questions as: How far should we go to secure something and is the cost justified? What are the indicators of good security performance? What are risks of not achieving our objectives? What do others do? and How do we compare against best practice?

The standards we are discussing are meant to be generic. Or in simple terms, they are appropriate to almost any conceivable security requirement and situation worldwide. The security categories in these models are also proactive, in the sense that they prescribe a typical set of actions that should be taken in order to provide active working security assurance in a given area of organizational functioning. Thus, for the purposes of implementation, they require an organization to develop and document an explicit statement of the approach that will be taken to address the specific security risks that have been identified for each aspect of the operation. That includes executing a process to prioritize the complete set of organizational information resources in terms of the level of protection required. Once the prioritization is done, the organization can specify evidence that will indicate that the appropriate level of protection has been successfully reached.

Finally, the implementation of every one of these standards requires a complete specification of the threats, vulnerabilities, and weaknesses that are associated with each asset. This is necessary in order to insure proper defense in depth. Therefore, there must also be a ranking of the relative priority and impact of each threat. Finally, these guidelines require that the organization itemize the measures that will be used to monitor and judge ongoing operational performance. If there are best-practice benchmarks involved in the actual determination of operational performance, those also have to be specified and their use clarified—for example, how they will be derived and used.

Establishing the Management System

As mentioned previously, the practical outcome of the implementation process is a tangible control-based system, which can be assumed to sufficiently protect ICT resource within the general security parameters of the organization. ISO 27000 dictates a specific process to develop that management framework, which it specifies in detail in ISO 27002. NIST 800-53 also has a process that is outlined in Federal Information Processing Standards (FIPS) 199. COBIT's implementation process is specified in the Information System Audit and Control Association's Management Guidelines. The documentation that is produced during the operation of this formal system of controls is what is referenced by the auditors in order to verify conformance to the principles of the given model. There are three different types of documentation artifacts involved in the process. The first of these are the documents that comprise the inputs to the implementation process itself. These inputs explicitly describe the various organizational context issues about which a policy decision must be made.

The initial documentation comes from the gap analysis. Using the recommended best practices as the point of reference, the organization identifies and prioritizes the threats it faces and the vulnerabilities that those represent. Essentially, any failure to comply with the recommendations of best practice represents a point of vulnerability. The organizations bases its decisions about the level of response to those identified vulnerabilities on its understanding of the harm that might come to its information and communication technology assets as a result of not responding to the threat.

Then, the substantive form of the response is structured based on the actual recommendations of the model. The response itself is operationalized through the standard procedures that the organization establishes as part of the implementation/tailoring of the generic practices of the model. The outcome of the tailoring amounts to the functioning security system with all of its controls and interactions in place. Finally, the documentation produced by the day to day operation of the controls drives the management of the overall security activity for the purposes of compliance oversight and audit.

The actual implementation of a standard is normally done in six practical phases, the first two of which involve the establishment of a formal security infrastructure that is based on the definition of comprehensive cybersecurity policy and the setting of the boundaries of control. Factors that might enter into this activity include such issues as: what is the level of criticality for each of the information assets within the scope of the system, and what is the degree of assurance required for each?

This is often expressed in the form of a 10-point asset classification rating that (for example) can range from "not needed" on one end of the scale all the way up to "the business would close without this" on the other end. Some other infrastructure considerations may include any foreseen strategic initiatives as well as any market or regulatory influences. The boundary setting element of this is particularly important since there is an obvious direct relationship between the resources required to establish the security level specified and the extent of the territory that must be secured (Figure 5.1).

The organization performs a risk assessment following this. The risk assessment may be the most important element in the process, because it captures and categorizes the actual threats to the business's information assets. Since a particular threat may not necessarily have much impact within a given situation, all risk situations are evaluated once they have been identified in order to distinguish only those circumstances that would enable specific and undesirable vulnerabilities. Then the resulting vulnerability picture is carefully examined with respect to the detailed organizational situation. The aim is to precisely describe the form and function of the specific weaknesses that has been identified and which the security controls need to directly target. As we have said before, these weaknesses are then prioritized so that the ones with the most critical impacts are dealt with first.

The next step in the process implements the actual risk controls. These substantive controls must provably address the findings obtained by the risk assessment. The deployment of controls is done in the order established by the priorities defined in the prior step. Moreover, so that these procedures can be monitored and assessed the appropriate measurement criteria are identified, operationalized, and referenced to each procedure.

Finally, a statement of applicability is written and documented for each control that is deployed. This statement itemizes the target asset to be secured along with the reasons for the control's selection, the quantitative measure that will be used to determine whether that control's objective's has been met, and the resources necessary to achieve that desired result. This establishes a history for each control and it

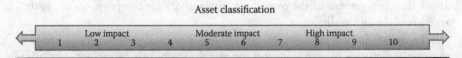

Asset classification

Figure 5.1 Asset classification continuum.

allows for rational modification as the organizational threat environment changes over time.

Standard Security Principles Derived from Standards

We have talked about these standards without discussing the various domains that comprise them. So in this section, we are going to factor out the common principles of security as represented by these models and then we examine each of these at some length. There are three influential control frameworks in the national and international space. These are the ISO 27000 model, which is a product of the International Organization for Standardization of Geneva, Switzerland. There is the FIPS 200 model that has been developed for federal information systems by the National Institute of Standards and Technology in Gaithersburg, Maryland. Finally, there is the COBIT model, which is a proprietary product of the Information Systems Audit and Control Association (ISACA) of Arlington Heights, Illinois. Each of these frameworks has an explicit set of security domains associated with it and each of those domains embodies a particular collection of underlying controls. Figure 5.2 provides a summary.

Please note that the much greater length of the third column (COBIT) in Figure 5.2 is due to the fact that the model is best represented by the high-level controls rather than the domains. There is considerable commonality between these three models. That allows us to tease out common principles of control coverage, which are shown in Figure 5.3 and specified in the following section.

Principle 1: Strategic planning-policy controls (FIPS 200–Planning–27000–Policy–COBIT–Planning and organization). Logically, the organization needs to develop a formal, comprehensive set of cybersecurity policies, which are promulgated organization wide in a customary policy stipulation document. In addition, there must be formal mechanisms in place to review, evaluate, and refine the policy set on a regular basis. This is the "big-picture" requirement that all frameworks enforce in order to prevent piecemeal solutions. The organization has to implement whatever management control it desires in a consistent, across the board manner. The aim is to ensure systematic deployment of procedure and operation of the security controls within the overall governance framework of the organization. Strategic planning and policy formulation is an intentional act. Therefore, it is sponsored and conducted at the top by the organization's policy decision makers. It is a future-oriented process that attempts to mitigate risk in the most cost efficient and effective manner possible. It is also a cyclical process, normally conducted on annual bases as all other forms of strategic plans are developed.

Principle 2: Operational security controls (FIPS 200–Accountability/integrity–27000–Process organization–COBIT–Delivery and support). The effect of this principle is to stipulate the need for day-to-day management of the controls that comprise the cybersecurity infrastructure that is created by the "Strategic Planning" principle (1). This includes the organization's commitment to formally organize

Security domains of three common standard models			
FIPS 200	**ISO 27002:2013**	**COBIT 5**	**COBIT 5 (continued)**
1. Access control (AC)	1. Information security policies	PO1. Define a strategic IT plan	DS9. Manage the configuration
2. Awareness and training (AT)	2. Organization of information security	PO2. Define the information architecture	DS10. Manage problems
3. Audit and accountability (AU)	3. Human resource security	PO3. Determine technological direction	DS11. Manage data
4. Certification, accreditation, and security assessments (CA)	4. Asset management	PO4. Define IT processes, organization, and relationships	DS12. Manage the physical environment
5. Configuration management (CM)	5. Access control	PO5. Manage the IT investment	DS13. Manage operations
6. Contingency planning (CP)	6. Cryptography	PO6. Communicate management aims and direction	ME1. Monitor and emulate IT performance
7. Identification and authentication (IA)	7. Physical and environmental security	PO7. Manage IT human resources	ME2. Monitor and emulate internal control
8. Incident response (IR)	8. Operations security	PO8. Manage quality	ME3. Ensure compliance with external requirements
9. Maintenance (MA)	9. Communications security	PO9. Assess and manage IT risks	ME4. Provide IT governance
10. Media protection (MP)	10. System acquisition, development, and maintenance	PO10. Manage projects	DS12. Manage the physical environment
11. Physical and environmental protection (PE)	11. Supplier relationships	AI1. Identify automated solutions	DS13. Manage operations
12. Planning (PL)	12. Information security incident management	AI2. Acquire and maintain application software	ME1. Monitor and emulate IT performance
13. Personnel security (PS)	13. Information security aspects of business continuity management	AI3. Acquire and maintain technology infrastructure	ME2. Monitor and emulate internal control
14. Risk assessment (RA)	14. Compliance	AI4. Enable operation and use	ME3. Ensure compliance with external requirements
15. System and services acquisition (SA)		AI5. Procure IT resources	ME4. Provide IT governance
16. System and communications protection (SC)		AI6. Manage changes	
17. System and information integrity		AI7. Install and accredit solutions and changes	
		DS1. Define and manage service levels	
		DS2. Manage third-party services	
		DS3. Manage performance and capacity	
		DS4. Ensure continuous service	
		DS5. Ensure systems security	
		DS6. Identify and allocate costs	
		DS7. Educate and train users	
		DS8. Manage service desk and incidents	

Figure 5.2 Security domains of three common standard models.

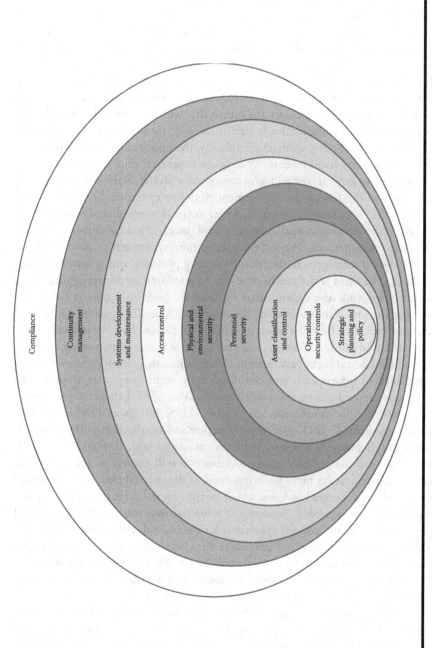

Compliance

Continuity management

Systems development and maintenance

Access control

Physical and environmental security

Personnel security

Asset classification and control

Operational security controls

Strategic planning and policy

Figure 5.3 Nine common principles of control coverage.

and coordinate its security functions by explicitly allocating the accountability for cybersecurity among its management personnel and units and then following up with oversight activities such as reviews as audits. That includes assigning housekeeping details such as the detailing of the authority for control of information processing facilities and the specification of how and where to seek advice on security from experts (e.g., consultants) and specialists. Finally, external issues such as the procedures for inter-organization cooperation and third-party access, as well as independent review of these procedures need to be specified in the form of explicit behaviors. This includes the means that will be employed to identify the risks associated with third parties as well as the security requirements, specifically with respect to third-party contracts. Explicitly, the policy and the mechanism for assuring the security requirements of outsourced contracts must be specified.

There are five general control issues associated with the establishment of operational security. The first is the requirement to define operational procedures and responsibilities in unambiguous terms. These range through such diverse areas as the mechanisms for operational change control, incident management, and external facilities management. The second issue is the requirement to develop procedures for system management, including capacity planning and system assurance procedures. The third is the means that will be employed to protect against malicious actions against the system. That includes the need to explicitly define the controls against malicious software. The fourth is the need for secure operational procedures including how and when to utilize a procedure, how the procedure will be validated, and assurance and the rules for operator threat assessment and reporting. The fifth control is the requirement for explicit management policies that can be embedded in information and communication technology system operations. That includes at a minimum the explicit specification of the behavioral controls.

Principle 3: Asset classification and control (FIPS 200–Identification–27000–Asset management–COBIT–Define architecture and relationships). This principle has two simple but very essential elements associated with it. First, the organization must spell out the rules and procedures; it will employ to account for its assets. Then these assets must be inventoried, uniformly labeled and formulated into rational and coherent baselines, which (as they are developed) are placed under formal change management. Second, the same rigorous process must be applied to the classification and control operations for the control set for those assets. This includes preparing a policy and procedure that itemizes how present and future information and its associated controls will be classified and managed as well as spells out how information assets will be labeled and handled. The controls themselves are also baselined and placed under change control.

Principle 4: Personnel security (FIPS 200–Personnel security–27000–Personnel security–COBIT–Manage human resources). This domain requires careful and rigorous control since over a third of the cybersecurity incidents perpetrated each year relate to human behavior exploits such as insider theft. Therefore, the organization has a responsibility to prepare and document the procedures that are required to insure the appropriate execution of the terms and conditions of employment for the organization. Much of the definition of the controls for this is embodied in the principles of Saltzer and Schroder (1975). That includes the necessary controls to ensure the effective definition of job responsibilities, effective screening of personnel and the arrangement of controls to protect sensitive material from unauthorized access, as well as the responsibility to undertake systematic cybersecurity education and training. This also involves the need to stipulate procedures that will ensure that personnel will respond appropriately to security incidents and malfunctions, report security incidents, and weaknesses that they encounter in their duties, report control, or system malfunctions and to develop lessons learned from incidents.

Along with all of these requirements, the organization must also formally define and publicize the disciplinary process that will apply to any personnel who breach those procedures. Of all of the issues embodied in personnel security, this is the one that might be the most important, since members of the organization have to be made to understand the consequences of security violations if the control system is to work at all. The aim of the enforcement process is to put consequences in place to ensure that violations of security are NOT the result of personnel simply ignoring correct procedure.

If security discipline is to be enforced, it will require a concomitant disciplinary process that details the exact consequences of violating controls over such humble day-to-day violations as not protecting passwords. In many cases, these violations can be attributed to sheer ignorance. But, since part of the purpose of a personnel security process is to ensure a proper level of security awareness among members of the workforce, something such as a defined and detailed disciplinary policy for security violations is a necessary adjunct, if nothing more than to get the staff's undivided attention.

Principle 5: Physical and environmental security (FIPS 200–Physical protection–27000–Physical security–COBIT–Manage facilities). This principle embodies the control objectives associated with traditional physical security. Since this area is often the only one that is actually allocated a set of tangible controls when an organization attempts to secure itself, this also serves to illustrate how necessary a complete specification of all of the elements of cybersecurity is. Although physical security is obviously important, it is only one of the aspects of complete cybersecurity. So, an organization that relies on securing just the physical elements of its operation might be considered to be unsecured.

The control objectives embraced by this area include the responsibility to define secure areas and the physical security perimeter, including the mechanisms for controlling physical entry, securing offices rooms and facilities, working in secure areas, securing isolated delivery and loading areas, and generally securing the equipment. This includes controls for properly protecting IT devices, as well as maintaining them, insuring uninterrupted power supplies, safeguarding the cabling, and protecting the equipment off site. Moreover, once the equipment has reached the end of its useful life, there must be controls in place that will ensure secure disposal or reuse.

Finally, there are two humble but very critical and often overlooked controls that are invoked by this security principle. That is the requirement for good security hygiene as well as the requirement that a policy for removal of property be made explicit and understood organization wide. Borrowing a laptop for a weekend is a potentially serious security violation, particularly if it contains sensitive data. And it is something that organizations as powerful and allegedly secure as the Pentagon and the National Security Agency (NSA) have suffered from. Nevertheless, in the absence of appropriate policy, it might seem logical for a zealous employee to see that act as a sign of commitment to the job rather than a critical breach of the organization's security protection.

Principle 6: Access control (FIPS 200–Access control–27000–Access control–COBIT–Ensure system security). This principle ensures accurate identification and authorization of system access. It involves six general control areas. The first of these is the classic access control policy definition process. For instance, will the access control be role based or mandatory, how will authorizations be maintained, and so on. And following logically along behind that first step is the requirement, that these policies be clearly stated and the enforcement mechanism publicized throughout the organization. That includes a specification of how users will be registered, how privileges will be assigned and managed, how passwords will be assigned, and how user access rights will be reviewed. The third requirement is for tangible user access management controls to be established and assured to be working correctly as well as effectively.

Then there are a series of electronically focused control requirements. The fourth requirement is for electronic access control to be created. This includes many detailed technical elements, such as user authentication procedures and node authentication, but it also requires that the organization formulate a policy toward the operation of network services. The fifth requirement looks at operating system access control. This includes such highly technical elements as automatic terminal identification policies, and use of system utilities. The sixth requirement involves the traditional definition of procedures to control application access. This makes this principle very important to the general purposes of securing information assets. It includes a number of traditional control elements, such as how access to information will be restricted as well as controls to ensure that sensitive systems will be isolated from access by mainstream users.

Principle 7: Systems development and maintenance (FIPS 200–System and services acquisition–27000–Information systems life-cycle management–COBIT–Entire acquisition and implementation domain). This area encompasses all of the lifecycle process related to the development and acquisition of systems and software. The control requirements for securing systems and software throughout the lifecycle must be spelled out including such high-level things as the specification of the rules for software engineering practice as well as simple things like procedures for data validation and message authentication. Because cryptography is an important aspect of electronic security that also includes the specification of cryptographic controls, this area includes all of the wonderfully elegant technical areas such as encryption, digital signing, and key management.

Another control element on the business side is the requirement that policies exist to assure the security of system files. That includes such things as how access to program and source code will be controlled and how system test data will be secured. However, there is also an implicit requirement for good software engineering management practice. So, there have to be process controls in place to ensure security in the development and sustainment activities of the organization including procedures for change control, technical reviews, and outsourced software development.

Principle 8: Continuity management (FIPS 200–Contingency planning–27000–Continuity–COBIT–Ensure continuous service). For the business side of the operation, this is an extremely important aspect of cybersecurity, since it requires that all aspects of business continuity management be considered and spelled out in the form of procedural controls. This includes the requirement that a business continuity management process, exist, ongoing business continuity, and impact analyses be performed and that continuity plans are written and implemented within a business continuity planning framework. This is another one of those frequently overlooked aspects of cybersecurity since it is not technical. Therefore, the continuity process is often conducted wholly on the business side of the strategic planning function. And, it takes place without reference to the technical issues that might be raised as part of the contingency planning. But, it is the backbone of insuring organizational survivability, which further serves to illustrate the practical importance of this principle.

Principle 9: Compliance (FIPS 200–Compliance–27000–Compliance–COBIT–Ensure compliance). Compliance is another business function, but it is also obviously a critical element of assuring information assets. Therefore, an integrated and effective set of controls are required. Compliance controls ensure that policies and procedures (primarily audit) exist that bring the organization into conformance with any and all external and internal legal requirements including intellectual property rights and privacy issues. The control set should also safeguard data and ensure technical compliance with regulatory standards.

The compliance principle is another example of why a comprehensive definition of security risks is a vital part of organizational survival. Since, generally speaking the people in the technical part of the business operation are neither aware of compliance concerns, nor do they consider it part of their responsibility. Nevertheless, failure to have controls in place to ensure due diligence in protecting the organization from violations in an applicable legal or regulatory area can lead to the sort of litigation that bankrupts businesses. Thus, a robust set of controls to ensure legal and regulatory compliance is an important part of any business's cybersecurity defenses.

Building the Security Control System

There is a standard generic process for implementing a control system. The form of this standard approach is dictated by the necessity to deploy a comprehensive set of systematic practices, not just address ad hoc problems. Because of the requirement to make the actual security solution complete and systematic there is an implicit order and logic to the implementation process based on the common goal, which is to ensure effective protection. Thus most real-world implementation processes follow the same general lines outlined here. Given the need to get to one common destination, most organizations implement the security control deployment process in nine stages (Figure 5.4).

Initial Setup and Tradeoffs

Information Gathering

The first stage understandably involves the gathering of all of the pertinent information necessary to define the form of the operational Cybersecurity Management System (CMS). That includes the identification, labeling, and valuation of all of the assets and the formulation of these into a comprehensive asset control baseline. This baseline is normally maintained under the dictates of rigorous, configuration management control.

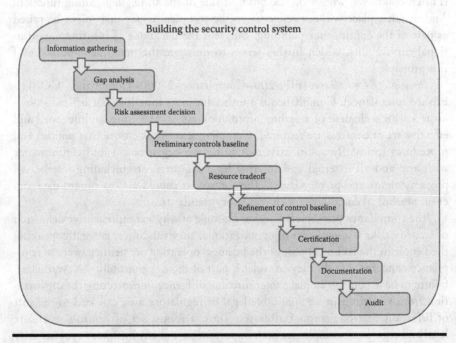

Figure 5.4 The security control deployment process.

Gap Analysis

Once all of the organization's information assets have been identified and baselined, the next step is to perform a security gap analysis. The purpose of this is to determine the exact status of the information protection safeguards that are already in place for each of the individual asset items in the baseline. This involves the identification of all of the direct threats, vulnerabilities, and weaknesses to the ICT base as well as any other contextual factors that might impact security, such as legal and contractual requirements and any current and projected business requirements.

Risk-Assessment Decision

This step requires the organization to make a considered decision about the findings of the gap analysis. As we said, this is not a simple matter of plugging holes, since it is likely that a comprehensive gap analysis will identify more existing vulnerabilities than the organization would ever have the resources to address. Consequently, a formally designated set of managers needs to perform a triage activity in order to prioritize and address the existing security concerns in such a way that the organization's critical functions will be adequately protected.

Preliminary Control Baseline

Once the management team feels as though it has gotten a handle on the security issues for their particular areas of responsibility, they will select a suitable set of control objectives from the reference model that they have adopted. Again, it needs to be stressed that there are a number of models for doing this. Nonetheless, there is an obligation to fully implement the recommendations of the one that is selected. This includes the development of a complete specification of all of the appropriate controls to address all of the threats and vulnerabilities identified in the gap analysis for any given area of best practice. In addition to the identified gaps, the controls must also satisfy any other legal, contractual, or business requirement that might have been identified.

Resource Tradeoff

Once the entire set of controls has been identified, the organization's decision makers undertake a rational and explicit tradeoff process that weighs the inherent impact of the threat against the resources required to address each item on the priority list. In simple terms, this means that the estimated cost of implementing the necessary controls is traded off against the potential business impacts of the threat.

This process is applied to the identified threats and vulnerabilities as well as any other identified legal, contractual, and/or business vulnerabilities. The rule that applies here is that the probability of the risk actually occurring must be balanced against the resources that would be required to eliminate it. The eventual outcome is a sliding scale set of recommendations called a risk reduction decision, which outlines the consequences of the range of viable responses to the problem, for example, a partial solution, against the estimated business cost should the expected impact materialize. This set of recommendations will range between not dealing with the threat at all, all the way up to deploying all of the resources required to completely eliminate it.

Selection of Final Control Set

Refinement of the Control Baseline

The next three steps are really aspects of the same activity. Once all of the elements of risk and resources are understood, it is time to refine the initial baseline of controls. As the title of this section implies that amounts to an iterative validation and enhancement process. The initial control deployment—the one for which the resource tradeoff was carried out—is a beta version of the operational control set. It is put in place as a sounding board for the evaluation of the selected controls over time. Over the initial setup period, the organization will decide on and fine-tune the eventual operational control set. These are the day-to-day behaviors that the organization's decision makers feel are the most effective steps for the assurance of its ICT assets.

Alterations to the operational set of controls are based on the feedback that is obtained from the users and stakeholders in the organization. Normally, the evaluation period will involve a significant period of time. During this time, changes are permitted based on the tenets of good configuration management practice. However, the long-term goal is still the finalization of the control set for long-term use. Once that final set is assessed and appears to be working properly, they are placed under a baseline configuration control, which is maintained under formal configuration management best practice. This is often the final stage in the assurance process unless the organization elects to move to the certification phase outlined next.

Certification

This stage is not necessarily the goal of the process in the sense that the purposes of the standards, we are discussing, are fulfilled by the completion of the prior stages. However, many organizations elect to pursue formal certification of their systems either to gain business advantage, as would be the case with ISO 27000 assessments, or because of compliance mandates such as those that are associated with NIST 800-53. If that is the case, it is necessary to prepare formal, written statements of applicability for every one of the control objectives that are selected and implemented in the operational systems as well as an explanation as to why all other standard controls have not been chosen.

Like threat assessment and control formulation processes, the justification process is also iterative. The organization examines all of its embedded controls and relates each of them to threat issues that substantiate their operation. One of the more important adjuncts to this process is the preparation of the justification for the controls that have *not* been selected. It is sometimes more important and difficult from an audit standpoint to be able to understand the lack of the presence of a control that has been recommended by the standard model. Therefore, the aim of the justification for *not* implementing the control has to provide the impact, likelihood, or economic justification for why the control was not included in the operational security system.

Properly done the documentation of the included controls along with the explanation for why a control has been omitted should provide a clear and unambiguous statement about the strategic security goals that underlies the implementation and operation of a particular cybersecurity system. This statement should serve as the lynchpin for the ongoing operation and sustainment of the security state that has been chosen by the organization, and it should also provide an authoritative road map for future security system development.

Once the organization is confident that it has its operational security system well in hand and functioning as intended a third-party auditor is contacted to perform the actual assessment for the purposes of certification. This assessment is normally carried out in the same fashion as any other compliance audit and it involves the presentation and evaluation of all forms of documentation relevant to and supporting the correctness of the operation.

There are currently a number of national bodies capable of granting certification depending on the standard. Generally, ISO certifies ISO 27000 implementation through agencies such as the United Kingdom Accreditation Service (UKAS), which is the national accrediting body of the United Kingdom. UKAS maintains that status through IRCA under EA-7-03 Accreditation Guidelines for Info Security Systems and ISO/IEC Guide 61:1996.

ISACA does not offer certification accreditation to COBIT. However, COBIT does provide the best practice basis for Sarbanes–Oxley (SOX) compliance under the SOX Act of 2002. The Public Company Accounting Oversight Board (PCAOB) defines the criteria for SOX compliance. And by convention the control objectives within the COBIT model are considered to be sufficient to demonstrate that those criteria have been satisfied. The audit is normally conducted by a licensed CPA firm against the stipulations of the COBIT controls and the certification of adequate control over financial reporting is based on the presence of any material weakness in control implementation.

The NIST 800-53 standard controls are the basis for the satisfaction of the legal requirements of the Federal Information Security Management Act (2002). The certification of system security as defined by those controls is required as part of the granting of an approval to operate any federal information system. That process is slightly different from the other two certifications in that there must first be an assessment of sensitivity of the information for classification purposes as defined by FIPS 199. Once the sensitivity has been defined, the baseline control formulation using the recommendations of FIPS 200/NIST 800-53 is undertaken using the appropriate control set.

Practical Implementation: How to Establish a Real, Working Control Framework

As we just said, the process of implementing a comprehensive set of controls entails the identification, prioritization, assurance, and sustainment of an effective response to every plausible threat. This control deployment function is not a one-shot "front-end" to setting up a static security solution. It is a constant and organized probing of the environment to sense the presence of and respond appropriately to any potential sources of harm to the organization's information assets (Figure 5.5).

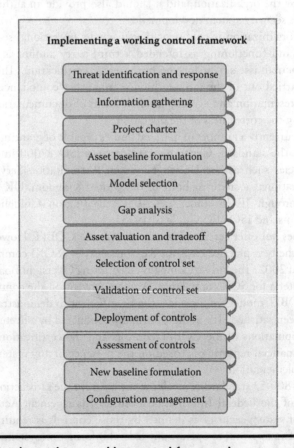

Figure 5.5   Implementing a working control framework.

Logically, the first step in formulating a correct security response is threat identification. That amounts to the systematic identification of **any** threats in the organization's technical or operating base that might lead to the loss of **any** information, of **any** value. And then the deployment of an effective set of controls to alleviate each vulnerability identified. There are two types of activities. The first type involves the steps to obtain corporate buy-in, the actual identification and labeling of the assets, the selection of an appropriate model of best practice and the subsequent strategic deployment of the controls based on resources available are the essential subfunctions of this phase. This part of the process drives the resource allocation decisions as well as the development and refinement of the optimum set of controls. It is termed the "threat identification and response" phase.

The second phase is aimed at the definition of the tangible cybersecurity system. We are going to discuss each of these phases in turn in detail. The threat identification and response phase is composed of the following four elements:

1. Information gathering and chartering
2. Asset baseline formulation
3. Model selection and gap analysis
4. Asset valuation and tradeoff

The aim of these four activities is to achieve an understanding of the security response that is appropriate to the precise situation. And which fits within the constraints of the organization. Properly executed, it is conducted in the background of day-to-day organizational functioning.

In practice, this activity employs methods and tools to identify, analyze, plan for, and control any potentially harmful or undesirable event. It should be noted that while the overall aim of the threat identification process is to prevent or minimize the impact of threats at the business level of the organization. Technical risks are also managed since they often constitute the root cause for business breaches or losses.

Threat understanding approaches must establish a disciplined environment for proactive decision making. They should regularly assess what could go wrong and then determine the approach and timing by which each potential threat will be countered. This all takes place within the constraints of practical business considerations such as resources available and time. Business constraints are an important consideration for a realistic solution since it is highly likely that more risks will be identified than can possibly be responded to. So, it is important to at least address the ones that pose the most potential harm to the corporation.

Finally, we want to stress that the form of the process as well as the scope of the solution is dictated by the type of control desired. Consequently, the substance of the identification, analysis, planning and control elements, and activities required is going to vary. It is also important to keep in mind that the actual business considerations vary with the focus and intent of the organization. Thus a project chartering prestep might be required. Charters are a form of contract. The drawing up of a charter often proceeds major engineering activities, that is because the creation of a comprehensive control system is expensive and can often be disruptive to the general flow of business. Therefore, the project requires up-front commitment. Operationally, the right set of representatives formulates the requirements for the control system into a statement of need. This is then documented and authorized by the appropriate executive decision makers and distributed to the business at-large.

The only purpose of this phase is to serve as a launch pad for the decision making with respect to the specific control model that will be utilized. So logically, the charter should generally define both the scope and extent of the desired control. In practice, this stage is probably the least substantive aspect in the sense that it does not really touch on any of the details of the requisite control scheme. Nonetheless, it might be the single likeliest point of failure. That is because everything that will happen downstream originates from this one point. As a consequence, it is important for everybody who will have anything to do with the control system understand and agree on the type and degree of protection at the beginning of the process.

In effect, a charter should accomplish two critical purposes. From a functional governance standpoint, it has to ensure that the project is properly targeted. More importantly, it should also support the education and buy-in of the people who are going to be actively involved in formulating the actual system. That is, because it is well documented that the long-term success of any solution is directly dependent on the level of support for the process. Comprehensive organizational control deployment is not an inconsequential exercise and it can be resource intensive. The execution of this process is generally based on generic business analysis approaches. So, there are numerous recognized ways of actually conducting this. However, there is only one absolute requirement, which is that the eventual outcome has to be sponsored at the highest levels of the company.

There have been a number of studies to support the idea that the ownership should be at the level of the board of directors or CEO. Notwithstanding that, the literature is unanimous in stressing that effective control solutions have to be thoroughly embedded in the everyday functioning of the organization. That requires across-the-board acceptance, which can only be enforced through executive sponsorship. One final point also must be stressed, which is that the information-gathering function should not degenerate into a detailed technical problem solving process. The only objective of this first stage is to define the general form of the problem for the purpose of determining an explicit strategic direction. There are many reasons why a complete framework solution may not be appropriate, ranging from a lack of resources all the way to knowledge of a specific targeted need. These must all be identified, brought forward, and agreed on in order to choose a proper scope and appropriate model for the eventual response. Since the decision makers are conventional executives, they are never interested in the details only in the assurance that the correct target will be hit. Consequently, the first phase has to be conducted with that single goal in mind.

Once the direction is chosen, the form of the rest of the process is dependent on the model selected and that activity constitutes the rest of this stage. The selection of an appropriate model is crucial, because the only way that the control scheme will work is if the model it is based on fits the organization's control needs. The only rule is that whatever is eventually developed should fit the particular requirements of the situation. This is both an intelligent design process as well as a political one. As such the findings of the information-gathering process must be rigorously adhered to in order to guide that decision-making process. And the eventual model selected should always meet the requirements that have been "bought into" by the whole organization through the chartering process. Since the next phase of the process starts the tactical implementation of the control solution, this initial stage is the point where the strategy is set.

This second stage is probably the least commonly understood of the control system implementation steps in that for most assurance tasks the substantive form of the assets to be controlled is known. In the case of information and communication technology, the asset base is an abstract construct, which could legitimately have many forms. Therefore, before control schemes can be devised, the boundaries and material form of the asset must be characterized. That involves gathering all of the pertinent information necessary to define the complete form of the assets that will be protected. This involves the meticulous identification and labeling of every item under control of the control system. It is a prerequisite for subsequent assessment of risk because it establishes the "day one" state of the organization's total set of information assets.

In practice, the aggregate set of assets is termed a "baseline." The individual components that constitute this baseline must be explicitly identified and labeled as part of the asset identification process. A precisely defined information asset baseline is an absolute prerequisite for the conduct of the rest of the process, since it is this explicit configuration that is maintained by the control system. And because it is a tangible structure, the classification and tagging of the asset elements that constitute it is usually based on their logical interrelationships with each other.

This is maintained as a top-down hierarchy of elements that ranges from a view of the ICT asset as a single entity down to the explicit items that constitute that resource at its basic functional level. The baseline scheme that emerges at the lowest level of decomposition represents the concrete architecture of the target information asset. It must be noted that the decisions that determine what this asset base looks like are normally made using the input of a number of different participants. That could range from the technical staff all the way up to executive owners of a given information item. The items defined at any level in the hierarchy are then given unique and appropriate labels that are explicitly associated with the overall organization of the information asset itself.

Once the asset baseline is established the next step is to do a gap analysis against the strategic model to be utilized. We have highlighted the three that are arguably the most popular, but there are a wide range of applicable models. The only condition is that one framework should be utilized, not a combination. That is because the specifications of the model are used to perform the gap analysis. The requirement for a gap analysis is common to most threat analysis situations. The gap analysis is always applied uniformly across the organization. That is, because the point of the gap analysis is to identify **risks** created by gaps in operating procedures. The gap analysis is arguably the most important element in any control implementation, because it identifies the places of potential weakness, assesses the harm that might ensue from each, and analyzes and categorizes options for response.

Operationally, this process is carried out by comparing the form of the current operation against the comprehensive set of control objectives specified in the selected control framework model. This is done to identify the gaps that exist. These gaps represent the deficiencies and material weaknesses that must be addressed by new procedures if the threat is to be mitigated. Since a particular gap may not have much impact for a given situation, it is important to only focus on priority gaps. Thus, once all of the gaps are identified, they are assessed to distinguish only those that would create specific and undesirable weaknesses.

Next, these weaknesses are carefully analyzed with respect to the particular organizational situation. The analysis is aimed at identifying the specific elements of the weaknesses that the control system needs to target directly. The weaknesses are prioritized so that the ones with the most critical impacts are dealt with first. The process can best be described by looking at it from the standpoint of the documentation that is utilized to carry it out. In fact, the tangible documentation set is so important that it is generally the only thing that an auditor uses to verify that a selected model has been implemented properly. This documentation will drive the activity in subsequent stages where the organization will make decisions about the actions that must be taken to address each identified weakness as well as how it will document the control system for the purposes of management oversight and audit.

The next subphase is the asset valuation and tradeoff process. The product of this phase is a concrete governance strategy. The input is derived from the outcomes of the prior three stages. The boundary setting element is particularly important to this consideration since there is a direct relationship between resources required to establish a control level specified and the extent of the territory that must be secured. Operational factors that enter into the development of this strategy include: what is the level of criticality of each particular information asset that falls into the asset baseline? What is the specific degree of resource commitment required to control it? Thus the most important aspect of this might lie in the simple valuation of the assets themselves.

This is the case because in the real-world, there are never enough resources to absolutely control every element of the information asset baseline. And since that baseline is overwhelmingly composed of abstract entities, the value of that asset base is also abstract, meaning not known. Therefore, it is essential for each organization to undertake a formal approach to systematically value and prioritize its information assets in a way that the most important assets are targeted first. Since, this is a resource decision the assumption is that the critical success factors are defined at the business level. And any form of operational asset valuation must be rooted in and reflect the vision, strategies, and purposes of that part of the organization.

The tradeoff process is a political one; however, it is necessary because the actual tradeoff is the fundamental element of strategic planning for control. This is not a scientific activity though. Nevertheless, with precisely targeted information decision makers can move ahead with some assurance that they are basing their strategies on the realities of the situation. The assumption is that the actual deployment of the control functions will meet the requirements of the project charter, which was drawn up at the front of the process. That decision making is based on knowledge of the financial equipment and personnel resources available to implement the desired level of control, and the pressing business concerns and the relative value of the asset. The point is to get a clear fix on the asset base so that the particulars of the deployment can be planned with precision. This should be both tangibly documented and publicized to the organization at large. This also effectively concludes the threat identification and response phase of the formal control system implementation process.

The next step in this process is the actual selection and validation of the control set. This phase involves tailoring, deploying, and validating an appropriate set of technical and behavioral controls. This is 99.999% of the time the same model employed to do the gap analysis, although not absolutely required. The only rule is that the control set has to address the priority requirements for control. The implementation is unique in the sense that the deployment is determined by the situation. However, there are three elements that must be carried out no matter which model is selected:

1. Assignment of controls to a control baseline
2. Assessment of the effectiveness of those controls
3. The formulation of the final control set into a control system

The necessary controls are deployed once the information asset baseline has been established and prioritized. This requires an item-by-item assessment of the information and communication technology resource baseline in order to design and formalize the appropriate control set. Nonetheless, in order to devise the appropriate and correct set of control procedures, it is necessary to return to the risk analysis to better understand the nature of the threat.

Basically threats can be characterized as physical or logical, from internal or external sources. Thus, the analysis considers the controls that are necessary to suitably address any and all anticipated threats from every given source. That includes steps to detect a threat as close to the time that it occurs (threat response). And a procedure to ensure that it will be either attended to by subsequent corrective action or that the loss that may arise from it will be effectively contained. Since adverse impacts of threats also inevitably fall into the financial arena, it is important to consider the applicable ROI issues.

One obvious example is that it ought to be a certainty that the cost of the control would be less than any anticipated dollar losses. Another consideration is the frequency with which the threat occurs. If the historical rate of occurrence is high than even a low ROI item could prove to be a good investment. The other issue is the *probability* that a threat might occur. Probability should never be confused with frequency. In essence, the question that has to be asked is, "What is the probability that harm might ensue if a threat occurs?" And, the answer would be how likely it is that a given occurrence will produce adverse results.

Finally, it must be recognized that there is always an uncertainty in all of these cases that dictates that baseline control formulation should always be an iterative function. Basically, uncertainty can be estimated as a level of confidence, from 0% to 100% on any control. What this expresses is the necessity or usefulness of the associated control. It should be noted that the failure to integrate uncertainty factors will reduce the overall level of trust in the effectiveness of the resultant control baseline.

It is necessary to validate the selected control set in order to assure the effectiveness as well as confirm the accuracy of the defensive scheme. This always takes place after it is operationally deployed. That is, it is formulated into an active baseline and placed under effective baseline control. From a control deployment standpoint, this activity is a standard beta-test function in the sense that the essence of the process is the ongoing comparison of expected performance with the actual result of executing the process.

The assessment process is planned, implemented, and monitored in the same fashion as any other testing activity. It normally embodies the criteria and factors considered during the threat analysis and baseline formulation process, but operational issues can be added at this point as well. The intention is to be able to say with assurance that the aggregate control set is effective within the aims of the control scheme. Operationally, this should be done within a specified time frame as well as a defined reporting and decision making structure. Because the overall purpose of this step is to produce a finalized baseline, the organization must treat it exactly like a project in the sense that the outcome of the process is a fully functioning control set for everyday use.

Once the project purposes and timelines are set, generally speaking each control must have a set of performance assessment criteria assigned. The purpose of this is to underwrite precise monitoring of the effectiveness of each component of the control baseline. Therefore, these criteria must be both measurable and able to be recorded. Then on execution of the process, the outcome data associated with each control is recorded. The organization uses the ongoing outcomes of the operational use of the control to assess its effectiveness.

This assessment is based on the performance criteria set for that particular control as well as the assumptions about cost and occurrence that were part of the baseline formulation process. Then, once the testing step is complete the aggregate set of results for the control baseline is assessed for the purposes of formalizing a finalized set of control objectives. These controls represent the operational realization of the control system. And their baseline representation is maintained under strict change control by the configuration management process. The released version of the information and communication technology asset baseline and its associated control baseline is managed by configuration management in the same manner as a software release. That is, no changes are allowed without authorization and subsequent verification of the correctness and effectiveness of the change.

Ensuring Long-Term Control Capability

The ISACA (COBIT), ISO, and NIST frameworks outline controls for a comprehensive set of logical domains within the IT environment. Each of these areas is intended to control some specific aspect of cybersecurity operation. In order to implement that control, there are high-level control statements for each domain and a variable number of explicit detailed control behaviors specified that operationalize the intent of each domain. However, given the number and complexity of the control procedures that might be developed and implemented to embody the desired level of control, there is a requirement that these procedures be evaluated for effectiveness. Or in simple terms, the fact that a control has been defined and documented does not de facto mean that it can be relied on. So, given the importance of organizational controls in each area of operational function, a mechanism to rate their effectiveness can be a useful tool, which is true both for reasons of assurance and also for the purpose of insuring continuous improvement of the security function. That is what we are discussing here.

It is possible to assess the effectiveness of each security control using a maturity rating scale. Logically, this is based on simple principles of best practice laid out in several similar capability models. The assumption is that capability is directly tied to the level of definition and execution of the process. Every one of the currently existing capability maturity frameworks assumes that a capable process is one that embodies the following five common elements:

1. Defined and documented policies and processes
2. Clear lines of accountability
3. Strong support and commitment from management
4. Complete and appropriate communication mechanisms
5. Consistent measurement practices

The levels of capability are normally expressed in terms of the performance of the practices associated with the control. Those practical performance levels are as follows:

1. Absent—not found or no response
2. Low—process is ad hoc and disorganized
3. Moderate—process follows a regular pattern but not documented
4. Contained—best practices documented and understood
5. Managed—process is monitored and measured
6. Optimized—change management is employed

These levels build on each other. For instance, the activities installed at the managed level are carried out in addition to the performance of the already existing best practices from the prior level.

The business can benchmark itself along this maturity rating scale both in terms of the effectiveness of individual control objectives and as a total entity. And it can aim to achieve higher levels of maturity by increasing the effort that it commits to the formulation and documentation of its controls. This can be supported by any explicit audit or review process that might be selected to augment performance. The advantage of a maturity framework in the implementation of effective organization-wide controls is that it provides a direction for the development of the overall cybersecurity governance function. This approach should be familiar to most IT organizations in that they do not build anything complex in a single pass. Instead they approach problems in an iterative fashion, continually refining their understanding and the relative quality of what they are creating. Implementing control through a defined maturity path provides the motivation for an organization to both start the process as well as continuously enhance its control systems. In that practical respect, a maturity framework could be as important to successful security protection as the control objectives themselves.

Chapter Summary

Standard frameworks, such as ISO 27000, COBIT, or NIST 800-53(4) can be adapted to serve as the template for defining a practical information governance infrastructure. And we discovered that auditable proof of conformance to the best-practice recommendations of such a framework is an excellent means of demonstrating that the business is both trustworthy and secure. That trustworthiness can be assumed, because the best practices that are embodied within such a standard model span the gamut of expert advice and consensus with respect to the correct way to ensure a given organizational application. Therefore, standard models such as 27000, COBIT, and 800-53 can be considered to be authoritative points of reference from which an organization's across the board cybersecurity approach can be evaluated for adequacy and capability.

The creation of a functioning, real-world control system requires the performance of an individually planned and intentionally executed control formulation process within the specific setting where the controls will be operated. That process must be able to help the business deal more effectively with the many demands and requirements of cybersecurity across the organization. And it should serve as the basis for getting that specific enterprise's information and IT-related assets under direct security control.

Managers have the responsibility to establish a tangible internal control system, which will explicitly protect the everyday functioning of the information processing and retrieval processes of the particular business. In that respect, there are seven universally desirable characteristics, which an information governance infrastructure should embody.

These generic qualities are operationalized through an explicit set of control behaviors that are executed in a practical, day-to-day systematic fashion. In the light of defined business aims, those behaviors offer the capacity to directly mitigate and control the design, development, maintenance, and operation of the operational ICT systems of the business. Moreover, since there are never enough resources to realistically fulfill the mandate for complete trustworthiness, the overall control system formulation process should allow decision makers to perform a sort of triage in prioritizing each of these elements. Decision makers satisfy the requirement for prioritization by explicitly defining the precise level of control required for every one of the ICT functions that they are attempting to secure.

The actual deployment of controls is driven by managerial decision making about the degree of control that is required within a particular setting. And the understanding that underlies this approach is that all situations are different. Thus, the requirements of all of these standards force companies to undertake a step-by-step assessment of their security needs and appropriate responsibilities with respect to their information assets.

The actual control formulation process centers on defining and deploying a set of rational actions that are designed to ensure that a given aspect of the company's information resources is secured. The process starts with the formulation of explicit policies toward each of the protected artifacts and elements that will fall within the secured space. Then it ranges down to the more detailed implementation issues, which are identified by the risk assessment and managed by the control objectives.

By developing concrete mitigation responses to the specification of control behavior requirements, the organization can ensure that a capable, real-world, control-based ICT security system is in place for any type of organization and at any level of security desired. The risk assessment that guides the implementation process is a necessary requirement for establishing that control. Management then uses the selected risk assessment approach to map where the organization is in relation to the best-practice requirements that are specified in the standard.

The documentation that is produced during the operation of this formal system of controls is what is referenced by the auditors in order to verify conformance to the principles of the given model. There are three different types of documentation artifacts involved in the process. The first of these are the documents that comprise the inputs to the implementation process itself. These inputs explicitly describe the various organizational context issues about which a policy decision must be made.

The initial documentation comes from the gap analysis. Using the recommended best practices as the point of reference, the organization identifies and prioritizes the threats it faces and the vulnerabilities that those represent. Essentially, any failure to comply with the recommendations of best practice represents a point of vulnerability. The organizations bases its decisions about the level of response to those identified vulnerabilities on its understanding of the harm that might come to its information and communication technology assets as a result of not responding to the threat.

Then the substantive form of the response is structured based on the actual recommendations of the model. The response itself is operationalized through the standard procedures that the organization establishes as part of the implementation/tailoring of the generic practices of the model. The outcome of the tailoring amounts to the functioning security system with all of its controls and interactions in place. Finally, the documentation produced by the day to day operation of the controls drives the management of the overall security activity for the purposes of compliance oversight and audit.

There is a standard generic process for implementing a control system. The form of this standard approach is dictated by the necessity to deploy a comprehensive set of systematic practices, not just address ad hoc problems. Because of the requirement to make the actual security solution complete and systematic, there is an implicit order and logic to the implementation process based on the common goal, which is to ensure effective protection. Thus, most real-world implementation processes follow the same general lines outlined here. Given the need to get to one common destination, most organizations implement the security control deployment process in nine stages.

This process is applied to the identified threats and vulnerabilities as well as any other identified legal, contractual, and/or business vulnerabilities. The rule that applies here is that the probability of the risk actually occurring must be balanced against the resources that would be required to eliminate it. The eventual outcome is a sliding scale set of recommendations called a risk reduction decision—which outlines the consequences of the range of viable responses to the problem, for example, a partial solution—against the estimated business cost should the expected impact materialize. This set of recommendations will range between not dealing with the threat at all, all the way up to deploying all of the resources required to completely eliminate it.

Alterations to the operational set of controls are based on the feedback that is obtained from the users and stakeholders in the organization. Normally, the evaluation period will involve a significant period of time. During this time, changes are permitted based on the tenets of good configuration management practice. However, the long-term goal is still the finalization of the control set for long-term use. Once that final set is assessed and appears to be working properly, they are placed under a baseline configuration control, which is maintained under formal, configuration management best practice. This is often the final stage in the assurance process unless the organization elects to move to the certification phase.

Like threat assessment and control formulation processes, the justification process is also iterative. The organization examines all of its embedded controls and relates each of them to threat issues that substantiate their operation. One of the more important adjunct to this process is the preparation of the justification for the controls that have **not** been selected. It is sometimes more important and difficult from an audit standpoint to be able to understand the lack of the presence of a control that has been recommended by the standard model. Therefore, the aim of the justification for **not** implementing the control has to provide the impact, likelihood, or economic justification for why the control was not included in the operational security system.

Given the number and complexity of the control procedures that might be developed and implemented to embody the desired level of control, there is a requirement that these procedures be evaluated for effectiveness. Or in simple terms, the fact that a control has been defined and documented does not de facto mean that it can be relied on. So, given the importance of organizational controls in each area of operational function, a mechanism to rate their effectiveness can be a useful tool. That is true both for reasons of assurance and also for the purpose of insuring continuous improvement of the security function. That is what we are discussing here.

It is possible to assess the effectiveness of each security control using a maturity rating scale. Logically, this is based on simple principles of best practice laid out in several similar capability models. The assumption is that capability is directly tied to the level of definition and execution of the process. Every one of the currently existing capability maturity frameworks assumes that a capable process is one that embodies common elements.

The business can benchmark itself along this maturity rating scale both in terms of the effectiveness of individual control objectives and as a total entity. And it can aim to achieve higher levels of maturity by increasing the effort that it commits to the formulation and documentation of its controls. This can be supported by any explicit audit or review process that might be selected to augment performance.

The advantage of a maturity framework in the implementation of effective organization-wide controls is that it provides a direction for the development of the overall cybersecurity governance function. This approach should be familiar to most IT organizations in that they do not build anything complex in a single pass. Instead they approach problems in an iterative fashion, continually refining their understanding and the relative quality of what they are creating. Implementing control through a defined maturity path provides the motivation for an organization to both start the process as well as continuously enhance its control systems. In that practical respect, a maturity framework could be as important to successful security protection as the control objectives themselves.

Key Concepts

- Controls are deployed to address substantively documented threats.
- Controls enforce governance.
- Controls are explicitly observable behaviors expressed as objectives.
- Strategic governance is enabled by a comprehensive set of controls.
- There is a generic process for applying all large control models.
- Every control deployment is tailored to every situation.
- The aim of practical tailoring is to create an everyday control set.
- Controls are implemented through gap analysis.
- Resource tradeoffs are necessary because all threats cannot be addressed.
- Control needs to be a living process updated by reviews and audits.
- Controls ensure a number of basic principles of security.
- Controls are arrayed in a baseline and managed under change management.
- The aim of capability maturity is to increase the effectiveness of organizational control models.

Key Terms

Control behavior—the actual operation of the control in real-world application.

Control framework—the specific array of controls utilized in the particular application.

Control model—a set of best practices arrayed in a commonly accepted general framework.

Control objective—a formally defined desirable outcome from the implementation and execution of an explicit control behavior.

Compliance—a state of agreement or alignment with formally expressed criteria.

Gap (gap analysis)—the process of estimating the presence of a threat based on the absence of a considered best practice.

Governance control—a strategic state where organizational actions are stated as explicitly auditable behavior.

Maturity model—a staged series of increasingly effective best practices arrayed for common application in a real-world setting.

Operational security—a predictable state of security enforced by an explicit set of controls.

Resource tradeoff—the process of decision making with respect to the cost and effectiveness of a given approach to control.

Risk analysis—an estimation of the level of harm that will result from the actions of a known threat.

Strategic planning—actions taken to ensure complete and comprehensive long-term deployment of a control set.

References

Information Systems Audit and Control Association. (2013). *Control Objectives for IT (COBIT) v5*. Arlington Heights, IL: ISACA.

International Organization for Standardization. (2012). *ISO 27000, Information Technology—Security Techniques—Information Security Management Systems—Overview and Vocabulary*. Geneva, Switzerland: ISO.

National Institute of Standards and Technology. (2006). *NIST Special Publication 800-53 Revision 4: Security and Privacy Controls for Federal Information Systems and Organizations*. Computer Security Division, Information Technology Laboratory, NIST. http://csrc.nist.gov/publications/fips/fips200/FIPS-200-final-march.pdf, Accessed July, 2015.

Privacy Rights Clearinghouse. (2014). *Chronology of Data Breaches Security Breaches 2005—Present*. San Diego, CA: PRC.

Saltzer, J.H. and Schroeder, M.D. (1975). The protection of information in computer systems. *Proceedings of the IEEE* 63,9, 1278–1308.

Chapter 6

Risk Management and Prioritization Using a Control Perspective

At the conclusion of this chapter, the reader will understand:

- That risk management is a formal organizational process
- That risk management is an integral part of strategic governance
- The classic elements that constitute the risk management process
- The principles for risk management
- The conventional steps involved in risk management
- The general steps and elements of risk response
- The business aspects of risk management
- The elements of risk management that drive control formulation

Ensuring that Risk Management Process Supports the Organization

Risk management ensures the continuing security of any business operation. It is essentially built around information and discrete controls. In effect, risk management gathers and utilizes information from all environmental and internal sources, in order to mitigate current risk and decrease the possibility of encountering future risks. That information gathering activity is aided by a set of formal processes and technologies. However, at its core, a successful risk management function depends on the ability to make certain that the knowledge that risk management acquires is incorporated as quickly and efficiently as possible into the organization's substantive business activities. That is the control part.

Identification is the first element of risk management. Identification describes the need to categorize all of the organization's information and communications technology systems in terms of their relative value. This is essentially an inventorying and valuation process that should produce a priority list of systems and their contents for defense-in-depth purposes.

The idea would be to identify those systems that contain the most valuable data and that are at the highest degree of risk. The ability to assign a priority to the systems that need to be monitored for risk ensures greater protection for them, as well as maximizes the use of the organization's security resources.

Once the organization understands what has to be protected, it is in a position to develop an integrated set of substantive security controls. This is the actual security infrastructure part of the process. The ideal would be to create an array of controls to manage the known risks to all of the priority systems identified by the first step.

These controls have to be comprehensive in their application as well as relevant and appropriate. The controls are typically detailed in a comprehensive control design and deployment document, which the organization develops through a formal process. The control architecture documented in that design document should embody a tangible set of electronic and process behaviors that can be evaluated for their effectiveness over time.

Once the controls that are embodied by that architecture have been precisely identified and explicitly designed, they have to be customized to fit the specific situation. Those designed control activities are then embedded in day-to-day practice. The intention of the control system is to make the identification, analysis, and response to risk a routine part of the standard operating procedure of the business. Accordingly, risk management controls should be put into place as an integral part of the functions that they support. In addition, there should also be provisions in the general process for maintaining and improving the effectiveness of risk controls over time.

Finally, the organization utilizes formal assessment methods to underwrite the need for continuous effectiveness. In this final step, prearranged tests and reviews are done to ensure that the risk management process as a whole is functioning as planned. In addition, targeted assessment methods are employed to evaluate the effectiveness of individual risk control functions. These targeted assessments are typically aimed at determining whether priority controls are operating as intended. The ideal outcome would be the ability to confirm through observation that the steps the organization has taken to ensure proper risk management remain effective.

If it can be confirmed that the risk management process is effective, then the information and communications technology (ICT) systems that fall under the risk management function can by-and-large be certified as secure. Obviously, because the risk picture changes that assurance is always subject to the restrictions of time and new priorities. Nevertheless, if all of the prior steps have been followed correctly and the monitoring of control functioning is sustained and accurate, the organization can generally assume that it has an effective risk management process in place.

The successful execution of this process requires the involvement of senior management and technical managers. The execution of the process is also likely to be influenced by external drivers such as laws and regulations. Nonetheless, if the organization takes the steps to ensure that the outcomes of the risk management process are properly aligned with the business goals and objectives of the organization, it is possible to have an institutionalized and systematic risk management function. With a formal function for risk management in place, senior management can then direct resources to ensure the proper level of risk management.

Five Elements of the Risk Management Process

Risk management is a complex organizational function whose general purpose is to underwrite the organization's obligation to identify and mitigate project risks. Risk management applies to every kind of organizational application from the assurance of technical vulnerabilities through ensuring the effectiveness of the company's management processes. The specific goal of the risk management process is to identify, analyze, mitigate, and monitor each currently active as well as latent risk that is known to exist within the organization. Therefore, at its heart, risk management is an information gathering and decision-making function. It focuses on understanding all feasible forms of risk, and then classifies and assesses those risks in order to determine their importance (Figure 6.1).

Risk management ensures that there is sufficient knowledge about each relevant threat available for decision making. And then risk management takes the necessary steps to react to and mitigate all priority risks. Risk management also monitors the effectiveness of those mitigations once they have been put in place. Risk management is assessment and analysis based. Therefore, the performance of a threat assessment is a prerequisite to the implementation of a formally executed risk management operation. Threat assessments ensure that all of the risks in the organization's risk environment are correctly identified and categorized. After the initial identification and characterization is done, the risk management process typically involves five generic steps:

1. Planning
2. Oversight
3. Risk analysis
4. Risk response
5. Continuous monitoring

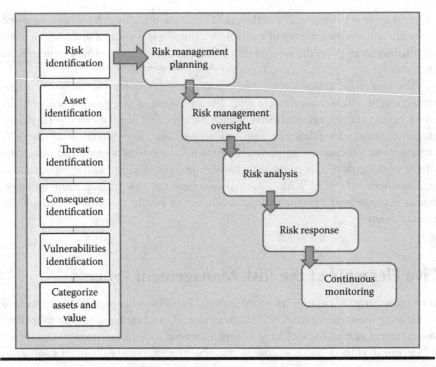

Figure 6.1   Risk management process.

Risk management planning: Because it is a formal organizational function, all of the operational steps of the generic risk management process have to be planned; that is, every one of the day-to-day activities that comprise the organization's explicit risk management strategy have to be scheduled right down to the who, what, when, and where of the execution of each practice. In addition to providing the information that helps guide strategic decision making about risks, risk management planning also makes certain that a commonly accepted and systematic set of policies and procedures are in place to handle known risks. These are operationalized through a standard set of everyday procedures. Those procedures ensure that the routine risk planning, analysis, response, and process management function are always directly aligned to the goals of the business operation. Nevertheless, the primary purpose of risk management is to sustain a disciplined and systematic set of controls that will respond to the risks that the organization considers a priority throughout the business operation.

That set of controls is conceived, organized, and managed by plan. A risk management plan is a high-level document that details the overall approach that will be employed to control the risks that the enterprise deems worth addressing. There might be any number of strategies embodied in that plan, but there is normally a specific approach captured in the plan.

Risk management process oversight: A formal oversight process has to be in place in order to ensure sustainment of the security strategy. The purpose of this process is to monitor and effectively report the organization's risk situation. Oversight procedures should be created to continuously and reliably depict the current status of all identified risks. Oversight should also be able to distinguish and report on new risks as they appear. All of the factors that comprise that organizational context have to be identified and understood in order to design an effective set of risk management controls. The definition of the scope of coverage and the required level of assurance are the primary influences that define that context. The overall purpose of the risk management function is to establish and maintain an appropriate set of risk controls. Because of that generic purpose, risk assessments are an especially critical part of the overall risk management process. Risk assessments ensure effective risk management response because they identify threats to the organization as they appear in the threat horizon and then decide how likely those threats are to have a meaningful impact, as well as the elements of the organization that are impacted by each threat. Correctly executed, the current threat environment is assessed on some agreed on periodic basis in order to ensure that the current risk mitigation schema is appropriate and is successfully mitigating threats.

Risk analysis: In order to maintain an effective understanding of risk, the organization has to deploy and maintain a comprehensive risk analysis function. The overall purpose of the risk management process is to mitigate risk. Risk analysis is the information gathering function that provides the necessary understanding of the nature of all identified risks. Risk analysis identifies and evaluates each relevant risk, determines that risk's potential impact, and itemizes the controls that will be needed to respond properly. Risk analysis is a prerequisite to the implementation of the risk management function. That is because a systematic risk analysis can specifically direct the prioritization of the steps that the organization will then deploy to do risk management.

The risk analysis function should also be able to carry out qualitative and quantitative analyses of any newly identified or emerging risk event. The risk analysis function should also be able to conduct all necessary analyses to confirm that presently active risks are fully characterized and contained. The ultimate outcome of the operation of the risk management function should be to confirm that the risks that the organization considers priorities are identified, agreed on, and addressed, and that any emerging risks will be recognized and dealt with as they appear.

Risk response: Once the analysis function is established and operating, the responses that the organization has chosen to utilize to ameliorate any meaningful risk have to be designed and deployed. The response to each significant risk should always be a substantive and correct set of operational procedures supported by the appropriate technology. Because the whole organization is involved in the response should be feasible and understandable to the general constituencies of the organization. Finally, the response should be shown to provably mitigate the predictable impacts of any identified risk.

Since there are an infinite number of risks in most projects, the targets of the risk response has to be precisely established within every organization. Essentially, this is a scoping process. It answers two distinct but highly related questions for the organization's decision makers. The first is: "What is the certainty of each identified risk occurring?" The second is: "What is its anticipated impact if it does occur?" The answer to those two questions is typically conveyed to decisions makers as an appraisal of the loss, harm, failure, or danger for every identified risk. The results of that assessment will then guide the deployment and subsequent conduct of the risk response process.

Once the risk response is appropriately targeted, a set of optimum risk management policies can be defined and implemented. The risks themselves are analyzed as they are identified and the priority that the mitigation ought to receive is determined. This is normally dictated by the danger of the risk and the resources required to ameliorate it. Then, once the risk mitigation decision has been made, the prescribed mitigations are designed, developed, applied, and then continuously evaluated in order to determine whether progress has been made toward the proper mitigation of the risk.

Continuous monitoring: The organization also has a duty to recurrently survey the existing risk environment. That is necessary in order to identify and mitigate any new threats that might arise. Constant vigilance is a central part of the risk management process because damaging risks can appear at odd times and in unanticipated places. The monitoring is typically underwritten by formal testing and reviews as well as periodic audits of the security function. Continuous monitoring must apply uniformly across the organization. Therefore, it is established through a strategic planning process. The strategic planning for risk management develops and implements the organizational policies about risk. These are documented in a detailed risk management plan. The plan is then utilized as a means to organize and run a rational risk management operation. In most cases, that planning process will dictate a set of specific actions to produce a desired outcome for every meaningful risk. Those outcomes are prioritized in terms of their criticality.

The aim of the strategic planning process for risk monitoring is maintain an effective set of formal controls to manage each risk. Along with those controls, strategic risk management planning is also responsible for assigning the specific employee roles and responsibilities required for the management of each risk. Finally, the plan provides a description of the process that will be used to evaluate and improve the overall risk management function, including how to use lessons learned to change the form of the response.

Because cost is always a factor in business decision making, a precise specification of the maximum degree of acceptable risk is necessary in order to guide decisions about the degree of risk the organization is willing to underwrite. A specification of the maximum level of acceptable risk drives the tradeoff process that is required to make a real-world planning decision about risk acceptance for each specific project. A decision about the degree of risk will also drive the decision about the practical form of the monitoring process. The actual response will typically be referenced to the level of practical acceptability of the risk. Consequently, the risk management planning process usually involves the formation of a substantive, usually resource-based, map between each risk and the various options for mitigating it.

How the Risk Management Plan Uses the Risk Profile

Strategic risk management works in conjunction with a risk profile. The risk profile establishes an explicit policy link between the overall risk management process and the constantly changing overall environment of the project. The link between the risk environment and the mitigations that have been deployed to address is actually maintained through a continuous risk management profile.

The risk management profile documents: the specific risk management context including the present threat status of each risk, its probability of occurrence, the consequences of occurrence, and the threshold where the occurrence will become active. The risk management profile also normally includes a description of stakeholder perspectives, organizational risk categories, and often involves the technical and managerial objectives, assumptions, and constraints laid out by stakeholders. The priority of each risk is then dictated by the general consensus of the stakeholders. That priority is based on the interpretation of the organization's risk acceptance policy along with the current status of the risk.

The risk management plan works with the profile. The plan provides the explicit policy guidance for the customization of the risk management process to meet the specifications of the risk environment. The priorities set in the general risk management profile are used to determine the specific application of resources for treatment. Since the assignment of priorities is a business decision, the profile is periodically disseminated to relevant stakeholders for feedback based upon their needs. Risk thresholds are then defined or adjusted, for each category of risk within the profile. Those thresholds dictate the conditions under which a level of risk may be accepted or escalated. The risk profile is updated when there are changes in an individual risk's state or form.

In addition to identifying and relating the various resource elements within the profile, each risk has to be categorized in terms of their general priority. Priority is directly related to the criticality of the organizational component being controlled. That is, it is essential to be able to know the sensitivity requirements of each component in order to decide how many resources to commit to its protection.

The determination of sensitivity is based on a simple understanding of each component's purpose. That description of purpose should convey the general importance of the element in the overall operating environment. The description of purpose satisfies two operational goals. First, it allows managers to make informed assignments of priorities for the protected components. Second, it allows managers to coordinate the implementation and subsequent execution of the control behaviors that are assigned to each component.

The targeted knowledge that the risk profile management process provides, ensures the most efficient use of security resources within the assumptions of the organization as a whole.

Because knowing where the priority risks are is a fundamental precondition for managing them, the term "risk analysis" is sometimes used interchangeably with the process of maintaining the risk management profile. However, those two are not the same activity. Risk analysis is a tool that supports the larger risk management function, rather than an end in itself. The risk management profile is unique to the particular organization. It is also maintained by the performance of the ongoing risk analyses, thus, it is a product in and of itself.

Risk profiles underwrite the operational plan that is used to manage risk. Risk profiles capture and maintain up-to-date knowledge about the risk situation. It does that by evaluating each identified threat against established risk thresholds. Those thresholds are stipulated in the profile. Risk management then documents mitigation strategies for every risk that is above its threshold. Risk management also entails any procedures that will be used to evaluate the effectiveness of potential mitigation alternatives.

Conducting a Risk Assessment in Support of Planning

The definition of the particular organizational approach to risk management should always address two distinct but highly related questions. The first is: "What is the certainty of the risk?" The answer to that question is typically expressed as likelihood of occurrence. The second is: "What is the anticipated impact?" The answer to that question is normally expressed as an estimate of the loss, harm, failure, or danger. Ideally, both of these questions can be answered in easily understandable terms. Making the estimate understandable and credible is a key factor because the results of the risk analysis will guide the deployment and subsequent conduct of the risk management process.

There is a logical order to how these two questions should be approached. Practically speaking, the first consideration has to be likelihood, since a highly unlikely event might not be worth the cost of further consideration. However, it is the estimate of the consequences that truly shapes the form of the response. That is because there is never enough money to secure against every conceivable risk and so the potential harm that each risk represents always has to be balanced against the likelihood of its occurrence.

Thus, the fundamental goal of the risk assessment process is to optimize the resources used for the operational deployment of security controls. It accomplishes that purpose by identifying risks with the greatest probability of occurrence and which will cause the greatest degree of harm. The options these represent are then arrayed in descending order of priority and addressed based on the resources that are available. Since all of the decisions about the tangible form of the risk management process will depend on getting the order of those priorities absolutely correct, it should be easy to see why a rigorous and accurate risk assessment process is so critical to the overall success of any security system.

Risk mitigation decisions are always built around tangible evidence. That evidence is usually obtained by conducting interviews and documenting observations of both organizational and human behavior, as well as auditing system logs and examining any other form of relevant technical or managerial record. Because the sources of data about risk are diverse, the collection process has to be systematic and coordinated. As a consequence, every risk assessment should embody a commonly accepted and repeatable methodology, which will produce concrete evidence that can be independently verified.

The gathering, compilation, analysis, and verification of data about risk can be time consuming and resource intensive. So, in order to ensure the effectiveness and accuracy of any particular risk assessment, the practical scope of the inquiry has to be precisely defined and should be limited to a particular problem.

Risk assessments typically target the various standard areas of threat in the organization's operating environment—electronic, human, and physical. The insight gained from each assessment is then aggregated into a single comprehensive understanding of the total threat picture, which serves as the basis for deciding how each threat will be addressed.

Operationally, it is perfectly acceptable to approach the understanding of risk in a highly focused and compartmentalized fashion, as long as the organization understands that the results of any particular risk assessment characterize only a part of the problem. In fact, the need to paint a detailed and accurate picture of all conceivable threats almost always implies a series of specifically targeted, highly integrated risk assessments that take place over a defined period of time.

Implementing a Managed Risk Control Process

As we said earlier, the steps to establish a risk control process involve five material considerations, planning, oversight, risk analysis, risk response, and continuous monitoring. The first consideration is implicit in all that we have said before; that is, all of the operational aspects of the risk management process have to be sufficiently planned. Operational planning is the essential ingredient in the organization of any kind of systematic process. Therefore, every step of the day-to-day practices that describe the organization's precise risk management approach have to be specified right down to the: who, what, when, and where of execution.

Then a well-defined, organization-wide and standard oversight process has to be conducted. Because continuity is a critical feature, this is done on an ongoing basis. Once routine risk management practices have been embedded in the organization's normal operation, they obviously have to be monitored for performance sake.

The aim of that oversight process is to always stay on top of the organization's risk situation. The oversight process should always be able to describe the present status of all identified risks. It should also be able to distinguish and report on new risks as they appear. Because it has to be continuous, that oversight process should be a regular management function.

In order to maintain a sufficient understanding of risk, the organization has to institute a specialized and well-organized performance reporting function. That function should be able to provide satisfactory qualitative and quantitative data to support the understanding of any novel or emerging risk event.

The performance analysis function should also be able to carry out the tests and reviews that are needed in order to confirm that currently existing risks continue to be understood and controlled. The ideal outcome of the execution of this function would be the continuous assurance that risks to assets that the organization considers priorities are properly understood and that any emerging risks will be identified and correctly described.

Once the performance analysis function has been defined and then properly staffed it is necessary to specify the series of prescribed responses that the organization chooses to make to the risks that currently exist. The responses should always be both substantive and correct. The responses should also be highly feasible and understandable. Finally, the responses should directly and provably target the known elements of an identified risk.

These responses are then implemented and employed as dictated in the plan. It is important to have a preplanned response in place for each known risk simply because the problems associated with risk can happen very quickly in cyber-space. Moreover, it is hard to decide what to do in the middle of an ongoing event. That is the reason why a planned response, which has been tested for effectiveness and drilled into the staff, is so useful. The deployment of the response can be validated through assorted "live-fire" hands-on drills and then updated as necessary.

The organization also has a duty to regularly monitor the changes in the operational risk environment. Constant vigilance is necessary because risks can appear at odd times and be in unanticipated forms in that environment. The monitoring can be done through systematic testing and reviews. Monitoring can also be carried out during day-to-day execution.

A formal testing and review plan is necessary in the case of the former approach. In the case of the latter approach, front-line users are among the best sources of information about new or emerging risks. That is because they use the technology in their day-to-day work and so users are often on the receiving end of the first probe or attack.

Accordingly, it is good practice to establish a direct, easy to utilize and clear reporting channel from the risk management function all the way down to the users in the organization. This channel can be maintained in many ways, but it is important that it be properly staffed and that the reports that come in are analyzed and acted on where appropriate.

Generic Approaches to Risk

There are four general approaches to risk (Figure 6.2). The first is to accept the risk and consequent losses. The second is to avoid the loss by performing the necessary actions to eliminate the risk. A third choice is to mitigate or reduce the effect of the risk. The last option involves transferring the risk to another party. That transfer can be achieved through contracts, insurance or a variety of similar mechanisms. All the same, no matter what approach is used the organization has to formulate a prescribed strategy to address each of its priority risks and make a decision about how they will be handled. Thus, regardless of the circumstances, the decision about what to do about the risk is purely in the domain of the designated decision maker for that organizational unit. The most common approach is probably the decision to accept the risk and the consequent losses. That is because many risks may pass through the risk management function unidentified or unacknowledged. Additionally, it is common practice to accept risks that are known to rarely happen or where there is little harm. That is because the cost of addressing the risk would not justify the potential cost of the harm.

The decision to accept a risk can also change as the risk situation changes. Risks that have been accepted are sometimes called residual risks. That is because the potential for harm exists, even though the present harm from the risk has been judged to be acceptable. Therefore, residual risks are still identified and tracked through the risk analysis process. Risk avoidance is aimed at preventing the risk from actually occurring. Cybersecurity has three standard components; prevention, detection, and response. The prevention element and all it involves are

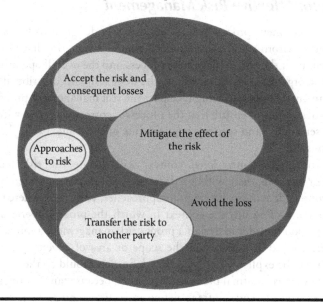

Figure 6.2 Approaches to risk.

examples of risk avoidance. Training programs, which are designed to increase employee ability to recognize and respond to incidents, are good examples of this type of risk handling approach. Because the least amount of harm will happen by addressing the risk directly, the cybersecurity process is heavily geared toward avoidance.

Risk avoidance approaches are the steps that an organization takes to minimize the potential loss in the event of the occurrence of a risk. For instance, an intrusion detection system will not prevent someone from actually intruding on the network. Instead, intrusion detection systems function as "burglar alarms" to limit the time that an intruder is allowed to roam undetected through a network. The limitation of time will not prevent damage. Instead the limitation of time is meant to restrict the damage that might occur.

The last two components of the cybersecurity process, detection, and response are embodied in the risk mitigation and risk transference approaches. In the case of risk transference, the response requires an outside party to assume the impact of the risk. Insurance is a prime example of this type of assumption. Obtaining insurance against specific risks does not prevent the risk from occurring, but it provides financial reimbursement to make up for a loss that will occur. Risk transfers work well when the risk is associated with a financial loss. Risk transfers are less effective when the loss is associated with intangible things, such as customer service/retention, organization reputation, or in some cases regulatory requirements.

Planning for Effective Risk Management

Every risk management process has to be purposely designed to fit its particular environment. Environmental considerations are the factors that have to be understood in order to fit the risk management process into the overall operating circumstances of the organization. Accordingly, the design should describe all technical and environmental factors that might impact the risk management process. In that respect, the design has to ensure that the process is correctly aligned with the environmental, sensitivity, and security requirements of the context that the organization functions in.

That is because organizational context will dictate the risk management approach. For instance, there will be a different set of risk management procedures where the context demands very rigorous approaches, versus one where the context is more relaxed. As a result, the context in which the process operates has to be clearly understood in order to design a proper risk management approach.

Once the context is understood the scope or area of coverage, of the actual assurance, has to be explicitly defined. That definition should be the result of a formal planning exercise. Formal planning is required because tangible organizational resources are involved. And failure to define an accurate and realistic scope for the risk management process could result in deficient protection and wasted resources.

Therefore, distinctive and meaningful boundaries have to be established for the risk management process.

In particular, logical interrelationships have to be understood between components, since the dependencies between the various elements that fall under the risk management process have to be factored into the assurance process. Since scope is always tied to the actual resources available, understanding which components will be a part of the risk management process and their actual interdependencies will allow the organization to be more realistic about what it will be able to protect.

The risk management process then develops a range of alternate solutions for identified risks. Risk management combines relevant technical, environmental, and stakeholder risk responses into a single coherent organizational response to risk. If stakeholders determine that a given action should be taken to make a risk acceptable, then risk response is developed and implemented. If the stakeholders accept a risk that exceeds its threshold, that risk is then continuously monitored by the risk management process in order to determine if any future actions will be needed. Every risk management process has to incorporate risk responses that are designed to address that specific risk in that particular environment.

Formal design of alternative risk mitigations is necessary because organizational resources are finite and a resource commitment is required to execute each mitigation step. Distinctive specifications have to be established for the risk response because the implementation and maintenance of the solution will always be limited to the actual resources available. Thus, the failure to define an accurate and realistic set of risk responses could result in wasted resources. For that reason, characterizing the components that will be a part of the risk management process for that specific risk management context and their actual interdependencies has to allow the organization to be more realistic about what it will be able to protect.

The roles and responsibilities that are defined for each of the actions that have been designated to mitigate each risk have to be explicitly assigned. This is a critical step in ensuring proper risk mitigation, since that definition designates specific personnel and financial resources to the activities that will be performed. It is also important to document assign the duties that are associated with each of those roles. Otherwise, participants are likely to use their own assumptions about what they are supposed to do and that could result in important risk mitigation activities falling through the cracks.

Roles and responsibilities are allocated by designating and then documenting explicit accountability for performance of each security task as well as all of the organizational reporting lines that are associated with each role. If third parties or contractors are responsible for any aspect of risk management, the responsibilities and reporting lines of both the contractor and the organizational unit also must be explicitly defined.

The assignment of accountability underwrites performance. Then continuous monitoring tells decision makers whether or not their objectives are being achieved, and whether their risk control management process is in line with expectations. The risk response architecture is monitored throughout its lifecycle in order to identify any new risks. This monitoring is an important element of good management practice. All risks that have been identified should be inspected for change, which includes the organizational context itself. Any new risk or one that has undergone change should also be evaluated.

Good risk management requires appropriate measures that accurately reflect the risk picture. Proper measurement relies on the availability of a set of meaningful standard measures of risk. As we said earlier, both qualitative and quantitative measures should be combined into a formal program of performance measurement. The qualitative and quantitative performance measurement program provides a series of snapshots of the risk picture and the succeeding analysis of those snapshots is used to manage risk.

Qualitative measures do not attempt to produce actual metrics, but rather focus on relative differences. Thus graphic scales, such as comparative risk levels are commonly used in qualitative analysis. In qualitative risk analysis, the measures that are used are typically a set of nominal values such as high, medium, and low. These categories are then given numbers so that the weights of relationships can be characterized.

Nonetheless, it is not possible to truly rank different elements of the same class. So the actual measurement itself is not precise. However, since one of the main purposes of the risk monitoring function is to determine priorities, qualitative analysis can be useful.

Quantitative analysis methods can also be used to measure risk. The value of quantitative methods depends on the quality of the data being generated. That is, the abstract and dynamic nature of information and communications technology operation will make the application of quantitative measures difficult. Therefore, in practice a blend of both quantitative and qualitative measures is often used to arrive at the desired understanding. Automated tools are frequently used to assist in the collection and analysis of any standard quantitative risk monitoring data. Automated tools ensure accurate risk monitoring data because they are not subject to fatigue or human error.

Sensitivity of the Information versus Rigor of the Controls

The aim of risk management is to capture a comprehensive picture of the risk environment. That picture will then comprise an all-inclusive record of the organization's assets, a statement of the acceptable levels of risk for each asset, and the constraints that will be placed on the protection against the risk by the technology or policies. The outcome of the risk environmental cataloging process is an alignment of the policies, procedures, and technologies that will be used for risk management with the business goals of the organization.

That alignment is needed to enable the tradeoff process. Tradeoffs will be used to decide the risk acceptance, risk avoidance, risk transference, or risk mitigation approach that will be used to ensure each asset against risk. When those tradeoffs are planned, they have to accurately reflect the organization's business objectives. An analysis of the priority of the information that enables those business objectives versus the risks that threaten that information is necessary in order to decide where to invest the organization's security resources. Defining risk levels needs to be done with respect to their impact on the confidentiality, integrity, and availability of the data in the organization's operational systems.

The determination of the appropriate level of control is based on a simple understanding of the requisite rigor of each control. That description of rigor should convey the general level of effort that is justified in order to protect that particular asset in the overall operating environment. The description of rigor satisfies two operational goals. First, it allows managers to make informed assignments of priorities for the allocation of assets. Second, it allows managers to coordinate the implementation and subsequent evaluation of the control functions that are assigned to the assurance of each asset.

Thus, it is essential to specify the sensitivity of each item of information within the system. That is because the sensitivity of the information determines the levels of confidentiality, integrity, and availability required. Thus this specification provides the necessary basis for determining the extent and rigor of the controls. The specification also forms the basis for designing the explicit controls that will be used to secure each component. That specification should not just be a guided by a consideration of technical standards and protocols. Minimally, the specification of the sensitivity should also consider the policies, laws, and any relevant constraints that might affect the confidentiality, integrity, or availability of information within the system.

The outcome of that specification should be a detailed recommendation of how the particular protection criteria will be addressed by a particular control. In addition, the recommendation for each control should provide a justification for why that particular approach was taken. The aim of that justification is to explain the type and relative importance of the effort to upper level managers. Each type of data and information processed by the system should be classified based on the severity of potential negative impacts on the organization and the degree to which the ability of the organization to perform its mission would be affected, should the information be compromised.

The sensitivity of information should be characterized based on the risks a compromise would represent. The highest risk would be associated with compromises that would adversely impact critical information, or which might result in loss of life, significant financial loss, threats to national security, or the inability of the organization to perform its primary mission.

Moderate risks would be those risks that might not compromise critical information, but where the losses would still have business impacts. Low risk items would be those risks where information might be lost, but it would not be vital to organizational functioning.

Writing the Risk Management Plan

The risk management plan shapes the risk management process. The primary role of the risk management plan is to create the framework for the detailed policies and procedures that will comprise the risk management process for that particular organization. The top level risk management plan provides the context that is needed to ensure that the organization's overall business objectives and goals are understood and then factored correctly into the decisions that are made about risk. In that respect then, the overall plan for risk management needs to be crafted in broad, organization-wide terms with the specific details of the approaches to be adopted left to lower level operational plans. It is important that this high-level document define the comprehensive processes and interrelationships needed to build a complete picture of the organizational risk situation. The ideal would be to create a road map that will let executive managers develop the strategies they will need to address existing risks.

First, the risk management plan should document the roles and responsibilities of the basic risk management team. The assignment of responsibility should be stated at a high enough level to allow the people on the risk management team to respond flexibly to situations covered in the plan. Nonetheless, the risk management plan has to assign specific authority to the team to act on those situations that are the responsibility of the risk management process. The assignment of high-level roles and responsibilities also ensures that the routine supervisory and budgetary authority, which is needed to conduct the process as a normal part of doing business, is expressly assigned to the individual members of the team.

Finally, the concepts associated with risk management have to be defined in clear organizational specific terms. That definition is necessary in order to align the organization's overall security objectives with its business objectives. In that respect, a comprehensive and detailed definition of key terms has to be provided as part of the planning setup process. The purpose of those definitions is to ensure a common vocabulary. Definitions are important because most people's understanding of what constitutes risk is subjective. Consequently, the organization has to provide a precise specification of what constitutes a risk, the levels of acceptable risk, and the attendant approaches that will be used to address each risk. Specific directives for how to report risks and the thresholds for acting on risk reports also have to be preestablished for the various risk elements. Those reporting requirements will also apply to active, residual, and accepted risks.

Coordinated Approach to Risk Management

Risk management coordinates three generic factors. Those factors are the risks that can be associated with the system, the business functions that are associated with the information in that system, and the extent of control necessary to manage those risks. The key to success lies in deploying the minimum number of controls to achieve a desired level of security, given the purposes of the affected business functions.

The risk management process can be carried out in two different ways. The most common way that risk management is conducted in most businesses is ad hoc. In the case of ad hoc risk management, security controls are created to fulfill specific security requirements. Those controls are generally created as the need is identified. Many organizations use an ad hoc approach to risk management simply because the deployment of a coordinated set of controls is a difficult undertaking. The ad hoc approach is cost efficient on a day-to-day basis because it only creates controls that are needed at the time. Nonetheless, it is almost certain to result in flawed protection. That is because the organization is reacting to events, rather than deploying coordinated protection.

The other approach to risk management is the coordinated approach. Because it is meant to provide comprehensive protection, the coordinated approach offers better security. The coordinated approach deploys a series of protection baselines in a defense in depth scheme. Those protection baselines are composed of a logical set of increasingly rigorous technical and behavioral controls. In most baselines, the electronic controls are automated, while the behavioral controls entail a series of human centered actions, which are intended to produce a desired outcome. In that respect then, each baseline is deployed to achieve specific security requirement. Those security requirements are prioritized in terms of the criticality of the data.

Nevertheless, the creation, deployment, and ongoing monitoring of the baselines is both time consuming and costly. Therefore, the degree of security justified under this scheme always has to be balanced against the level of effort and cost that is required to implement it. The aim of the coordinated approach is to identify the priority risks to the organization and then create and maintain an effective array of controls to manage those risks. Because cost is a factor, a precise specification of the maximum degree of acceptable risk is necessary in order to ensure a realistic plan. The specification of the maximum level of risk is necessary because much of real-world planning typically involves deciding what level of risk the organization is willing to accept.

A decision about the degree of risk that the organization is willing to accept will lead to an assignment of priorities. Understanding the value of an item enables an explicit decision about its priority. Those priorities then drive decisions about the practical form of the response. That value is typically expressed as the level of acceptability of the risk. Consequently, acceptability is typically expressed in operational terms such as, "Spend whatever it takes to ensure that this risk does not occur," all the way down to: "The harm the risk would cause does not justify the cost of addressing it." Nonetheless, in order to decide about that level of risk, the decision maker has first to know the value of the information the organization possesses.

Decisions about the acceptability of risk lead directly to a coordinated security response. Therefore, the risk management process always involves a technique that establishes a substantive, usually resource-based, link between the each risk and the benefits of managing it. Operational factors that enter into that analysis of risk acceptance include such issues as: "What is the level of criticality of each particular information asset and what is the specific degree of resource involvement?" Therefore, at a minimum risk evaluations have to answer one key question: "What is the tradeoff between accepting the risk and the harm it can cause?"

Ensuring an Effective Set of Risk Controls

The overall purpose of the risk management function is to maintain an appropriate set of risk controls. Therefore, all control sets have to be periodically assessed to ensure that their protection is relevant and maintains its effectiveness. Control assessments are a particularly critical part of that overall purpose. Control assessments are important because they continue to calibrate the effectiveness of the response to the specific threats to the current organizational operation. Control assessments underwrite the strategy that is used to deploy the overall risk management process. Control assessments let managers deploy the relevant reactive behaviors to respond to a risk. Control assessments also monitor the effectiveness of those controls once they have been put in place. Thus, the control assessment process ensures effective and up-to-date knowledge about the status of the security situation.

Control assessment is a prerequisite to the sustainment of the risk management function. That is because a systematic control assessment can specifically evaluate the performance of the control set that the organization has planned and deployed to carry out the substantive risk management. That targeted knowledge ensures the most efficient functioning of the control scheme across time. Control assessment is an information gathering function that focuses on understanding the performance of the assigned mitigations for any feasible risk. Control assessment identifies and evaluates each relevant action taken to mitigate risk, determines that the control that has been set to respond is in place and functioning correctly and as planned. In that respect, control assessments should always answer three relevant questions. The first is: "Is the control working as intended?" The answer to that question is typically expressed as an expression of effectiveness, usually on a percentage scale—for example, "the control appears to be eighty percent effective." Because controls are often not entirely effective the second question is: "What is the anticipated harm of the percentage of control failure?" The answer to that question is normally expressed as an estimate of the ongoing loss or harm resulting from the control's lack of effectiveness. The third question logically follows from the first two. That is: "Does the cost of the loss justify the cost of improving the control?"

All three of these questions have to be answered in practical terms in order to ensure ongoing sustainment of an effective security response. In particular, the cost benefit calculation that ensues from the control effectiveness estimate is going to guide the deployment and subsequent management of the new control.

Therefore, this process has to be both comprehensively conducted and rigorous in its application.

Risk Management Controls

The controls for risk management differ in their purpose and specificity. It is important to keep this difference in mind when designing and then assigning control processes because the people who will actually be executing each control need to know exactly how to perform all of the tasks that are required to make the control effective. As a consequence, it is important to ensure that managers are not asked to perform highly technical tasks, just as it is equally critical that technical people are not asked to perform managerial activities. In both cases, there is potential that the activities that underlie the control will either be misunderstood or misapplied.

It is also important to understand the operational status of the control. Knowing the existing operational status of the control is important in the design process because some controls will already exist in the overalls scheme while others will not be in place. Therefore, it is essential to have a complete understanding of where a procedure has already been implemented and where it has to be developed. This understanding is based on whether each necessary control item is operational and effective, or planned, but not actually operational.

It is also common to have part of the control in place while other parts are still missing. If some parts of the control are implemented and others have been planned, there should be an explicit specification of the parts of the control that are in place and the parts that are not. Where there are planned measures, this description should also include a list of resources required to make them operational and the expected date.

Finally, situations will exist where controls would be desirable, but it would neither be cost effective nor feasible to implement them. If that is the case then those controls should be noted for future planning as well as potential long-term monitoring of the risk that the measure was meant to manage.

Control Types: Management Controls

Management controls are behavioral. They are based on policies and implement the organization's risk management procedures. They manage risks through human-based actions rather than technology. These controls are typically designed based on a risk analysis, which should support a comparison between the costs of the applicable controls and the value of the information resource they are designed to protect. Management controls are always deployed based on the impact of the threats that they have been designed to address. It is important to design the appropriate administrative, physical, and personnel security controls into the risk management process from its inception. Because risks come in a number of forms, there can be an extensive range and variety of risk management controls. Management controls are primarily enforced by the testing and review process. Therefore, the design must ensure that tests are performed during the development of the risk management process. The aim of those evaluations is to confirm that all of the necessary controls are an established part of the risk management process.

Control Types: Technical Controls

Just as with the management process, the technical controls should also be well defined, understood, and followed. From a risk management standpoint, the most obvious technical controls are those that underlie the access control system. Technical controls are important and should be monitored closely. The monitoring of technical controls is an essential aspect of management accountability as well as a technical issue. As a consequence the monitoring of technical controls from a managerial standpoint is often associated with audit procedures. A complete audit trail and a chronological record are evidence of adequate monitoring. The use of system log files is an example of this type of control.

Practical Steps to Implement a Security Control

The implementation of an effective security control requires the ability to focus the activity at a stratum in the organization that was far lower and more detailed than most people imagine. The design of a control itself is modular in the sense that it is a well-defined behavior with a high degree of boundary integrity. The control design also should evidence defense in depth in that those spaces were controlled in increasingly rigorous fashion. Finally, the security system that the design created must be unmistakably cost efficient in that the priority areas that were identified by stakeholders were secured by resources in a progressive fashion, from most vital to least important.

The control architecture has to be carefully targeted; that is, the targets for control and their associated behaviors ought to be stated in concrete terms. Risks represent a threat to some aspect of organizational functioning. Moreover, the management of risk is a complex process with lots of inherent detail. Therefore, in order to implement a rational set of risk management controls, it is necessary to classify and understand the nature of the risks that will present themselves in the organization's current operating environment.

In general, risks can be classified into two categories, known and unknown. Unknown risks, also known as asymmetric risks, are not predictable and are not subject to management by standard risk management methods. Because of their unpredictability, they do not lend themselves to specific techniques for analysis. Known risks are those that should be logically expected to occur. Thus, another name for known risk is intrinsic risks. In many cases, the probability of occurrence and subsequent impact of an intrinsic risk can be estimated. Intrinsic risks can be managed and minimized by an effective risk management program. Accordingly, the organization has to adopt and follow some kind of structured process to designate, classify and provide a meaningful response to the intrinsic risks that fall within the scope of the risk management process.

Risk breakdown structures typically provide the needed structure. Risk breakdown structures can be employed to organize and coordinate the risk identification, analysis, and planning activities of a comprehensive risk management program. Risk breakdown structures classify areas of intrinsic risk into three standard categories: strategic (or policy level), operational (or ongoing) and process execution risks (Figure 6.3).

Using these categories in some form of checklist, managers can systematically work their way through a practical operational situation and evaluate the status of each of the identified threats and their associated risks and place a priority. These risk categories encompass all of the potential ways that an organization's information and communication technology assets and documentation can be threatened, as well as any of the risks that are associated with the failure to carry out some aspect of the process correctly. These are very large areas of organizational functioning and so their analysis requires extensive coordination. And because of the sheer scope of each of these areas, the analysis process itself usually requires a large number of participants.

Managers can use a risk breakdown checklist as a road map to guide the deployment of resources to evaluate the threat potential of each of the risks in each of these categories. In addition, managers can use a risk breakdown checklist to organize the raw data from each of these areas into logical categories for analysis once that data has been obtained.

The second category includes all of the operational risks. These types of risk are much more focused and detailed. Operational risks involve failures in the operational security activities that the organization carries out, such as identify management, identification and authentication processes, auditing, malicious code protection, and long-term system maintenance and communications security. These areas require the coordination of complex managerial and technical activities. Because of that complexity, the analysis of those areas has to be detailed and closely

Figure 6.3   Three categories of risk.

controlled. A risk management checklist allows managers to both coordinate the data collection effort as well as aggregate the huge amount of data that are normally collected into a description of the risk to the operation of the organization.

Finally, there are the risks that are associated with the technical controls. Those include the predictable risks to electronic systems; however, they also include any electronic controls over media and the physical and personnel security environment. The technical risk category even includes risks that reside in the security education, training, and awareness function. Because of their diversity and inherent complexity, every technical risk area has to be very well defined in order to be properly analyzed. A checklist of categories for analysis provides the necessary structure for the analysis. It will ensure that the right data are captured for each category as well as ensure that the eventual analysis is appropriate.

Modeling Risks for Prioritization

The entities that comprise an organization, their relationships to each other and the potential actions that could adversely impact them, can be modeled using a formal modeling technique. An exact understanding can be derived from the application of such a method. That understanding will let the organization describe in graphic terms the things that threaten it, what those threats are likely to impact and their likelihood of occurrence. That understanding can then facilitate the development of precisely targeted controls for each threat.

Threat modeling is a structured method that is used to analyze risk related data. A successful threat modeling process requires a lot of "creative" thinking, in that every conceivable threat should be put on the table and assessed. Threat modeling allows risk data to be modeled and subsequently communicated among team members. The major steps of threat modeling begin with a determination of the scope of protected space that the model corresponds to. Then threats that might impact the components of that space are enumerated and specific details as to the potential likelihood and impact of the threat are collected.

In order to ensure that the analysis is comprehensive, data flow diagrams or similar information flow diagrams such as Unified Modeling Language (UML) based use-case diagrams are employed to help visualize and describe the target space. Those diagrams will help to ensure inclusive coverage. Descriptions of potential attack vectors and the impacts of each of those vectors on the protected space are used to think through and then describe the actual attack behavior. In that respect then, all potential attack vectors should be able to be described and examined from an adversary's point of view. And controls can be crafted to mitigate a given line of attack.

Once the threats are characterized, they are entered into a database. That database will contain the detailed information about every attack depicted in the threat model. Then, the implications of each threat have to be analyzed. This analysis is typically based on assigning a criticality score. A standardized criticality score is an important part of the threat modeling process because it allows analysts to classify each identified threat in terms of its likelihood and potential harm.

That classification can then lead to a priority ordering of known threats from most dangerous to least dangerous. The ordering will allow management to concentrate resources on controlling the threats that have the greatest potential for harm. It will also let managers assign fewer resources to lower priority threats. It is this classification process that allows managers to build logical and substantive defense in depth control schemes.

A focus on priority differs from the typical low hanging fruit approach. Nevertheless, the implementation process has to be based on some kind of quantitative or rational method for assigning priorities. Without priorities to guide the implementation it is likely that the easiest to understand or most obvious threats will be addressed first. That approach would, in essence, disregard the business value of what was being protected. Given the requirement for thorough understanding in order to assign practical priorities, it is important to have a commonly agreed on starting point to base the comparisons. That is the role of threat modeling. Threat modeling goes a long way toward putting implementation based on a quantitative and systematic footing.

Risk Management and Operational Evaluation of Change

Because the business environment is constantly changing, it is necessary to do continuing operational assessments of the risk situation in order to assure the validity of the risk management strategy. Operational risk assessments are established by plan. The planning has to be aligned with business goals and their accompanying strategies. The outcome of the planning process must be a relevant response to the current risk picture, within business constraints.

All plans for any form of risk management should be based on consistent standard data. Consistency is important because management will use that data to make decisions about the degree of risk exposure, as well as the types of controls that will have to be deployed. Accordingly, all of the metrics included in the risk evaluation process must be unambiguously defined in the plan. Those definitions can then be used to ensure that the data from the assessment process is consistent.

Consistency is a critical factor because stakeholders have to share a common understanding of the precise nature of the threats the organization faces in order to deploy an appropriate and trusted response. As a result, it is important to make certain that there is reliable understanding of what a given piece of information means. If the various people who are involved in the risk management process interpret the information differently, there is a potential for uncoordinated and ineffective operational responses. Also, there is the issue of credibility when it comes to the data itself. If there is no clear definition provided, to function as the basis for measurement, then it is hard for decision makers to rely on the data.

The activities that are involved in operational assessment are planned and implemented in the same way as other types of organizational assessment activities; that is, the operational risk assessment process employs risk evaluations to decide about the nature of emerging threats.

Even so, rather than producing an overall risk management strategy, the goal of the operational risk assessment is to say with certainty that the currently deployed set of controls properly address the right threats. The assessment also seeks to prove that those controls continue to be effective given the overall aims of the business.

If the controls that are currently deployed do not address the aims of the business, then the operational risk assessment should provide all of the information necessary to allow decision makers make the changes that are needed to achieve the desired state. Thus, any review report that contains recommendations for change is typically passed along to the people who are responsible for maintaining the risk management process instead of the top level planners who initially formulated the response. The aim of that report is to provide explicit advice about changes that must be made to the current risk management process.

Planning for operational risk assessments involves the establishment of a standard schedule for each assessment, as well as a defined process for problem reporting and corrective action. The routine nature of these reviews means that the organization should treat operational risk assessment exactly as it would any other continuous organizational process. That is, the process should be resourced and staffed to ensure that it functions as a part of the everyday business operation. Operational risk assessment does not typically entail the sort of strategic planning focus that was involved in the formulation of the security strategy. Instead, it makes use of a defined set of performance criteria to evaluate the performance of the routine operation of the risk management function.

Those criteria are typically laid down during the formulation of the initial risk management strategy. Consequently, every risk control that is deployed should have an explicit set of standard criteria built into its specification. These criteria should be both measurable and capable of being recorded in some meaningful fashion. In addition, the assumptions about cost and occurrence that were part of the original decision to deploy each control should also be stated as a means of maintaining perspective on the operational intent of that control. The purpose of standard performance criteria is to allow decision makers to judge whether that control is performing as desired and continues to achieve its intended purpose. The organization will use the data produced by the operational assessment process to ensure the effectiveness of its risk management scheme.

Evaluating the Overall Policy Guidance

The real proof of a risk management program's success lies in the execution of the policies and procedures for risk management. The test is whether those policies and procedures have achieved the desired business outcomes. Security assessments and evaluations can be used to verify that policies and procedures are functioning as designed. Moreover, assessments can produce evidence that those policies and procedures are effectively controlling risk. Actual operational assessment of risk management plans is done in a multiphase process involving assessments, evaluations, and red team exercises.

The assessment process itself is mainly a "paper drill" designed to verify through interviews and records checks that policies and procedures have successfully covered the essential elements of risk management. Thus, there is no hands-on testing in an assessment. Assessments focus at the policy/procedural level. An assessment is an examination of a set of policies and procedures, together with records associated with the operation of those policies and procedures over time, to evaluate whether the organization is actually operating as planned. The assessment also attempts to characterize the effectiveness of each procedure based on the historical data that are recorded about its execution. An evaluation is similar to an assessment in that it too seeks to do a comprehensive examination of the effectiveness of a risk management system, but evaluation add a series of planned tests of the actual functioning of the process in order to confirm that features are functioning as they were designed to so. Both assessments and evaluations are designed to cover the entire breadth of the business.

Assessments and evaluations are general in focus and comprehensive. They do not go into sufficient depth to be able to address a particular focused target. As the scope of an evaluation narrows, it is possible to deepen the specific analysis at strategic points. That is the basis for a final technique. That technique is known as a "red team" approach. Red team approaches are often used to perform deeper dives into a particular aspect of risk management. Red team approaches, which are sometimes also known as pen-testing, assess the actual performance of a security control in the operational environment. A red team evaluation is narrow in scope, but designed to probe deeply enough to assess the actual effectiveness of a control against a specific type of attack. The aim of a red team approach is to accurately judge the effectiveness of a particular control. These are time-consuming, resource intensive exercises as they rely heavily on skilled operators, who attempt to violate the security in such a manner as to mimic real-world attacks.

Program Management Reviews

Periodic reviews are necessary for any program. They are needed to ensure that the program is still meeting the objectives established by management. Risk management programs are no different. One of the important elements of the risk management process is to perform a series of reviews, which are designed to assess the overall performance of the program. Two types of review are commonly used, a time-based review and an event-based review. It is generally a good idea to utilize both types of reviews in practice, in order to ensure complete coverage.

A time-based review is one that occurs at regular intervals, ranging typically from 1 to 3 years between reviews. These are top-down, comprehensive reviews that are designed to examine all aspects of the risk management program against the business objectives that are currently in place. The purpose of these time-based reviews is to ensure that the risk management program stays current with respect to both the controls that implement it and the ever changing business objectives of the enterprise.

An event-based review is designed to be less comprehensive, but much more focused on a particular aspect of the risk management process. Like lessons-learned and after-action reviews, event-based reviews are meant to capture and record information about a particular element of the risk management program. For instance, if a business unit is reorganized, then business objectives may change. Because that change would represent a significant modification of the operating environment, it would be a good idea to make sure that the risk management program continues to support the goals of the business. For the same reason, it is also important to evaluate the risk management situation after an actual incident has occurred in order to ensure that the outcomes of the incident reflect the desired results.

The objective of both of these kinds of reviews is to ensure that the risk management program stays in-step with changes in the business environment. Regardless of the type of review conducted, there are some common elements that should be looked at as a part of each review. The first of these elements are the security controls themselves. In essence, the review should determine how effective these controls were in responding to the occurrence that they were designed to prevent. In addition, the review should confirm that there was not a need for additional controls for that particular incident.

In conjunction with the assessment of the actual control set, the reviews should also examine the effectiveness of the policies and procedures that guide the implementation and routine operation of those controls. Those policies and procedures should be proven to align with the residual risk levels within the environment, as well as address all of the known threats and vulnerabilities. If the need to add additional controls, policies, procedures, or modify existing ones is identified then the review report should itemize what those changes should be.

In addition to operational reviews, a standard operating procedure should be defined for conducting audits. As most organizations have an internal audit function, the audit of risk management processes and procedures should be built into their regular internal audit function. Conducting an audit of the risk management process as part of regular internal audit activity is an appropriate way to address the need for periodic audits of the risk management process. Rolling the assessment of the risk management function into regular internal audit activities is yet another way to institutionalize reviews of the risk management process.

Information should be collected throughout the project's life cycle for purposes of improving the risk management process. There should be designated points in the risk management process where the process itself is reviewed in order to evaluate its effectiveness. Also, the risk management evaluation process can generate useful lessons learned. Risk management data includes such things as risks identified, their sources, their causes, their treatment, and the success of the treatments selected. Information on the risks identified, their treatment, and the success of the treatments can then be used to stay on top of systemic project and organizational risks.

Periodic reviews ensure that the project is still meeting the objectives established by management. Risk management programs are no different than any other organizational function in that they can wander off their initial purpose. Thus, one of the important elements of the risk management process is the execution of a series of reviews that are designed to assess whether the process continues to achieve its objectives. Two types of review are commonly used to do this, a time-based review and an event-based review. It is generally a good idea to utilize both types of reviews in practice, in order to ensure complete coverage.

A time-based review is one that occurs at regular intervals in a project. The intervals are typically set during project planning. These are top-down, comprehensive examinations that are designed to assess all aspects of the risk management program against business objectives. The purpose of these time-based reviews is to ensure that the risk management program stays current with respect to both its treatments and the ever changing risk environment. An event-based review is less comprehensive, but much more focused on a particular aspect of the risk management process. Like lessons-learned and after-action reviews, event-based reviews are meant to capture and record information about a particular element of the risk management program.

The objective of both of these types of review is to ensure that the risk management program stays in-step with changes in the risk environment. Regardless of the type of review conducted, there are some common elements that should be looked at as a part of each review. The first of these elements are the risk treatments themselves. In essence, the review should determine how effective these treatments continue to be in responding to the risks that they were designed to prevent. In addition, the review should confirm that there was not a need for additional measures for that particular incident.

In conjunction with the assessment of the actual treatments, the reviews should also examine the effectiveness of the policies and procedures that guide the implementation and routine operation of the risk management program. Those policies and procedures should be proven to align with the environment's understood, residual risk levels, as well as address all of the known risks. If the need to add additional treatments, policies, procedures, or modify existing ones is identified then the review report should itemize what those changes should be.

Chapter Summary

Risk management ensures the continuing security of any business operation. Risk management gathers and utilizes information from all environmental and internal sources, in order to mitigate current risk and decrease the possibility of encountering future risks. That information gathering activity is aided by a set of formal processes and technologies. However, at its core a successful risk management function depends on the ability to make certain that the knowledge that risk management acquires is incorporated as quickly and efficiently as possible into the organization's substantive business activities. Risk management applies to every kind of organizational application from the assurance of technical work through ensuring the effectiveness of the company's management processes.

The specific goal of the risk management process is to identify, analyze, mitigate, and monitor each currently active as well as latent risk that is known to exist within the organization. Therefore, at its heart, risk management is an information gathering and decision-making function. It focuses on understanding all feasible forms of risk and then classifies and assesses those risks in order to determine their importance. Risk management ensures that there is sufficient knowledge about each relevant threat available for decision making. And then risk management takes the necessary steps to react to and mitigate all priority risks. Risk management also monitors the effectiveness of those mitigations once they have been put in place.

In addition to providing the information that helps guide strategic decision making about risks, the risk management process also makes certain that a commonly accepted and systematic set of policies and procedures are in place to handle known risks. That responsibility is operationalized through a standard set of operating procedures. Those procedures ensure that the risk planning, analysis, response, and process management function are always directly aligned to the goals of the business operation. Nevertheless, the primary purpose of risk management is to ensure a disciplined and systematic set of controls that will respond to the risks that the organization considers a priority. That set of controls is conceived, organized, and managed by plan. A risk management plan is a high-level document that details the overall approach that will be employed to control the risks that the enterprise deems worth addressing. There might be any number of strategies embodied in that plan, but there is normally a sequence of six standard elements involved in risk management.

All of the factors that comprise that organizational context have to be understood in order to design an effective set of risk management controls. The definition of the scope of coverage and the required level of assurance are the primary influences that define that context. The overall purpose of the risk management function is to establish and maintain an appropriate set of risk controls. Because of that generic purpose, risk assessments are an especially critical part of the overall risk management process.

Risk assessments ensure effective risk management response because they identify threats to the organization as they appear and then decide how likely those threats are to have a meaningful impact, as well as the elements of the organization that are impacted by each threat. Correctly executed, the current threat environment is assessed on some agreed on periodic basis in order to ensure that the current risk mitigation schema is appropriate and is successfully mitigating threats.

The aim of the strategic planning for risk monitoring is to initially identify the priority risks and then create and maintain an effective set of formal controls to manage each risk. Along with those controls, strategic risk management planning is also responsible for assigning the specific employee roles and responsibilities required for the management of each risk. Finally, the plan provides a description of the process that will be used to evaluate and improve the overall risk management function, including how to use lessons learned to change the form of the response. Because cost is always a factor in business decision making, a precise specification of the maximum degree of acceptable risk is necessary in order to guide decisions about the degree of risk the organization is willing to underwrite. A specification of the maximum level of acceptable risk drives the tradeoff process that is required to make a real-world planning decision about risk acceptance for each specific project.

Good risk management requires appropriate measures that accurately reflect the risk picture. Qualitative measures do not attempt to produce actual metrics, but rather focus on relative differences. Thus graphic scales, such as comparative risk levels are commonly used in qualitative analysis. In qualitative risk analysis, the measures that are used are typically a set of nominal values such as high, medium, and low. These categories are then given numbers so that the weights of relationships can be characterized.

Quantitative analysis methods can also be used to measure risk. The value of quantitative methods depends on the quality of the data being generated. That is, the abstract and dynamic nature of information and communications technology operation will make the application of quantitative measures difficult. Therefore, in practice a blend of both quantitative and qualitative measures is often used to arrive at the desired understanding. Automated tools are frequently used to assist in the collection and analysis of any standard quantitative risk monitoring data. Automated tools ensure accurate risk monitoring data because they are not subject to fatigue or human error.

The overall purpose of the risk management function is to maintain an appropriate set of risk controls. Therefore, all control sets have to be periodically assessed to ensure that their protection is relevant and maintains its effectiveness. Control assessments are a particularly critical part of that overall purpose. Management controls are behavioral. They are based on policies and implement the organization's risk management procedures. They manage risks through human-based actions rather than technology. These controls are typically designed based on a risk analysis, which should support a comparison between the costs of the applicable controls and the value of the information resource they are designed to protect. Management controls are always deployed based on the impact of the threats that they have been designed to address. It is important to design the appropriate administrative, physical, and personnel security controls into the risk management process from its inception. Because risks come in a number of forms, there can be an extensive range and variety of risk management controls.

Just as with the management process, the technical controls should also be well defined, understood, and followed. From a risk management standpoint, the most obvious technical controls are those that underlie the access control system.

Technical controls are important and should be monitored closely. The monitoring of technical controls is an essential aspect of management accountability as well as a technical issue. As a consequence the monitoring of technical controls from a managerial standpoint is often associated with audit procedures. A complete audit trail and a chronological record are evidence of adequate monitoring. The use of system log files is an example of this type of control.

The entities that comprise an organization, their relationships to each other and the potential actions that could adversely impact them, can be modeled using a formal modeling technique. An exact understanding can be derived from the application of such a method. That understanding will let the organization describe in graphic terms the things that threaten it, what those threats are likely to impact and their likelihood of occurrence. That understanding can then facilitate the development of precisely targeted controls for each threat. Threat modeling is a structured method that is used to analyze risk related data. A successful threat modeling process requires a lot of "creative" thinking, in that every conceivable threat should be put on the table and assessed. Threat modeling allows risk data to be modeled and subsequently communicated among team members. The major steps of threat modeling begin with a determination of the scope of protected space that the model corresponds to. Then threats that might impact the components of that space are enumerated and specific details as to the potential likelihood and impact of the threat are collected.

Because the business environment is constantly changing, it is necessary to do continuing operational assessments of the risk situation in order to assure the validity of the risk management strategy. Operational risk assessments are established by plan. The planning has to be aligned with business goals and their accompanying strategies. The outcome of the planning process must be a relevant response to the current risk picture, within business constraints.

Key Concepts

- Risk management is driven by information.
- Risk management requires effective channels of communication.
- There are five principle activities in the risk management process.
- Risk management is made more effective by risk profiles.
- Risk management is enabled by a strategic planning function.
- The risks in the risk environment must be categorized in order to be addressed properly.
- The aim of practical tailoring of controls is to address priority risks.
- There are two types of controls—managerial and technical.
- Risks can be modeled using threat models.
- The risk management program must be continuously assessed for relevance.
- Periodic reviews ensure continuing effectiveness of the risk management function.

- There are four approaches to risk—accept, mitigate, transfer, or avoidance.
- Risk management controls are managed through a baseline configuration.

Key Terms

Acceptable risk—a situation where either the likelihood or impact of an occurrence can be justified.

Annual rate of occurrence—the frequency per year that a known event takes place.

Asset valuation—an assessment of the overall worth of a given possession, usually in dollars.

Benchmarking—establishing a basic point of comparison for evaluation of an item.

Business impact analysis—an assessment of the effect on the organization of the occurrence of a given event.

Likelihood determination—an assessment of the probability that an event will occur.

Operational process model—depicts the sequence of interconnected activities and their relevant inputs and consequent outputs which make up a business or operational process.

Organizational process framework—a mechanism for managing organizational complexities. It uses five architected views: alignment, process interdependence, governance, organizational operations, and process traceability.

Residual risk—an intrinsic weakness that is currently not exploited by a threat.

Risk analysis—the assessment of the overall likelihood and impact of a threat.

Risk control—electronic or behavioral actions designed to prevent or mitigate an adverse event.

Risk level—the degree of likelihood and impact that is considered acceptable before a response is required.

Risk management—a set of formal organizational process that are designed to respond appropriately to any identified adverse event.

Risk mitigation—a set of formal organizational processes that are designed to slow down or minimize the impact of an adverse event.

Risk profile—a categorization of the known risks for a particular instance presented as a unified baseline.

Risk response—the specific mitigation that is planned for a given adverse event.

Threat—adversarial action that could produce harm or an undesirable outcome.

Threat modeling—representation of the risk environment using a commonly accepted graphic modeling approach such as data flow or UML.

Vulnerability—a recognized weakness that can be exploited by an identified threat.

Chapter 7

Control Formulation and Implementation Process

At the conclusion of this chapter, the reader will understand:

- The fundamental practices of control formulation
- The common types of control requirements for an organization
- Examples of the various types of behaviors embedded in controls
- How to implement a control in a practical setting
- The top-down process of designing and implementing controls
- The common types of documentation produced by controls
- The process of tailoring controls to the business environment
- The variety of control types and their application

The Control Formulation Process

A properly functioning control process will ensure the overall value and productivity of the information and communication technology (ICT) operation while ensuring all legal and regulatory requirements for performance of the business process are met. The function of an established set of discrete behavioral and technical controls is to assure the status of some aspect of the ICT operation at a given point in time. This is accomplished by identifying organizational functions that require protection by controls and then deploying them. A concrete framework of best practice behaviors is deployed in order to ensure a desired level of organizational assurance. That framework is usually based on a standard model, which is appropriate to the control target.

The resultant control set is then assess or audited in order to determine the status of the target function with respect to its desired state. The resultant reviews or audits should provide sufficient knowledge about the performance of the assigned control set in order to judge their effectiveness.

The actual control is enabled by a set of discreet behavioral and technical activities that operationalize the intended assurance requirements. In addition, a systematic reporting function is also established as the formal means of feeding control status information back to the organization. Accountability for the control system is enforced through regular assessments. The purpose of these assessments is to sustain the desired state of assurance for the entity under control.

Proper assurance of ICT assets requires the performance of an explicit inventory management function, including an identification and labeling scheme, prior to the decision about the form of the control set. This scheme provides an explicit description of the objects in that inventory and the rules for control as well as a plan for how the ongoing status assessment will be conducted.

The common mechanism that is employed by a business to ensure its proper operation is a set of formally designed and implemented control set. The question facing every manager, though, is "How do you judge the suitability and adequacy of those controls." With cybersecurity, there are three generic requirements that a proper control set will seek to satisfy:

1. Controls that ensure only authorized access to information
2. Controls that ensure against the incorrect entry or maintenance of erroneous information in the business operation
3. Controls that ensure that the right information is available to the right decision makers as it is needed

Those three meta-requirements underwrite seven desirable end-qualities (Figure 7.1).

In essence, all of these generic qualities must be to some extent present in order to assure suitable overall security of the ICT system. All of these qualities are abstract in nature. But their presence can be judged by explicit outcomes or effects, which result from the practical operation of the controls that have been set to achieve them. As mentioned previously, these seven qualitative outcomes are as follows:

1. *Confidentiality*—concerns the protection of sensitive information from unauthorized disclosure. It ensures that only authorized access is given.
2. *Integrity*—relates to the accuracy and completeness of information as well as to its legitimacy in accordance with business values and expectations. It ensures that all information is valid and correct.

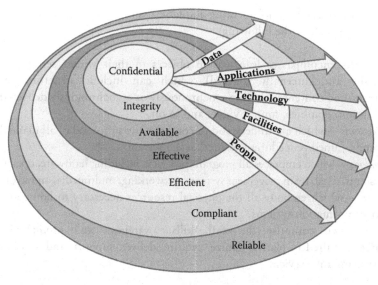

Desired characteristics for all ICT of value

Figure 7.1   Seven desirable end qualities with combined factors.

3. *Available*—relates to information being accessible when required by the business process now and in the future. It also concerns the safeguarding of necessary resources and associated capabilities.

4. *Effective*—deals with information being relevant and pertinent to the business process as well as being delivered in a timely, correct, consistent, and usable manner. It guarantees that the control set will achieve its purpose.

5. *Efficient*—concerns the provision of information through the optimal (most productive and economical) use of resources. It ensures that the control set operates as capably as possible.

6. *Compliant*—deals with conforming to those laws, regulations, and contractual arrangements to which the business process is subject, that is, externally imposed business criteria. It ensures that the control set conforms to all laws, regulations, and standards.

7. *Reliable*—relates to the provision of appropriate information for management to operate the entity and for management to exercise its financial and compliance reporting responsibilities. It ensures that the control set performs consistently as intended.

In that respect then, these are the universally desirable characteristics that the control system should exhibit. The goal of these combined factors is to systematically dictate the requirements for implementing auditable assurance of all ICT items of value. Those items include the following:

1. *Data*—this encompasses information objects in their widest sense (i.e., externally and internally sourced), which can include structured or nonstructured content including synchronously or asynchronously delivered information, graphics, sound, video, and so on.
2. *Applications*—which are understood to comprise the sum total of all manual and programmed procedures executed in the system.
3. *Technology*—which embraces all programmed logic including hardware, operating systems, database management systems, networking, multimedia, and so on.
4. *Facilities*—which embody all the physical resources necessary to house and support information systems.
5. *People*—which comprise the staff skills, awareness, and productivity resources required to plan, organize, acquire, deliver, support, and monitor ICT systems and services.

Control Frameworks

As we have seen, control frameworks are large strategic models which specify standard, well-defined, and commonly accepted practices for suitable ICT management and protection. They are normally structured as a set of high-level control objectives, which are then elaborated by a collection of well-defined underlying activities or control objectives. These control objectives represent the explicitly desired behaviors that will implement the control process and which can be observed and audited.

The underlying aim of a control framework is to provide best practice for three generic levels of ICT work. Another way to view and organize standard control requirements can be described from three generic points of view:

1. Operational—in terms of discretely auditable performance requirements/criteria
2. Managerial—in terms of functions deployed to fulfill the business requirements
3. Organizational—in terms of logically related organizational functions

Operational Activities: Starting from the most focused perspective, there are the fundamental work-related activities that comprise the day-to-day tasks that the business carries out to produce measurable outcomes. Activities within the operational domain have an applied orientation, thus they have a life-cycle focus.

The lifecycle orientation necessitates that the control requirements underwrite the performance of standard information and communications technology tasks. Those tasks tend to have a predefined outcome associated with them. Thus, they represent a discrete set of operational work instructions, rather than process descriptions.

Management-level processes are then defined conceptually one layer up. The control recommendations at the management level can be viewed as a series of logically related ICT functions with natural partitions with respect to the form of the control. In essence, controls at the management level provide the functional definition of information and communications technology governance requirements, such as, general project and risk management processes. This level forms the basis for the policy and procedure definitions that guide the design and deployment of the explicit controls at the operational level.

At the organization level, management processes are grouped into support of the generic business functions, such as financial system controls or manufacturing system controls, and so on. That natural grouping into business processes often defines the global factors that an organization has to consider in order to be effective. It is the presence or absence of important elements of these generic factors at any level of the organization's functioning that dictates the relative performance of the company or the business unit.

Standard Control Requirements

Figure 7.2 shows the four business factors for standard control requirements.

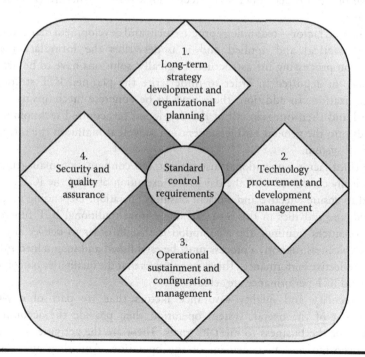

Figure 7.2   Standard control requirements.

In their most universal form, there are four generic business factors that involve some type of control requirement:

1. Long-term strategy development and organizational planning
2. Technology procurement and development management
3. Operational sustainment and configuration management
4. Security and quality assurance

The first factor relates to the business's development of comprehensive organization-wide long-term strategy and shorter-term tactical plans to manage and direct the ICT function. This factor specifically centers on the identification of the best way that the organization's ICT operation can contribute to the achievement of business goals.

This factor's global responsibility is to assure that the organization's strategic ICT vision is both well-defined and properly attained. This inevitably involves a comprehensive long-range planning function. Likewise, it also involves execution of a prescribed process to ensure that long-term strategies are sufficiently communicated to the organization as a whole, sufficiently to execute the plans. It also ensures that feedback from the different constituencies within the organization is usefully integrated going forward. Finally, this factor assures that a capable organizational process and technological infrastructure is created and maintained.

The second factor—technology procurement and development management—is more practical and applied and it underwrites the formulation of the information processing infrastructure. Logically, solutions have to be designed, developed, or acquired in order to underwrite the planned ICT strategies of the organization. In addition, there have to be concrete mechanisms in place to install and then integrate all of the developed or acquired technologies and processes into the general business operation as well as maintain the integrity of the overall system.

The third factor—operational sustainment and configuration management—is then logically concerned with the day-to-day execution of all of the ICT functions required to ensure effective and efficient business operation. Depending on context and need, the activities in this area can range from traditional ICT functions to human resources training. The assumption is that in order to deliver any of the necessary business support, a process must be established and maintained sufficient to ensure effective performance. This factor ensures that the qualitative outcomes that define good ICT performance are achieved.

The security and quality assurance factors that are part of day-to-day management of the overall system operation then provide the accountability necessary for the business to meet its goals. These are the activities that ensure proper oversight and management of the operation. And they are closest to the control elements of the organization. Those activities perform the regular updating, verification, and validation of both the system and its discrete controls over time.

The focus of that operational assessment is on ensuring the capability and compliance of all of the controls with that particular area of responsibility. Therefore, this is the factor enforces the organization's commitment to assure continuous and ongoing management control over all of its ICT objects and processes.

Creating and Documenting Control Objectives

Control objectives provide a precise and clear definition of the activities necessary to ensure effectiveness, efficiency, and economy of resource utilization. Thus, the operation's control objectives define the control framework concepts that have to be translated into specific actions applicable within the ICT process. Control objectives specify the actions of ICT managers and staff for any interested reviewers or auditors, both internal and external. More importantly, they also communicate best practice to the business process owners.

Detailed control objectives are identified for each process defined by the control framework. These control objectives are by definition the minimum control set required to ensure effective outcomes. Control objectives are enabled by control statements. In that respect, each control statement specifies a set of applicable control behaviors that are assumed to fulfill a given goal or purpose of the ICT operation.

Each control objective specifies the desired behaviors and expected results or outcomes to be achieved by implementing a given control procedure. The control objectives in all of the frameworks we have discussed are generic in that respect. So the actual specification and implementation of the behavior have to be tailored. This simply means that the actual control statement has to be crafted to precisely fit the application within the particular environment.

For instance, in the process of creating an information infrastructure, it would be necessary to specify a model of the underlying database architecture, as well as to create a data dictionary and syntax rules and classify all of the items of data in the system in terms of the requisite protection levels. The definition of the database and its rules is a specific set of steps within the overall operational requirement to define an information architecture for the business. That definition is a generic requirement of any information architecture formulation. Nevertheless, the actual control objective might be operationalized in a specific business such as the following:

> Senior management will responsible for developing and implementing the information architecture. Therefore, under the direction of senior management the ICT staff will identify and classify all relevant discrete items of business information. The outcome of this classification

process will be an explicit infrastructure of data items and their defined relationships with associated business activity requirements. This architecture will be periodically audited to confirm compliance with operational needs.

Control objectives are implemented by means of an individualized set of control statements. This particular statement supplies the specification of the desired outcomes needed to structure those procedures. There is a desired behavior written for each control objective. These control behaviors are documented as a coherent set which is applicable to a single given organizational setting. Along with the necessary procedure description, the qualifications for the person performing it should be listed. The recommendations of these control statements are intended to represent organizational best practice for that particular purpose.

The purpose of a control statement is to communicate how a given function is to be performed. Figure 7.3 shows the six procedure specifications.

This has to be expressed on a well-defined, systematic, and ongoing basis. Each procedure specifies, at a minimum, the following:

1. Expected input criteria
2. Expected output criteria
3. Interrelationship with other procedures

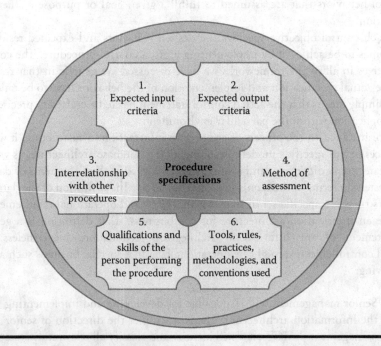

Figure 7.3 Procedure specifications.

4. Method of assessment
5. Qualifications and skills of the person performing the procedure
6. Tools, rules practices, methodologies, and conventions used

Each procedure must be accompanied by explicit work instructions or requisite behaviors. These designate specifically how each objective will be formally executed. Generally, these work instructions are captured and displayed in some auditable fashion within a standard organizational concept document which is conventionally termed a control specification. This control specification outlines all of the work that must be done to achieve the aims of the particular control objective. In addition to detailing how the procedure will be executed, the control specification details the activities necessary to judge whether each behavior has been carried out properly.

The procedural specification explicitly itemizes each task, the skills required, and the organizational resources needed to accomplish this. Since the specification might be subject to change, it has to be maintained under strict management control, which means that it has to be associated with an organizational stakeholder. And it has to be updated on a regular basis. In that respect, the specification has to provide a complete set of procedures for review, approval, change, distribution, withdrawal, and tracking of its recommendations. Because some parts of the specification may be vague or incomplete at the outset, it must be a "living" document.

Creating a Management-Level Control Process

The general principles of an IT security control policy includes a well-defined process for implementation. The implementation process is primarily centered on identifying and controlling information flows, along with the assignment of control responsibilities for the fulfillment of the requirements of control specified by the selected generic framework or standard.

Security control responsibility, from a management point-of-view, is defined as the requirement to determine and judge what is being accomplished. In essence, management's function is to evaluate the performance of the security control set and if necessary apply corrective action in such a way that control operation takes place according to a defined plan.

Without reliable ICT systems and effective control activities, public companies would not be able to perform even routine business functions. Control is embodied through the policies, procedures, and practices that are put into place to ensure that business objectives are achieved and risk mitigation strategies are carried out. Control activities are developed to specifically address each control target in such a way that it mitigates the identified risks.

There is no one way to group controls; however, a popular grouping of ICT controls are in three broad groups: general controls, application controls, and management reporting (or process) controls. The first two control types have specific application to the ICT management function.

General controls are designed to ensure that the information generated by an organization's ICT systems can be relied upon. That includes the following four categories of control:

1. Data center operation controls—routine operational controls such as job setup and scheduling, operator actions, and data backup and recovery procedures.
2. System software controls—controls designed to ensure the effective and efficient acquisition, implementation and maintenance of system software, database management, telecommunications software, security software, and utilities.
3. Access security controls—controls that prevent inappropriate and unauthorized use of the system.
4. Application system development and maintenance controls—these are the controls that enforce accountability in the development and maintenance of software. These provide explicit control over the development or maintenance processes including system design and implementation criteria, documentation requirements, change management, and approvals and checkpoints.

Application controls are embedded within software programs to prevent or detect unauthorized transactions. When combined with other controls, application controls ensure the completeness, accuracy, authorization, and validity of processing transactions. Some examples of application controls include the following:

■ Check digits within an application—these values are calculated to validate data. A company's part numbers contain a check digit to detect and correct inaccurate ordering from its suppliers. Universal product codes include a check digit to verify the product and the vendor.
■ Predefined data listings—provide the user with predefined white lists of acceptable data. For example, a company's intranet site might include drop-down lists of products available for purchase.
■ Data reasonableness tests—which compare data captured to a present or learned pattern of reasonableness. For example, an order to a supplier by a home renovation retail store for an unusually large number of board feet of lumber may trigger a review.
■ Logic tests—which include the use of range limits or value/alphanumeric tests. For example, credit card numbers have a predefined format.

General controls are needed to support the functioning of application controls. Both are needed to help ensure effective and efficient information and communication technology system processing, as well as the integrity of the resulting information that is generated to manage, govern, and report on the organization.

As computerized system controls increasingly replace manual controls, general controls are becoming more important. Information about the functioning of an organization's systems is needed at all levels of an organization in order to run the business and achieve the entity's purpose. However, the identification, management, and communication of relevant information represent an ever-increasing challenge to the ICT function.

The determination of which information is required and its communication requirements are a quality concern that involves ascertaining which information is

- Appropriate—is it the right information?
- Timely—is it available when required and reported in the right period of time?
- Current—is it the latest available?
- Accurate—are the data correct?
- Accessible—can authorized individuals gain access to it as necessary?

In addition to developing security controls appropriate to the environment, the development of reporting requirements is also necessary. This includes establishing reporting deadlines and the format and content of monthly, quarterly, and annual management reports. At the activity level, this includes the development and communication of standards to achieve corporate policy objectives and the identification and timely communication of information to assist in achieving business objectives, as well as the identification and timely reporting of security violations.

In general, both of these activities require consistent and effective monitoring of the control set, which encompasses the oversight of internal control by management. This is enforced through continuous and point-in-time assessment processes. Typically, there are two types of monitoring activities: continuous monitoring and separate evaluations.

ICT performance and effectiveness can be monitored using defined performance measures, which are designed to indicate if an underlying control is operating effectively, such as the following.

Defect identification and management—which involves establishing metrics and analyzing the trends of actual results against metrics. This can provide a basis for understanding the underlying reasons for processing failures. Correcting these causes can improve system accuracy, completeness of processing, and system availability.

Security monitoring—security controls reduce the risk of unauthorized access to an ICT infrastructure. Improving security can reduce the risk of processing unauthorized transactions and generating inaccurate reports. And if applications and ICT infrastructure components have been compromised it can ensure the consistent availability of key systems. Additionally, an organization can implement a variety of activities that can function as security monitoring to include:

- Internal audits
- External audits
- Regulatory examinations
- Attack and penetration studies
- Independent performance and capacity analyses
- IT effectiveness reviews
- Control self-assessments
- Independent security reviews
- Project implementation reviews

At the corporate level, the following types of activities can also be implemented:

- Centralized continuous monitoring of computer operations
- Centralized monitoring of security
- IT internal audit reviews (while the audit may occur at the activity level, the reporting of audit results to the audit committee is at the company level)

At the IT departmental level, the following may be expected:

- Defect identification and management
- Local monitoring of computer operations or security
- Supervision of local IT personnel

Management reporting controls and procedures: denote the processes in place that ensure the timely and effective reporting of operational information from the ICT systems, up and down the organization's management ladder. Reports about the effectiveness of a company's internal control over its ICT operation can take many forms. However, the general focus is on identifying and characterizing all of the material weaknesses that exist in the ICT operation.

From an effectiveness standpoint, any identified new deficiencies in the established control set, as well as any significant changes, must be communicated to the organization's managers in a timely manner. An organization's principal executive officers need to understand how effective their internal control functions are. That would be the case even if an identified internal control problem had already been mitigated and the control had been satisfactorily tested to determine whether it was effective management controls, certify such essential qualities as

- Completeness
- Accuracy
- Validity

- Authorization
- Segregation of duties

Most of the relevant controls are directly embedded in the ICT operation, such as program development and change management, computer operations, and access control. However, there are also organization level controls over the general control environment which include

- Enterprise policies
- Governance
- Collaboration and information sharing agreements

General controls and application controls are becoming more integrated because a greater number of organizations are focusing on alignment between the business and the ICT function. Traditionally, general controls were needed to ensure the proper functioning of application controls that depended on computer processes. While this continues to be true, general controls increasingly supplement application and business process controls.

A number of application and business process control objectives, such as system availability, may be achieved only through the operation of general controls. So general controls are becoming more integrated into the specific functioning of application controls. And both are needed to ensure complete and accurate ICT operation.

Also, general controls and application controls have become important as the requirement for security protection and error detection receives more attention. For example, it may have been acceptable in 2000 to wait several weeks to detect an intrusion. However, in an age where cyber-crime is big business, this kind of impossible delay is totally unacceptable. A network intrusion attempt must be detected within 5 minutes or less in order to have any chance of responding. Therefore, a manual control like reviewing system logs can no longer be the key control. Accordingly, there will be an increasing focus on automated general and application controls.

The control formulation process consists of four steps. First, a standard of desired performance is specified for a given control process. Then, a systematic management method of sensing and determining what is happening in the process is developed. Third, the management method that has been employed compares control set performance with business expectations in the light of the requirements of the standard. Then, if what is actually happening with the control set does not conform to expectations and the specifications of the standard, the management method will define corrective action and direct that it be taken. This is conveyed as corrective action back to the process.

As we have seen, the standard that is selected can be from a variety of sources. However, the requirement is that the selected standard is high level enough to formulate comprehensive high-level plans and strategies, down to detailed measurable performance factors. In that respect, a clearly documented, maintained, and communicated standard framework is a must for a good control process formulation. For this model to work properly, the responsibility for the management of the selected information and communications technology process must be clear and the accountability must be unambiguous. If not, control performance information will not flow to the right source and corrective action will not be acted upon.

The control process must be well documented with clear responsibilities. An important aspect is the clear definition of what constitutes a deviation from acceptable norms, that is, what are the limits of acceptable performance. Ensuring the timeliness, integrity, and appropriateness of control information flows, as well as other relevant information, is basic to the good functioning of the overall control process and is something the organization must address in control process formulation.

Both control information and corrective action information will have requirements as to the evidence that is required in order to establish accountability for action after the fact. The following 10 generic steps are performed in order to ensure control process performance as well as to identify corrective action that might be required:

1. Unambiguously state all business requirements and associated risks
2. Unambiguously specify the form of the organization structure
3. Clearly state roles and responsibilities
4. Clearly specify relevant policies and procedures
5. Clearly specify all relevant laws and regulations
6. Document any control measures currently in place
7. Define management reporting lines (status, performance, action items)
8. Document the process-related information and communication technology resources that are affected by control performance
9. Document all relevant aspects of the control process, including the measurable performance indicators of the process and all control implications
10. Routinely assess the effectiveness of control measures or the degree to which the control objective is achieved and recommend corrective action where needed

Factors that can effect control formulation include: business requirements and associated risks, general organizational structure, personnel roles and responsibilities, relevant policies and procedures, laws and regulations, existing control measures already in place, and existing management reporting requirements. The following five evaluation criteria are used to assess the performance of control measures within a control process:

1. A documented control processes exists
2. Appropriate deliverables can be identified
3. Responsibility and accountability are clear and effective

4. Relevant controls behaviors have been specified where applicable
5. The control set satisfies all relevant business objectives

Assessing Control Performance

It is the universal intention of all ICT control frameworks to specify some form of control over

- The ICT resource environment
- General computer operations
- Access to programs and data
- Program development and program change procedures

These control requirements apply to all types of systems; from mainframe through client–server environments. Subsequently, the correctness and applicability of the control set are evaluated by means of a control assessment. Control assessments look at a wide range of practical concerns including past weaknesses, risks to the organization, known incidents, new developments, and potential strategic choices.

Although the selected control framework and its control objectives provide direction, the practical guidance for the day-to-day management of control performance is dependent on the formal assessment process that is employed by the organization. In that respect then, the key to successful performance of that control assessment lies in the steps that are taken to ensure the routine evaluation of the control set. In essence, the organization has to execute an assessment process on a systematic basis in order to ensure operational effectiveness of the control set.

The routine oversight of control performance is the active element of control process management. The following are the three requisite steps that need to be carried out in order to ensure that the control measures that have been established are working as prescribed:

1. Obtain direct or indirect evidence to ensure that requisite control procedures have been performed for the period under review. This is done using direct and indirect evidence.
2. Perform a review of the adequacy of the control process outcomes and deliverables.
3. Determine the level of substantive testing and additional work that might be needed to provide assurance that the control process is adequate.

The aim here is to identify and evaluate the risks that might be associated with the circumstance of the control process not being properly carried out. In that respect, the assessment process needs to document any known control weaknesses and any relevant threats that might exploit that weakness. From the assessment and documentation of known vulnerabilities, the organization should be able to identify and document the actual and potential impact of any known threat as well as the root cause.

The practical purpose of the threat assessment is to assure management that the formal control process is sufficient or to advise management where processes need to be improved. From a management perspective, the obvious question is: "Am I doing all right in securing my assets? And if not, how do I fix it?" Therefore, the overall control process is studied in order to

- Obtain an understanding of business requirements–related risks and relevant controls
- Evaluate the appropriateness of stated controls
- Assess control compliance by testing whether the stated controls are working consistently and continuously as prescribed
- Substantiate the risk of control objectives not being met by the use of analytical techniques and/or consulting alternative sources

When assessing control processes, reviewers should be aware that controls operate at different levels in the organization from high-level managerial to low-level technical, and thus they have intricate relationships up-and-down the organizational ladder. Therefore, the assessment of control processes has to take this added complex dimension into account.

Measurement-Based Assurance of Controls

Basically the term "measurement-based assurance" just means that confidence in a given organizational function can be assured through measurement and evaluation of the control set. This requires the organization to utilize a range of standardized metrics that allow it to assess the performance of a given control, at a given point in time, in a given situation. Management requires focused understanding of the performance of its various operations. So over the past 20 years, there has been a growing trend toward quantitative measurement of control functioning. Measurement is the term for a mathematical process, algorithm, or function used to obtain a quantitative assessment of a product or process. The actual numerical value produced is called a measure. Thus, for example, probability of occurrence is a metric. But the value of that metric is the percentage estimate.

There are two general classes of metrics: management metrics, which assist in the oversight of the control process and quality metrics, which are predictors or indicators of the performance of a discrete control. Management metrics can be used for assessing control over any industrial production or manufacturing activity. They are used to assess resources, cost, and task completion. Quality metrics are used to estimate performance characteristics or qualities of a control set. By their nature, some metrics can serve both management and quality purposes, that is, they can be used for both management oversight and control performance assessment.

The primary disadvantage with control performance measurement is the lack of one standard scale to ensure consistent interpretation. This is particularly true of metrics for control performance. That is, measures like effectiveness, efficiency, maintainability, reliability, and usability are not tied to a commonly accepted definition. These measures must be interpreted by comparison with contract requirements, similar projects, or similar components within the organization.

Also while some control metrics are mathematically-based, most, including probability models, have not been proven. Since there are an infinite number of possible metrics, users need to adopt criteria to decide which control metric best fits the needs of their organization.

Ideally, a metric should possess five characteristics (Figure 7.4):

1. *Simple*—definition and use of the metric is simple
2. *Objective*—different people will give same value
3. *Easily collected*—the cost and effort are reasonable
4. *Robust*—metric is insensitive to irrelevant changes
5. *Valid*—metric measures what it is supposed to

These types of primitive metrics can be collected throughout the operation of the control process. These metrics can be plotted using bar graphs and histograms as part of statistical process control. The plots can be analyzed by management to: identify the control activities that are most error prone, suggest steps to prevent

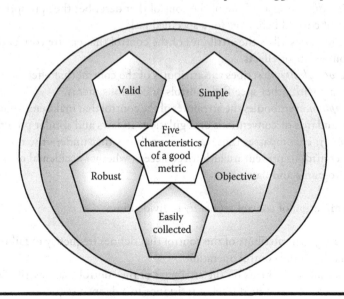

Figure 7.4   Five characteristics of a good metric.

recurrence of similar errors, suggest procedures for earlier detection of control failures, and make improvements to the development process.

Nevertheless, these metrics apply to the assessment and characterization of the overall performance of a control set, rather than in evaluating a specific performance characteristic of an individual control. For this reason, managers will need to assign weights to the evaluation process for any individual control that reflects business requirements. The manager may also need to align the control performance with conventional management criteria such as schedule delay or cost overrun. That is an essential requirement because he/she wishes to optimize control effectiveness within limited cost, human resources, and time frame.

Given this, the six standard characteristics for a properly defined individual control are (Figure 7.5)

1. Functionality
2. Reliability
3. Usability
4. Efficiency
5. Maintainability
6. Portability

For the purposes of designing relevant metrics, these generic characteristics are broken down into subcharacteristics that will allow specific metrics to be designed and deployed. For instance, the determination of control *functionality* is divided into

1. *Suitability* is the attribute of the control that describes the appropriateness of a set of control behaviors for a specified task.
2. *Accuracy*: describes the attributes of the control that ensure correct or agreed upon results or effects.
3. *Interoperability*: describes the attributes of the control that effect its ability to interact with other specified controls or control systems.
4. *Compliance*: embodies the attributes of the control that make ensure adherence to standards or conventions or regulations in laws and similar prescriptions.
5. *Security*: encompasses those control attributes that underwrite the ability of the control to prevent unauthorized access, whether accidental or deliberate, to programs and data.

The determination of control *reliability* is divided into

1. *Maturity*: The attribute of the control that defines frequency of failure caused by faults in the control operation.
2. *Attack tolerance*: bears on the attributes of the control that describe its ability to maintain a specified level of resistance to a defined set of attacks.

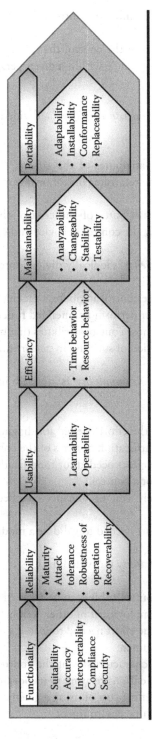

Figure 7.5 Six standard characteristics.

3. *Robustness of operation*: The number of control failures per unit of time, usually month.
4. *Recoverability*: The attributes of the control that effect its capability to reestablish a given level of performance within a given period of time and effort investment.

The determination of control *understandability* is divided into its two basic components:

1. *Learnability:* Describes the attributes of the control that ensure the users' ability to learn and apply the requisite control behavior (e.g., routine logging of building access).
2. *Operability:* Describes the attributes of the control that dictate the effort required by the user to apply the control behavior and operate the control.

The determination of control *efficiency* is logically divided into two items:

1. *Time behavior*: includes those control attributes that characterize how quickly the control will respond to or perform its intended function.
2. *Resource behavior*: includes those control attributes that bear on the amount of resources used and the duration of such use in performing a control function.

The determination of control *maintainability* is divided into four operational measures:

1. *Analyzability*: characterizes the effort needed for diagnosis of deficiencies or causes of failures, or for identification of parts of the control to be modified.
2. *Changeability*: describes the effort needed for modification, fault removal, or for environmental change for a control.
3. *Stability*: describes the likely risk of unexpected effects resulting from a modification.
4. *Testability*: describes the effort needed to validate a modified control.

The determination of control *portability* is divided into

1. *Adaptability*: bears on the control's ability to be adapted to different specified environments without the employment of other actions or means.
2. *Installability*: characterizes the effort needed to install a normally functioning control in a specified environment.
3. *Conformance*: describes the characteristics of the control that ensure that it adheres to standards or conventions relating to its portability.
4. *Replaceability*: bears on the effort cost of using a given control in the place of another control within the same environment.

Assessing and Remediating the Control Environment

The ICT control environment includes all governance processes, as well as the monitoring and reporting processes responsible for ensuring that the ICT operation is aligned with business requirements. According to the Public Corporation Accounting Oversight Board (PCAOB), a critical level of weakness in a control set will cause an ineffective control environment. And an ineffective control environment can lead to many forms of harm to the organization and its ICT operation.

The proper response depends on the conventional operation of the ICT operation. The question is whether the organization has adequately documented and evaluated its ICT control requirements and is adequately prepared to respond to the specific control challenges that the organization might face. Furthermore, it is also based on whether the executive management—including the chief information officer (CIO)—appreciates the impact that a comprehensive set of ICT controls has on the security and productivity of their organization.

The overall ICT governance process, which these individuals sponsor, is the entity that ensures effective and efficient organizational functioning. And as we have discussed, the ICT governance process always involves a particular set of standard elements or functions, including

- Information systems strategic plan
- ICT risk management process
- ICT compliance and regulatory management
- ICT policies, procedures, and standards

Practically, there are a number of layers of controls within the ICT operation. All of these have to be considered and addressed in creating, installing, and evaluating an organization's internal control system. That includes program development, program changes, computer operations, and access to programs and data.

Logically, in order to enable the technology support for a properly functioning ICT process, it is necessary to understand the routine flow of transactions and processing that takes place as part of the business operation. That includes understanding how transactions are initiated, authorized, recorded, processed, and reported.

Information flows commonly involve the use of application systems for automated processing in order to support high volume and complex transaction handling. The reliability of these application systems is in turn reliant upon various ICT support systems, including networks, databases, operating systems, and more.

Collectively, these technological elements all define the ICT systems that support the business processes of the organization. And, as a result, every one of these elements should be included in the design and evaluation of internal controls for the business's ICT function.

On the other hand, from a practical controls management standpoint, it also has to be determined whether the ICT operation currently documents, evaluates, and remediates its controls set on an a regular basis. If controls are regularly evaluated then it has to be determined whether the ICT operation itself has a formal mechanism in place to identify and respond to any identified control deficiencies.

During the course of this overall review, it is possible that control process performance defects might be identified in the existing system. Those might include

- Intentional violations of established management policy
- Intentional violations of regulatory requirements
- Deliberate circumvention of existing controls
- Unauthorized use of assets or services
- Negligence
- Unintentional illegal acts

Because it can be expected that control defects are going to be identified, we are going to look at the generic performance considerations with respect to their remediation. Management is responsible for designing, implementing, and maintaining a system of internal controls. Nevertheless, management cannot guarantee that all irregularities will be detected.

To ensure a responsible degree of functional coverage, management must design and then routinely execute tests that can reasonably be expected to detect

- Performance defects that could have a material impact on either the effectiveness of the specific control or the business function as a whole
- Weaknesses in internal control status that could result in control malfunctions which are either not prevented or detected

Even when a management review or audit is appropriately planned and performed, control defects could go undetected. Therefore managers must be able to identify risk factors that may contribute to the inability to detect a defect. That might include such factors as (Figure 7.6) the following:

- The types of assets held, or services offered, and their susceptibility to control failures
- The strength of relevant controls
- Applicable regulatory or legal requirements
- Findings from previous reviews or audits
- The industry and competitive environment in which the organization operates
- Findings of outside reviews or investigations
- Findings that have arisen during the day-to-day course of business

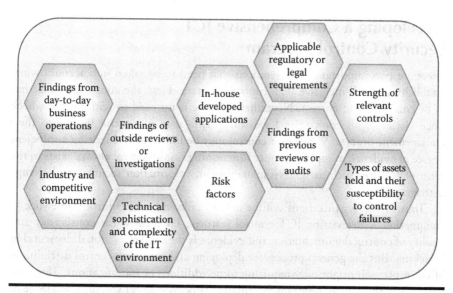

Figure 7.6 Risk factors.

- The technical sophistication and complexity of the information system(s) supporting the operational area under control
- Existence of in-house developed/maintained applications systems, compared with packaged software, for core business systems

Management should use the results of their risk assessment to determine the rigor of the testing required. The aim is to obtain sufficient documented evidence to provide reasonable assurance that

- Control defects that could have a material effect on the performance of the control will be identified
- Review weaknesses that would fail to prevent or detect material defects in the control process have all been identified

If defects or weaknesses have been detected, the manager should assess the effect of these performance issues on the business operation and on the reliability of control process functioning. If the documented evidence indicates that defects or weaknesses have occurred, the manager should recommend that the matter be investigated in detail or the appropriate actions be taken. This advice should be communicated to appropriate persons in the organization in a timely manner. The notification should be directed to a level of management oversight above the organizational level where the control irregularities are suspected to have occurred.

Developing a Comprehensive ICT Security Control Program

There are two important considerations that need to be taken into account when establishing an all-inclusive ICT control program. First, the control coverage has to be complete and correct. Nevertheless, there is no need to reinvent the wheel; since virtually, all companies have some semblance of control built into their management process. While that control may be informal and lacking a sufficient degree of evidence to support proper functioning, some control always exists in the form of features such as quality management, information security, and change management.

Thus, many organizations will be able to tailor a broad control framework in conjunction with existing ICT control features. Frequently, the consistency and quality of control documentation and evidence is the single functional element that is lacking. But the general process for deploying and enforcing control discipline is often in place, it might only requiring some additions or modifications. Thus, the first step in the control program formulation process is to get specific knowledge of the shape of the current control landscape.

The work involved in executing a thorough review of ICT control processes and then maintaining adequate documentation of them as the enterprise moves forward is a time-consuming and resource-intensive assignment. Nonetheless, without appropriate knowledge and guidance, organizations run the risk of doing either too much or too little in their control setup. That risk is amplified when those people responsible are not experienced in the design and assessment of ICT controls or they lack the necessary skill or management experience to identify and focus their attention on the areas of most significant risk.

While some industries, such as financial services, are familiar with stringent regulatory and compliance requirements of public market environments, most industries are not. Thus, in order to put together and effective control program, most organizations will require a change in their overall culture. More likely than not, enhancements to ICT systems and processes will be required, which will most notably lie in the area of additional steps required in order to document and retain control evidence and to evaluate the ICT controls themselves. That will seem like additional bureaucracy to most workers.

Nonetheless, because the cost of a successful cyber-attack can be devastating to an organization, it is crucial for a business to adopt a proactive approach. That means that it must take on the challenge of implementing a comprehensive control system. The most basic level in that process is the need to establish control over the activities of the business's conventional ICT processes. Those processes encompass all of the current areas of management control within the existing ICT infrastructure and includes all of the established processes that might be dedicated to operational

- Acquisition
- Configuration management
- Systems integration
- Installation sustainment and maintenance

Controls over the routine ICT operation encompass the day-to-day delivery of information services, including:

- Service level management
- Management of third-party services
- System availability management
- Customer relationship management
- Configuration and systems management
- Problem and incident management
- Operations management
- Scheduling and facilities management

The system management controls for the operation include all of the organizational actions that are dedicated to

- Control over the acquisition implementation, configuration, and maintenance of operating system software
- Control over the deployment and operation of database management systems
- Control over the deployment and operation of middleware software
- Control over the deployment and operation of communications software
- Control over the deployment and operation of security software
- Control over the deployment and operation of utilities that run the system and allow applications to function

In addition, from a specific information security standpoint, the function of the control process is to provide authentication and authorization controls, incident tracking, system logging, and system monitoring. In fact, in many respects, the aim of organizational control environments can be summed up in those two words, "access control."

In essence, the entire ICT control process is centered on ensuring that only authorized individuals have access to programs and data within the organization. Effective access security controls have to be able to provide a reasonable degree of assurance against inappropriate access and unauthorized use of programs and data. And control over access to proprietary programs and data assumes even greater importance as internal and external business connectivity is allowed to grow.

If access controls are well designed, they can intercept unethical hackers, malicious software, and other intrusion attempts. Adequate control is demonstrated by preventing unauthorized use of, and changes to, the system. Satisfactory access controls include such things as secure passwords, internet firewalls, data encryption, and cryptographic keys. User accounts and related privilege controls restrict the applications or application functions to just those authorized users who might appropriately need to have access within the appropriate division of duties in the workforce. In the larger sense, controls enforce two fundamental information security principles, separation of duties, and least privilege. In the case of the former, the control environment is structured in such a way that no one has control over a critical business function. In the case of the latter, authorization ensures that every worker only has access to information that they need in order to carry out their job.

Explicitly Controlling ICT Work

ICT work embodies three general activities—technology acquisition, application resource development, and sustainment. The first activity involves the simple acquisition and implementation of new applications. The second purpose involves the development and coding of new applications and the maintenance of existing applications. The third area involves managing systems in such a way that their efficiency of operation and their effectiveness in furthering business goals is optimized.

The fact remains that these latter two areas, program development and sustainment and ongoing system management, have historically been an area characterized by a high degree of failure. Many implementation projects are considered to be outright failures, or they do not fully meet business requirements and expectations, are not implemented on time, or do not fall within budget.

In order to reduce the well-known set of system management risks, most ICT organizations employ a well-defined and standard set of development practices, along with a quality assurance methodology. Both of these assurance approaches are built around the execution of formal control behaviors, which are aimed at process control and improvement. These methodologies are often supported by standard software tools and IT architecture components.

In the case of new software applications, the methodology provides structure for the identification of automated solutions that can be acquired rather than built, and if that is not the case these methods embody a rational set of development and implementation practices. These methodologies also support the necessary documentation requirements, testing and test cases, approvals, project management and oversight, and project risk assessments.

Much of the development and ongoing sustainment of application software is governed by the organization's patching, change control, and configuration management processes. These processes enable control over the change and evolution of the system. They exist to help ensure that all changes to the configuration are made properly. With these processes, there is also a need to determine the extent of testing that will be required to underwrite the release of a new system.

For example, the implementation of a major new software release may require

- Evaluation of the enhancements to the system
- Extensive testing
- User retraining
- The rewriting of procedures and business processes

Controls for this process may involve

- Required authorization of change requests
- Review of the changes
- Approvals
- Documentation
- Testing
- Assessment of changes on other IT components
- Implementation protocols

Finally, the program change management process also has to be fully integrated with other ICT processes, including

- Incident management
- Problem management
- Availability management
- Infrastructure change control

Assessing the Adequacy of ICT Controls

In order to manage the control process properly, organizations need to be able to document, evaluate, monitor, and report on the status of their ICT controls. The first step in this process is to assess the overall IT organization using the framework of choice. In this book, we have focused on three of those: International Organization for standardization (ISO) 27000, National Institute for Standards and Technology (NIST) 800-53, and Control Objectives for IT (COBIT). This is done by considering the following questions. First, does the executive leadership understand the risks that are intrinsic in ICT systems and their impact on the organization as a whole? Second, have the business process owners defined their requirements for control for their sectors of the organization? Third, has ICT management implemented an identifiable and suitable set of documented controls to meet business requirements? And finally, do policies governing security, availability, and processing integrity exist, and are they documented and communicated to all members of the organization? If all of those conditions are met then the next step is to ensure that all of the people who are involved in ICT work understand their roles and responsibilities. In order to do this properly, those roles and responsibilities have to be well-defined and documented, as well as satisfactorily understood.

In addition, some form of active training has to take place in order to ensure that all of the members of the ICT operation, and all of the workforce that is involved in information technology use understand their specific job roles. Of course, this has the precondition that all ICT workers have to be proven to have the knowledge and skills necessary skills to effectively carry out their job responsibilities.

Dealing with Control Risks

No single risk assessment methodology can be expected to be appropriate to all controls in all situations. In addition, the conditions affecting the results of a risk assessment may change over time. Therefore it is important to periodically reevaluate the appropriateness of the controls that have been chosen for a given purpose. Managers should use a well-defined set of risk assessment practices in order to develop the overall control deployment plan and in following up with targeted reviews and audits of control performance over time.

Control risk should also be considered in making decisions about the nature and timing of control procedures, the sensitivity of the business function to be controlled, as well as the amount of time and resources to be allocated to control development and implementation.

In general, there are six areas of risk that have to be considered when evaluating controls. The first area of risk would be that the control might fail due to improper design or execution. The second area of risk would be that there might not be a control in place to detect and respond to an adverse event. The third area of risk would be that a risk identification process used to classify and evaluate risks and their potential effect is missing. The fourth of area of risk would be that requisite tests of detailed activities and transactions are not carried out. The fifth area of risk would be that tests that are designed to characterize the completeness, accuracy, or existence of risk activities or transactions are not done. The sixth and final risk is that processes are not consistently applied and/or executed.

The ICT manager should consider each of the following three types of risk when performing a risk analysis. The aim is to determine the overall degree of

1. Inherent risk
2. Control risk
3. Detection risk

Inherent risk denotes the susceptibility of a given area of ICT functioning to exploitation, error, or misuse. An inherent risk be a significant factor either individually or in combination with other errors. For example, the inherent risk associated with operating system security is ordinarily high. That is because operating system security weaknesses could result in loss of information integrity and/or competitive disadvantage. By contrast, the inherent risk associated with security for a stand-alone PC not used for business-critical purposes is ordinarily low.

Inherent risk for most ICT areas is ordinarily high. That is because the potential effect of exploitations and errors ordinarily spans several business systems and many users. In assessing the inherent risk for ICT operations, the manager needs to consider the impacts of both pervasive and detailed information system control risks.

In the case of pervasive ICT risks, the manager should consider such things as the general capability of ICT process managers. Their relative level of management experience and knowledge and the contextual factors and factors that might affect the organization's industry as a whole. Specifically, it is necessary to ensure that ICT management does not attempt to conceal or misstate information, for instance to hide business-critical project over-runs or hacker activity. It is also necessary to consider such factors as the nature of the organization's business and systems, for instance, plans for Internet commerce.

Larger technical considerations like the lack of effective systems integration, or changes in technology, or ICT staff availability. With outsourcing a consideration might be something like the level of third-party influence on the control of vital systems development work. At the detailed control level, managers have to consider such particulars as the complexity of the systems involved and the level of manual intervention required. In addition, considerations like the susceptibility of impotent systems to loss or misappropriation of the assets for instance inventory and payroll. In addition, because technology is constantly being used, the actual control issues are cyclical; that is, the likelihood of adverse activity peaks at certain times in the use of the system.

Activities outside the day-to-day routine of ICT processing also have to be considered: for instance, the accessing of applications or operating system utilities to alter data. Finally, there is the consideration of the capability, experience, and skills of the ICT management and staff in the application and use of the specified controls.

Control risk is the risk that an error will not be prevented or detected and corrected in a timely manner by the internal control system. For example, the control risk associated with manual reviews of computer logs can be high. That is because of the volume of data and the timeliness requirements needed to comb through the logs to hopefully detect an incident after the fact. The control risk associated with testing and data validation procedures is ordinarily low. That is because those processes are normally consistently applied and executed. ICT management should assess the control risk as high unless relevant internal controls can be assured to be identified, evaluated as effective, tested, and proven to be operating appropriately.

Detection risk is the risk that the auditor's substantive procedures will not detect an adverse event or error. For example, the detection risk associated with identifying breaches of security in an application system is ordinarily high. That is because there are so many potential ways that a system can be breached. The detection risk associated with identification of lack of disaster recovery plans is ordinarily low since existence is easily verified.

In determining the level of substantive testing required to characterize detection risk, ICT management should consider both the inherent risk associated with the entity, as well as the level of identified control risk following compliance testing. The higher the assessment of inherent and control risk the more evidence management ought to obtain from the performance of the prescribed review and audit procedures.

The ICT should also consider documenting the risk assessment technique or methodology used for a specific review or audit. The documentation should ordinarily include

- A description of the risk assessment methodology
- Identification of significant exposures and corresponding risks
- Risks and exposures the audit is intended to address
- The audit evidence used to support the assessment
- The risk of giving an incorrect audit opinion
- Tests of controls designed to obtain audit evidence

That recommendation applies to both the evaluation of the effectiveness of the controls as well as their operation during the period of assessment. Detection risks are normally classified as

1. The risk that an error which could occur in an audit area will not be detected and corrected on a timely basis
2. Controls over the acquisition, implementation, delivery and support of IS systems, and services are effective
3. The risk that the auditor's substantive procedures will not detect an error which could be material, individually or in combination with other errors.

Chapter Summary

The function of controls is to ensure the precise status of some aspect of the ICT operation at a given point in time. This is accomplished by identifying organizational functions that need to be protected by controls and by assessing or auditing the status of the target function with respect to its desired state. The resultant reviews or audits should provide sufficient understanding of the performance of the assurance controls in order to ensure their correctness.

This requires building a framework of controls, usually based on a standard model, which enforce a set of purposes that are appropriate to the control target. This is accomplished through the creation and deployment of concrete behavioral controls, which operationalize the purposes/requirements of that model. In addition, a systematic reporting system has to be built to feed that status information back to the organization. Accountability and control is enforced through systematic reviews and audits. The mission of these reviews and audit is to describe the exact status of the entity under control.

Thus, proper control and assurance of ICT assets require an explicit inventory management framework including an identification and labeling scheme, a description of the objects in that inventory, and the rules for control and a plan for how the ongoing status assessment will be conducted.

ICT resources are deployed to produce a given set of desired business outcomes. In order to effectively and efficiently achieve those outcomes, the organization as a whole has to be controlled in a rational, predictable manner. In addition to these generic factors, a properly functioning control process will also ensure the overall value and productivity of the ICT operation while ensuring all legal and regulatory requirements for performance of the business process are met.

Control frameworks are large strategic models which specify standard, well-defined, and commonly accepted practices for proper ICT technology management and protection. They are normally structured as a set of high-level control objectives, which are then elaborated by a collection of well-defined underlying activities or control objectives. These control objectives represent the explicitly desired behaviors that will implement the control process and which can be observed and audited.

Control objectives provide a precise and clear definition of the activities necessary to ensure effectiveness, efficiency, and economy of resource utilization. Thus the operation's control objectives define the control framework concepts that have to be translated into specific actions applicable within the ICT process. Control objectives specify the actions of ICT managers and staff for any interested reviewers or auditors, both internal and external. More importantly, they also communicate best practice to the business process owners.

Detailed control objectives are identified for each process defined by the control framework. These control objectives are by definition the minimum control set required to ensure effective outcomes. Control objectives are enabled by control statements. In that respect, each control statement specifies a set of applicable control behaviors that are assumed to fulfill a given goal or purpose of the ICT operation.

Each control objective specifies the desired behaviors and anticipated results or outcomes to be achieved by implementing a given control procedure. The control objectives in all of the frameworks we have discussed are generic in that respect. So the actual specification and implementation of the behavior has to be tailored. This simply means that the actual control statement has to be crafted to precisely fit the application within the particular environment.

Control objectives are implemented by means of an individualized set of procedures. This particular statement supplies the specification of the desired outcomes needed to structure those procedures. There is a desired behavior written for each control objective. These control behaviors are documented as a coherent set which is applicable to a single given organizational setting. Along with the necessary procedure description, the qualifications for the person performing it should be listed. The recommendations of these control statements are intended to represent organizational best practice for that particular purpose.

The purpose of a control statement is to communicate how a given function is to be performed. This has to be expressed on a well-defined, systematic, and ongoing basis.

Each procedure must be accompanied by explicit work instructions or requisite behaviors. These designate specifically how each objective will be formally executed. Generally, these work instructions are captured and displayed in some auditable fashion within a standard organizational concept document which is conventionally termed a control specification. This control specification outlines all of the work that must be done to achieve the aims of the particular control objective. In addition to detailing how the procedure will be executed, the control specification details the activities necessary to judge whether each behavior has been carried out properly.

In general, there are three broad groupings of ICT controls. From a terminology standpoint, these are called "general controls" "application controls," and "management reporting (or process) controls."

General controls are designed to ensure that the information generated by an organization's ICT systems can be relied upon.

Application controls are embedded within software programs to prevent or detect unauthorized transactions. When combined with other controls application controls ensure the completeness, accuracy, authorization, and validity of processing transactions.

ICT performance and effectiveness are increasingly monitored using defined performance measures, which are designed to indicate if an underlying control is operating effectively.

Most of the relevant controls are directly embedded in the ICT operation, such as program development and change management, computer operations, and access control. However, there are also organization level controls over the general control environment, which include

- Enterprise policies
- Governance
- Collaboration and information sharing agreements

Management requires focused understanding of the performance of its various operations. So over the past 20 years, there has been a growing trend toward quantitative measurement of control functioning. Measurement is the term for a mathematical process, algorithm, or function used to obtain a quantitative assessment of a product or process. The actual numerical value produced is called a measure. Thus, for example, probability of occurrence is a metric. But the value of that metric is the percentage estimate.

The primary disadvantage with control performance measurement is the lack of one standard scale to ensure consistent interpretation. This is particularly true of metrics for control performance. That is, measures like effectiveness, efficiency, maintainability, reliability, and usability are not tied to a commonly accepted definition. These measures must be interpreted by comparison with contract requirements, similar projects, or similar components within the organization. Given this, the six standard characteristics for a properly defined individual control are

1. Functionality
2. Reliability
3. Usability
4. Efficiency
5. Maintainability
6. Portability

There are two important considerations that need to be taken into account when establishing an ICT control program. First, the control coverage has to be comprehensive and correct. Nevertheless, there is no need to reinvent the wheel; since virtually all companies have some semblance of control built into their management process. While that control may be informal and lacking a sufficient degree of evidence to support proper functioning, some control always exists in the form of features such as quality management, information security, and change management.

Thus, many organizations will be able to tailor a broad control framework in conjunction with existing ICT control features. Frequently, the consistency and quality of control documentation and evidence is the single functional element that is lacking. But the general process for deploying and enforcing control discipline is often in place, it might only requiring some additions or modifications. Thus, the first step in the control program formulation process is to get specific knowledge of the shape of the current control landscape.

In addition, from a specific information security standpoint, the function of the control process is to provide authentication and authorization controls, incident tracking, system logging, and system monitoring. In fact, in many respects, the aim of organizational control environments can be summed up in those two words, "access control."

In essence, the entire ICT control process is centered on ensuring that only authorized individuals have access to programs and data within the organization.

Effective access security controls have to be able to provide a reasonable degree of assurance against inappropriate access and unauthorized use of programs and data. And control over access to proprietary programs and data assumes even greater importance as internal and external business connectivity is allowed to grow.

The fact is though that these latter two areas, program development and sustainment and ongoing system management, have historically been an area characterized by a high degree of failure. Many implementation projects are considered to be outright failures, or they do not fully meet business requirements and expectations, are not implemented on time, or do not fall within budget.

In order to manage the control process properly, organizations need to be able to document, evaluate, monitor, and report on the status of their ICT controls. The first step in this process is to assess the overall IT organization using the framework of choice. In this book, we have focused on three of those: ISO 27000, NIST 800-53, and COBIT. This is done by considering the following questions. First, does the executive leadership understand the risks that are intrinsic in ICT systems and their impact on the organization as a whole? Second, have the business process owners defined their requirements for control for their sectors of the organization? Third, has ICT management implemented an identifiable and suitable set of documented controls to meet business requirements? And finally do policies governing security, availability and processing integrity exist, and are they documented and communicated to all members of the organization?

No single risk assessment methodology can be expected to be appropriate to all controls in all situations. In addition, the conditions affecting the results of a risk assessment may change over time. Therefore it is important to periodically reevaluate the appropriateness of the controls that have been chosen for a given purpose. Managers should use a well-defined set of risk assessment practices in order to develop the overall control deployment plan and in following up with targeted reviews and audits of control performance over time.

Control risk should also be considered in making decisions about the nature and timing of control procedures, the sensitivity of the business function to be controlled, as well as the amount of time and resources to be allocated to control development and implementation.

Key Concepts

- Controls enforce management accountability
- Controls are arrayed in a framework
- There are a number of general frameworks including ISO 27000 and COBIT
- There are three classes of controls—management, technical, and process
- There are six qualitative criteria associated with a good control
- There are general controls, application controls, and management reporting controls

- Controls must be tailored to the specific organizational application
- Measurement is an important part of control management
- Measurement is underwritten by metrics
- Frameworks focus at three levels: operational, managerial, and policy
- Control reviews have to be consistently executed on a periodic basis
- Controls are enabled by control statements
- There are three types of risk—inherent, control, and detection

Key Terms

Access controls—specific authentication and authorization behaviors

Accountability—the assigned responsibility for control performance

Application controls—behaviors designed to assure application software operation

Asset—an item of value within the ICT operation

Compliance control—standard actions designed to assure an external requirement

Control alignment—assurance that the control will satisfy business requirements

Control monitoring—routine assessment of control performance with reporting

Control risk—probability of failure by control type

Control statement—specification of behavior with anticipated outcomes

Control target—the entity to which a control objective applies

Disclosure risk—risk associated with a false reporting

General controls—behaviors designed to assure the operational computer and information technology process

Impact analysis—an assessment of the effect of control failure

Inherent risk—an intrinsic weakness at the operational level

Threat—adversarial action that could produce harm or an undesirable outcome

Threat assessment—estimate of likelihood and impact for control formulation purposes

Threat environment—the specific dangers that the control system must address

Threat identification—the explicit inventory of environmental risks

Threat response—a set of formal organizational controls that are designed to slow down or minimize the impact of a defined threat

Chapter 8

Security Control Validation and Verification

At the conclusion of this chapter, the reader will:

- Understand what security control validation and verification is, and how it fits into the scope of the system development life cycle (SDLC)
- Understand the security control assessment as specified by National Institute for Standards and Technology (NIST)
- Be familiar with common security control assessment testing methodologies
- Be familiar with common security control assessment examination methodologies

Today, the evaluation of information and communication technology (ICT) systems security in accordance with business requirements is a vital component of any organization's business strategy. The problem is that while many organizations understand what security controls are, few understand the importance of ensuring their effectiveness through verification and validation techniques. Likewise, even fewer organizations understand the process associated with testing the effectiveness of security controls, much less able to integrate such a process into their underlying risk management strategy. As a result, in many cases, the entire process gets performed haphazardly or skipped entirely, causing an increase in the potential of security attack. "Testing and assurance is a critical step in creating a secure ICT product and it should be obvious that it has to be done. The challenge is that the realities of timing and unanticipated problems seldom permit the testing process to move ahead on a rational schedule. Instead, components come up to testing as they are completed and those things are often completed based on the 'hardest to execute last' principle. So in many cases the most critical and complex items in a system are either not tested because of pressures to release the product, or not tested in a serious fashion. The conditions of this inevitable trap are best avoided if the producer wants to create a trustworthy product" (Shoemaker and Sigler, 2015).

To further complicate things, the process is referred to differently depending upon the person you talk to or resource on the topic. We titled this chapter "Security Control Verification and Validation." The NIST Risk Management Framework (RMF) refers to it as "Security Control Assessment and Testing." Some resources call it "verification analysis," "security assessment," "security audit," or "security testing"; while others refer to it as "risk assessment." Taking the latter reference a step further, the question is begged, does risk assessment not take place in the early stages of the risk management process?

If you find yourself confused about this discussion, you are not alone; and that is why many organizations skip this part of the risk management process entirely. One rationalization to that question is that as ICT professionals, we tend to think from the perspective of life cycles. Once a phase of the process is complete, we move on and do not return until we need to perform that phase on a separate project. This demonstrates the cyclical nature of a risk management strategy. The verification and validation (V&V) of security controls should take place when very few controls exist and the organization is attempting to determine where risks and vulnerabilities exist in order to implement the proper controls to mitigate those risks. V&V of security controls should also take place after new controls are implemented (in the same way as systems and software are tested during development and before deployment) to ensure that the implemented controls provide the level of effectiveness as prescribed in the organization's risk management plan.

The point to be made is that all of the ways in which this facet of risk management is identified are correct. Nevertheless, the V&V of security control is an important part of the organization's risk management strategy; and to be done to the extent that it can be effectively managed, the activities must follow a defined process.

In this chapter, we begin by providing some fundamental concepts about security control assessment. We continue our discussion by providing a summary of the control assessment and testing process based on the steps defined in NIST SP 800-53A *Assessing Security and Privacy Controls in Federal Information Systems and Organizations*. Last, we provide some insight into some of the technical aspects of the security control V&V process.

Security Control Assessment Fundamentals

It may be wise to begin by defining some of the terminology we have already used in the introductory paragraphs of this chapter. Based on NISTIR 7298 *Glossary of Information Security Terms* V&V can be defined as follows:

- Verification: Confirmation, through the provision of objective evidence, that specified requirements have been fulfilled (e.g., an entity's requirements have been correctly defined or an entity's attributes have been correctly presented; or a procedure or function performs as intended and leads to the expected outcome).
- Validation: The process of demonstrating that the system under consideration meets in all respects the specification of that system. Or the confirmation (through the provision of strong, sound, objective evidence) that requirements for a specific intended use or application have been fulfilled (e.g., a trustworthy credential has been presented, or data or information has been formatted in accordance with a defined set of rules, or a specific process has demonstrated that an entity under consideration meets, in all respects, its defined attributes or requirements).

(Kissel, 2002)

Further, the glossary of terms goes on to define security control assessment as: "The testing and/or evaluation of the management, operational, and technical security controls in an information system to determine the extent to which the controls are implemented correctly, operating as intended, and producing the desired outcome with respect to meeting the security requirements for the system." Or "The testing and/or evaluation of the management, operational, and technical security controls to determine the extent to which the controls are implemented correctly, operating as intended, and producing the desired outcome with respect to meeting the security requirements for the system and/or enterprise"(Kissel, 2002).

Recall our discussion from Chapter 4. The activities associated with selecting the security controls that meet the needs of any given organization is an important step within the underlying risk management process that has an impact on the operations and assets within the functional areas of an organization as well as third-party suppliers and customers that have established interconnections through technological artifacts of an ICT system. Security controls are the defense mechanisms and countermeasures specified for an ICT system and its entire supply chain that are implemented to protect the confidentiality, integrity, and availability of its information.

"Once employed within an information system, security and privacy controls are assessed to provide the information necessary to determine their overall effectiveness, that is, the extent to which the controls are implemented correctly, operating as intended, and producing the desired outcome with respect to meeting the security and privacy requirements for the system and the organization. Understanding the overall effectiveness of implemented security and privacy controls is essential in determining the risk to the organization's operations and assets, to individuals, to other organizations …" (NIST, 2014a,b).

Fitting Security Control Assessment within the SDLC

We mentioned in the opening remarks of this chapter that there is no one specific place within the risk management process that security assessment activities are performed. In fact, to be proactive and assured proper security measures are implemented, the activities should be performed within multiple steps of the process. It is important to remember that the activities and tasks of the risk management process and those of the SDLC run in parallel. As such, security control assessment tasks can and should be performed at several different phases within the SDLC to promote confidence within the organization and supply chain that the system-specific or common security controls implemented within the ICT system provide the level of effectiveness necessary to defend and counter against security attack.

"Some of the benefits of integrating security assessment into the SDLC include the following:

- Early identification and mitigation of security vulnerabilities and problems with the configuration of systems, resulting in lower costs to implement security controls and mitigation of vulnerabilities
- Awareness of potential engineering challenges caused by mandatory security controls
- Identification of shared security services and reuse of security strategies and tools that will reduce development costs and improve the system's security posture through the application of proven methods and techniques
- Facilitation of informed executive decision making through the application of a comprehensive risk management process in a timely manner
- Documentation of important security decisions made during the development process to inform management about security considerations during all phases of development
- Improved organization and customer confidence to facilitate adoption and use of systems, and improved confidence in the continued investment in government systems
- Improved systems interoperability and integration that would be difficult to achieve if security is considered separately at various system levels."

(Radack, 2009)

In many cases, security control assessments are conducted by system developers during the development/acquisition and implementation phases of the life cycle.

For those organizations that have implemented defined system life-cycle process standards such as ISO12207:2008 would include assessment activities within the tasks prescribed within the technical processes of that standard (Figure 8.1).

By assessing controls within system development and implementation phases, the organization can be assured that the required controls for the system are properly designed and developed, and correctly implemented, while also providing evidence of consistency with the organization's ICT security architecture before the system moves into operations and maintenance phase. The main objective is to identify any security risks that may exist through nonexistent deficient controls as early as possible within the SDLC in order to employ remediation activities in a quick and cost effective manner.

Security assessments are also conducted during the operations and maintenance phase of the life cycle to ensure that security and privacy controls continue to be effective in the operational environment and can protect against constantly evolving threats. "Many times when a system transitions to a production environment, unplanned modifications to the system occur. If changes are significant, a modified test of security controls, such as configurations, may be needed to ensure the integrity of the security controls. This step is not always needed; however, it should be considered to help mitigate risk and efficiently address last-minute surprises" (Kissel et al., 2008). It is through the performance of security control assessment during operations and maintenance that this part of the risk management process gets its cyclical identity.

The key point of this discussion is that the organization must continuously assess all implemented security controls on an ongoing basis in accordance with its information security continuous monitoring strategy. The frequency in which the assessments get performed determined by the organization and affected third-party

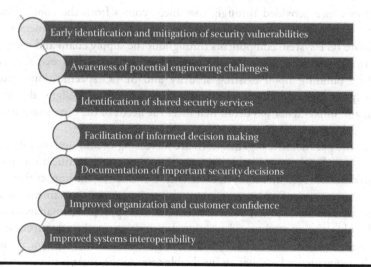

Figure 8.1   Benefits of integrating security assessment into the SDLC.

suppliers and documented within the approved risk management plan. Last, the disposal/retirement phase of the life cycle is the final point at which security assessment activities take place. Such related tasks are necessary to ensure that important organizational information is purged from the information system prior to disposal.

Adequate Control Implementation: The Proof Is in the Pudding

The question often arises to the extent at which the expense of performing control assessment is justified in terms of the organization's underlying security posture. The answer is obvious. Through assessment, an assurance case is being made that the necessary security controls are implemented to the extent that priorities established in the organization's security strategies are effectively achieved. Building a compelling case involves

- "Compiling evidence from a variety of activities conducted during the SDLC that the controls employed in the information system are implemented correctly, operating as intended, and producing the desired outcome with respect to meeting the security and privacy requirements of the system and the organization
- Presenting this evidence in a manner that decision makers are able to use effectively in making risk-based decisions about the operation or use of the system."

(NIST, 2014a,b)

The evidence provided through assessment comes from the conclusions that appropriate system-specific and common controls have been implemented in the appropriate ICT system components throughout the supply chain and corresponding management structures. As the assessment activities progress, the assessor should be building upon existing security and SDLC specifications that have previously established management and ICT requirements, designs, development criteria, and implementation detail that meet the needs of the organizations underlying security assurance strategy.

Over the past decade, organizations are increasing becoming "data-driven." In doing so, no decisions are made without the appropriate justifications provided through data collected internally or externally. Considering the impact that security has on the success of an organization, through security assessment processes, assessors obtain the required evidence to allow the appropriate management staff to make objective proactive and reactive decisions about the effectiveness of the security controls and the overall security posture of the ICT system. Moreover, the collected evidence becomes an invaluable asset to the organization during ICT security audit processes.

The assessment evidence needed to make such decisions can be obtained from a variety of mechanisms, for example, ICT component and system assessments. ICT component assessments (also known as component testing, evaluation, and validation) are normally performed by third-party assessment organizations. Such assessments are intended to examine the security functions of the system components in an effort to establish a set of appropriate configuration settings. In many cases, assessments are performed as a means of demonstrating compliance to regulatory requirements, or industry, local, national, or international ICT security standards and guidelines.

System assessments, one the other hand, provide a larger scope of evidence of effectiveness. These assessments are normally performed by members of the system development team, user representatives from the functional units that use the system, common control providers, assessors, and system auditors. When these types of assessments are performed, the assessment team collect as much documentation as possible about the ICT system including specifications, security plan, risk management plan, and other such information collected from organizational knowledge bases. Additionally, the results from individual component product assessments are useful in conducting system-level assessments using predetermined assessment methods (some of which we discuss in a later section of this chapter). The vital goal of system assessments is to collect and assess the evidence necessary for management to determine the effectiveness of security controls deployed in the ICT system and throughout the organization in terms of their likelihood of mitigating risk. Important to note is that when we speak of evaluating security controls, all three implementation control types (management, technical, and operational) must be considered.

Security Control Validation and Verification Procedures and Methodologies

While there are many methodologies in existence aimed at performing V&V on security controls. We recommend that organizations utilize the most effective approach for the set of security controls they have implemented and the security priorities the organization has established. For simplicity sake, we will carry forward in this discussion and remaining topic of this chapter using NIST SP 800-53A and NIST SP 800-115 as a basis for explanation.

NIST defines a verification and validation (assessment) procedure as "a set of assessment objectives, each with an associated set of potential assessment methods and assessment objects" (NIST, 2014a,b). Recall from our discussion in Chapter 4, assessment procedures are analogous to a test plan developed within the traditional SDLC. Test plans provide predefined statements and scenarios (called test cases) that are evaluated to test the validation and verification criteria of an ICT system or software component. Each test case is further specified to the level of detail describing the approach to be taken in order to generate adequate test results and document evidence. In much the same way, NIST defines assessment objectives as a set of predefined statements related to the particular security control under assessment. When performing quality assurance (QA) activities associated with ICT systems or software components, the individual that develops the associated test plan ensures that the statements contained within the plan can be effectively traced back to the requirements specification of the system or software. Likewise, the security control assessment objectives must be linked to the content of the security control being assessed to ensure traceability of assessment results back to the prescribed control requirements. The outputs from performing the assessment procedures become the evidence that determines the level of effectiveness provided by the control being assessed. These findings in turn should be documented in an effort to provide management the knowledge it needs for decisions made that impact the underlying security posture of the organization.

Assessment methods define *how* the assessment objects are evaluated. Although there are numerous methodologies that exist, and organizations are encouraged to identify and employ the approach that meets their own particular needs, NIST guidelines provide three primary methods, which include the following:

■ "*The examine method:* is the process of reviewing, inspecting, observing, studying, or analyzing one or more assessment objects (i.e., specifications, mechanisms, or activities). The purpose of the examine method is to facilitate assessor understanding, achieve clarification, or obtain evidence.

■ *The interview method:* is the process of holding discussions with individuals or groups of individuals within an organization to, once again, facilitate assessor understanding, achieve clarification, or obtain evidence.

■ *The test method:* is the process of exercising one or more assessment objects (i.e., activities or mechanisms) under specified conditions to compare actual with expected behavior."

(NIST, 2014a,b)

Regardless of the varying degree to which the methods are employed, the end result is to achieve the objective defined by each individual control assessment procedure. Figure 8.2 summarizes each method provided by the NIST guidelines and examples of objects associated with them.

NIST assessment methods and their objects	
Method	Object
Examine	• Specifications such as security policies; security and risk management plans; protection, detection, recovery and response procedures, system requirements, designs • Mechanisms such as hardware and software functionality • Activities such as system-level operations, system-level administration, security process management
Interview	• Individuals or groups of individuals that have a direct impact on security and control existence, functionality, correctness, completeness, and potential for improvement over time
Test	• Mechanisms such as ICT hardware, software, and telecommunications • Activities such as system security operations, system security administration, security policy and process management

Figure 8.2 NIST assessment methods and their objects.

Important to note is that each of the security controls defined in NIST SP 800-53 has an associated assessment procedure defined within NIST SP 800-53A, thereby eliminating the need for an organization to develop their own procedure for each control. This is not to suggest that an organization should feel obligated to adopt the controls specified within NIST SP 800-53. However, the guideline does serve as a basis from which the organization can build its security control framework.

Each of the assessment methods provided by NIST guidelines has a set of associated attributes that are described from the perspective of depth and coverage. These attributes assist the assessor in determining the amount of effort required of employing that method. The depth aspect of each attribute identifies the level of detail and precision is required when applying that method. Values for the depth attribute include: basic, focused, and comprehensive. All three methods provide their own definition of what constitutes each value. The coverage attribute defines the scope at which each method is employed. The guidelines accomplish this by including the number and type of specifications, mechanisms, and activities to be examined or tested, and the number and types of individuals to be interviewed. In the same way that depth was identified as basic, focused, and comprehensive. The same values are assigned to each method as they relate to the level of coverage each method provides to the overall assessment process. The organization must make the decision as to the appropriate level of depth and coverage of each method it must employ to adequately verify and validate the security control implemented within the organization and its supply chain. Figure 8.3 provides a summary of each depth and coverage level defined by NIST.

NIST Security Control Assessment Process

It should be noted, up front, that there is a variation in terms of how NIST has defined the tasks in NIST SP 800-37 *Guide to Applying the Risk Management Framework to Federal Information Systems* and how they are subsequently defined in NIST SP 800-53A. Nevertheless, what gets accomplished through the assessment process, according to both guidelines, does not change. NIST SP 800-37 simply defines the process in four distinct tasks, while NIST SP 800-53A uses four tasks that differ slightly from the other guideline and provide key inputs to each task, activities, and expected outcomes. For consistency purposes, we will continue to use NIST SP 800-53A as a basis for explaining the process (Figure 8.4).

Task 1: Preparing for Security and Privacy Control Assessments

In every ICT management book ever written, the statement is made that successful completion of ICT projects requires the cooperation and collaboration among all parties having a vested interest in the scope of that project. This includes ICT

NIST assessment attribute levels summary for depth and coverages		
Level	Depth	Coverage
Basic	• High-level reviews, observations, or inspections of the assessment objects, discussions with ICT professionals, or tests on the basis of no previous knowledge of internal control implementation details. • Conducted using limited evidence, generalized questions, or functional control specifications. • Results are basic assessments providing a high-level of understanding of the security control necessary for determining whether the control is implemented and error free.	• Uses a sample set of assessment objects that provide just enough coverage necessary for determining whether the security control is implemented and error free.
Focused	• Greater depth of analysis is performed on each assessment object. • Conducted using a substantial amount of evidence, detailed questions, or high-level design and process descriptions for controls. • Provide the level of understanding for determining whether the control is implemented, error free, and the assurance that the control is implemented correctly and operating according to specification.	• Uses a sample set of assessment objects and other pertinent assessment objects considered important to achieving the assessment objective to provide a higher level of coverage necessary for determining whether the security control is implemented, error free and there exists assurance that the control is implemented correctly and operating according to specification.
Comprehensive	• Activities that can range from basic or focused levels to a very detailed depth of analysis of the assessment object. • Conducted using an extensive amount of evidence, in-depth interview questions, or detailed technical control specifications. • Provide a level of understanding of the security control necessary for determining whether the control is implemented, error free, and the assurance that the control is implemented correctly and operating as intended on an ongoing and consistent basis. • There is evidence that supports continuous improvement in the effectiveness of the control.	• Uses a large sample set of assessment objects and other pertinent assessment objects considered to be important to achieving the assessment objective to provide the greatest level possible of coverage necessary for determining whether the security control is implemented, error free, and there exists assurance that the control is implemented correctly and operating according to specification, and that there is support for continuous improvement in the effectiveness of the control.

Figure 8.3   NIST assessment attribute levels summary for depth and coverages.

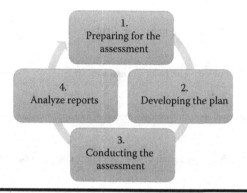

Figure 8.4 NIST security control assessment process.

professionals, system users, and senior executives. By establishing an appropriate set of expectations before, during, and after the project is important to achieving an acceptable outcome. The preparation for security control assessment is not different. This task comprises activities associated with preparing for assessments and developing security assessment plans. Security control assessors develop security assessment plans for each ICT system; however, care must be taken to complete the necessary organization-level preparation activities in addition to system-specific preparations. In combination with the criteria provided in guidelines such as NIST SP 800-53A, many organizations find it useful to develop their own assessment procedures specifically tailored to their organizational requirements, operating environments, and risk tolerance levels while making these procedures available for use in ICT systems. Moreover, organizations may choose to develop templates for recording control assessment results and producing security assessment reports as part of their ICT security program. Still other organizations deploy automated assessment tools or other mechanisms to facilitate persistent assessment activity across the organization and throughout the supply chain.

In much the same way as other ICT projects, the security control assessment process begins with information gathering, the identification of assessors and necessary resources (external and internal), and other activities to confirm that the system, its operating environment, and its resources are ready for the assessment. NIST identifies assessment preparation activities conducted prior to any planning taking place (Figure 8.5), which include:

- "Ensuring that appropriate policies covering security and privacy control assessments, respectively, are in place and understood by all affected organizational elements
- Establishing the objective and scope of assessments
- Ensuring that security and privacy controls identified as common controls (and the common portion of hybrid controls) have been assigned to appropriate organizational entities for development and implementation

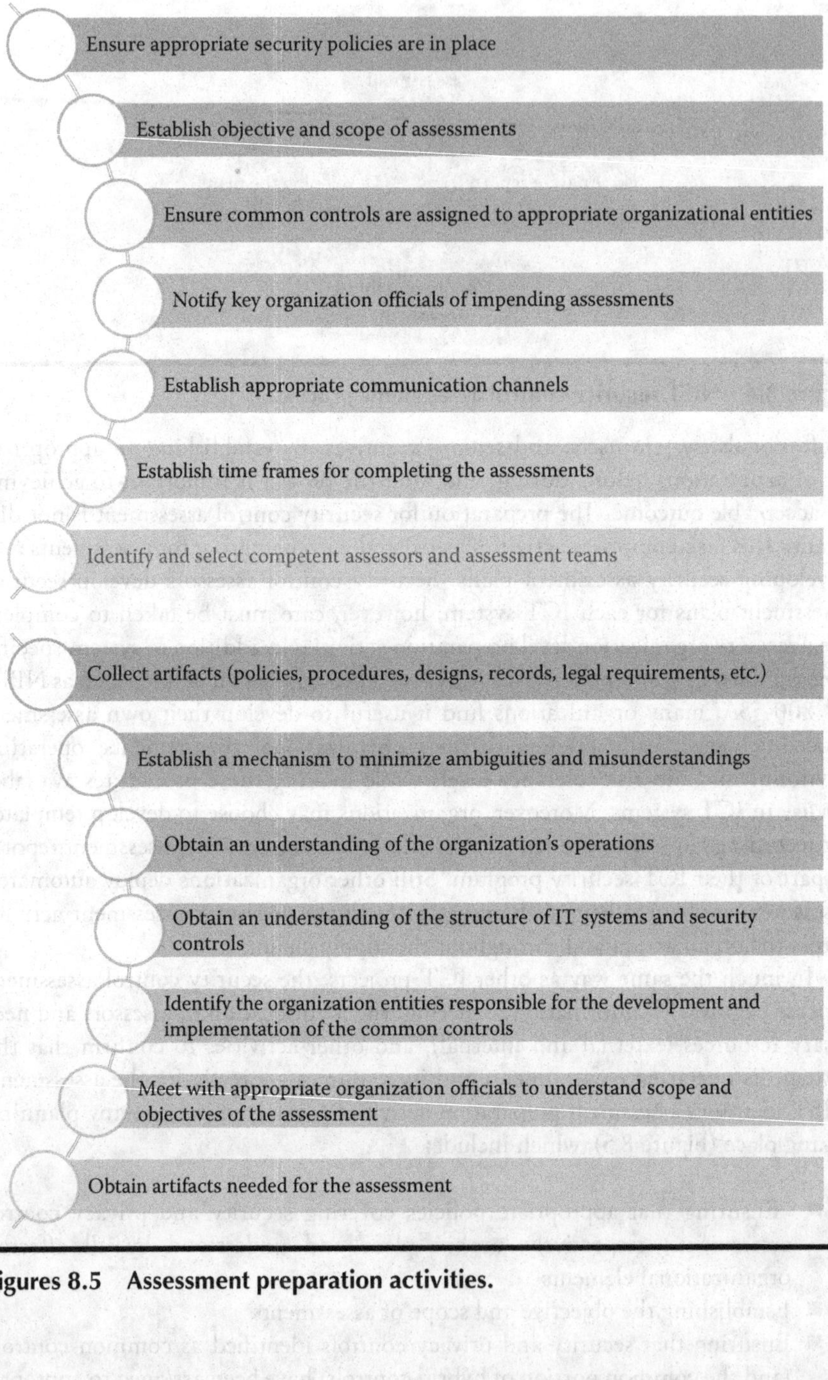

Ensure appropriate security policies are in place

Establish objective and scope of assessments

Ensure common controls are assigned to appropriate organizational entities

Notify key organization officials of impending assessments

Establish appropriate communication channels

Establish time frames for completing the assessments

Identify and select competent assessors and assessment teams

Collect artifacts (policies, procedures, designs, records, legal requirements, etc.)

Establish a mechanism to minimize ambiguities and misunderstandings

Obtain an understanding of the organization's operations

Obtain an understanding of the structure of IT systems and security controls

Identify the organization entities responsible for the development and implementation of the common controls

Meet with appropriate organization officials to understand scope and objectives of the assessment

Obtain artifacts needed for the assessment

Figures 8.5   Assessment preparation activities.

- Notifying key organizational officials of impending assessments and allocating necessary resources to carry out the assessments
- Establishing appropriate communication channels among organizational officials having an interest in the assessments
- Establishing time frames for completing the assessments and key milestone decision points required by the organization to effectively manage the assessments
- Identifying and selecting competent assessors/assessment teams that will be responsible for conducting the assessments, considering issues of assessor independence
- Collecting artifacts to provide to the assessors/assessment teams (e.g., policies, procedures, plans, specifications, designs, records, administrator/operator manuals, information system documentation, interconnection agreements, previous assessment results, legal requirements)
- Establishing a mechanism between the organization and the assessors and/or assessment teams to minimize ambiguities or misunderstandings about the implementation of security or privacy controls and security/privacy control weaknesses/deficiencies identified during the assessments
- Obtaining a general understanding of the organization's operations (including mission, functions, and business processes) and how the information system that is the subject of the particular assessment supports those organizational operations
- Obtaining an understanding of the structure of the information system and the security or privacy controls being assessed (including system-specific, hybrid, and common controls)
- Identifying the organizational entities responsible for the development and implementation of the common controls (or the common portion of hybrid controls) supporting the information system
- Meeting with appropriate organizational officials to ensure common understanding for assessment objectives and the proposed rigor and scope of the assessment
- Obtaining artifacts needed for the assessment (e.g., policies, procedures, plans, specifications, designs, records, administrator and operator manuals, information system documentation, interconnection agreements, previous assessment results)
- Establishing appropriate organizational points of contact needed to carry out the assessments
- Obtaining previous assessment results that may be appropriately reused for the current assessment
- Develop the security assessment plans"

(NIST, 2014b)

As may be expected, the amount of effort necessary to properly prepare for a security control assessment is contingent upon the scope of the assessment. In this context, the assessment scope is measured by the number and types of security controls to be assessed, which assessment procedures are to be performed, and the extent to which evidence is needed to support the objectives of the methods of those procedures. NIST recommends that the following three factors be considered in the selection of procedures:

- The system security categorization
- The set of security controls selected for the system that falls within the scope of the assessment
- The level of assurance the organization needs to satisfy to determine the effectiveness of implemented security controls

The first step for planning and preparing for assessment is to identify the controls that are to be assessed. As mentioned in an earlier section, NIST SP 800-53A contains assessment procedures for every control and control enhancement in the security control catalog of NIST SP 800-53 Rev 4. While that may give some organizations incentive to use NIST's control catalog, it is not uncommon for organizations to adapt proprietary- or industry-based assessment procedures to achieve the intended assessment objectives. However, regardless of the means by which assessment methods are chosen, the selection of those procedures must take into consideration criteria such as the impact level of the system and assurance requirements that must be satisfied.

Once the organization has effectively established the scope of the assessment, other factors can be considered. At this point, a timeline for activities performed throughout the assessment can be established. Additionally, the organization can make the necessary decisions regarding the allocation of sufficient resources to the assessment, including the decision about how many assessors should be assigned to the project. When multiple assessors are assigned, it is important that each assessor has sufficient expertise to evaluate their assigned controls and that all assessors have a common understanding of what constitutes a "satisfied" finding.

Task 2: Developing Security and Privacy Assessment Plans

The security control assessment plan is intended to provide the necessary details about the controls being assessed. The plan should define the scope of the assessment (determined in the previous task), in particular indicating if the intention is to perform a complete or partial assessment. Additionally, it should specify if it provides assessment planning criteria for a new or significantly changed system or criteria for ongoing assessments of operational systems. The plan must also describe the procedures (including the selection of assessment methods and objects and assigned depth and coverage attributes) to be used for each control; whether that be from NIST SP 800-53A or another source tailored as necessary to satisfy organizational or system-specific security requirements. Finally, the assessment plan should include sufficient detail to clearly indicate the schedule for completing the project, the individual or individuals responsible (assessor or assessment team), and the assessment procedures planned for assessing each control. It is important that the information contained within the plan be clear and concise since organizations rely on the information within the plan to allocate appropriate resources to the assessment process (Figure 8.6).

Regardless of the circumstances surrounding the need for creating the assessment plan, in order for an organization to develop a complete and comprehensive NIST compliant document requires the following steps to be completed in order:

1. "Determine the set of security controls and control enhancements to be included in the scope of the assessment
2. Select the appropriate assessment procedures to be used based on the set of controls and control enhancements within scope and on organizational factors such as minimum assurance levels.
3. Tailor the assessment methods and objects to organization or system-specific requirements and assign depth and coverage attribute values to each selected method.
4. Develop additional assessment procedures to address any security requirements or controls implemented that fall outside the scope of the security control catalog in Special Publication NIST SP 800-53 Rev 4.

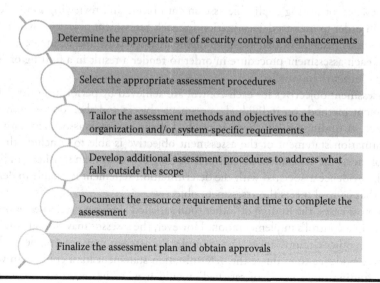

Determine the appropriate set of security controls and enhancements

Select the appropriate assessment procedures

Tailor the assessment methods and objectives to the organization and/or system-specific requirements

Develop additional assessment procedures to address what falls outside the scope

Document the resource requirements and time to complete the assessment

Finalize the assessment plan and obtain approvals

Figure 8.6   Assessment development activities.

5. Document the resource requirements and anticipated time to complete the assessment, considering opportunities to sequence or consolidate procedures to reduce duplication of effort.
6. Finalize the assessment plan and obtain the necessary approvals to execute the security control assessment according to the plan."

(NIST, 2014a,b)

After completing those six activities, the security control assessor (or lead assessor) submits the assessment plan to the appropriate authority within the organization for approval prior to beginning the actual assessment of controls.

Task 3: Conducting Security and Privacy Assessments

Once the assessment plan has progressed through the appropriate approval process, management oversight must ensure that security control assessment proceeds according to the schedule and approach specified in the plan. As mentioned previously, the assessment should adequately verify the implementation of security controls documented in the system security plan by examining evidence produced through interviewing members of the security implementation team with knowledge of specific aspects of the system, and testing the controls based on the criteria specified in the assessment plan to validate that they function as expected, and verify that evidence shows that the security controls continue to meet documented requirements.

Progression through the assessment process should follow the predetermined procedures specified for each control in the security assessment plan, examining, interviewing, or testing applicable assessment objects and reviewing available evidence in order to make a determination for each assessment objective. Recall from our previous discussion that the goal of the assessor is to find adequate evidence within each assessment procedure in order to render a result in a finding of "satisfied" or "other than satisfied."

Assessment objectives for each control are achieved by performing the defined assessment methods on individual assessment objects and then documenting the evidence. A finding of "satisfied" is reached if the evidence associated with each determination statement of the assessment objective is able to conclude that the control meets the assessment objective. A finding of "other than satisfied" indicates that the evidence associated with the determination statement is unable to demonstrate that control meets the assessment objective.

In most cases, the finding of "other than satisfied" indicates weaknesses or deficiencies in a control's implementation. However, the assessor may provide the same finding in other circumstances. For example, the assessor may not be able to obtain adequate evidence to evaluate the determination statement for a control; in which case a finding of "other than satisfied" would have to be recorded. Each "other than satisfied" finding must be documented with details that include what aspects of the security control were considered to be unsatisfactory or were unable to be assessed, and how the control implementation is different from what was planned or expected.

Regardless of the procedure, it is important that security control assessment findings be objective, evidence-based indications of the way the organization has implemented each security control. Since documentation and observation are generally used as a source of evidence for assessed controls, such evidence must be correct, complete, and present a level of quality that provides its own evidence of accuracy. Moreover, documentation of security control assessment results should be presented at a level of detail appropriate for the type of assessment being performed and include required criteria consistent with organizational policy.

One of the benefits of following the NIST guidelines is that they provide recommendations to assessors in terms of what actions to take and what sequence of steps to follow. However, they do not define what constitutes a satisfactory assessment objective implementation.

Task 4: Analyzing Assessment Reports

The initial result of the security control assessment process is a draft security assessment report. Included within the report are the assessment findings and indications of the effectiveness determined for each security control implemented for the ICT system. For ease in creating the report and ensuring that it contains the correct content, we recommend the general format provided by NIST in Special Publication 800-53A. To effectively communicate the conclusions drawn from engaging in the assessment process, the report should, at a minimum, document assessment findings and provide recommendations for correcting control weaknesses, deficiencies, or other-than-satisfied determinations made during the assessment. NIST SP 800-53A recommends the following content be included:

- The information system name
- The impact level assigned to the system
- Results of previous assessments or other-related documentation
- The identifier of each control or control enhancement assessed
- The assessment methods and objects used and level of depth and coverage for each control or enhancement
- A summary of assessment findings
- Assessor comments or recommendations

We need to emphasize that organizations and associated common control providers rely heavily on the technical knowledge and judgment of security control assessment team to accurately assess the controls implemented for ICT systems, and provide recommendations as to how corrections can be made to alleviate weaknesses or deficiencies identified during the process. The assessment team normally provides their assessment results in an initial security assessment report in order to communicate missing evidence or provide corrective actions for identified control weaknesses or deficiencies before the security assessment report is finalized. Likewise, it is common for the assessment team to reevaluate any security controls added or revised during this process and include the updated assessment findings in the final security assessment report.

Control Testing and Examination Application

Recall from previous discussions in this and other chapters, that control types can be characterized by the way they get implemented. To that extent, management controls use the fundamental practices of planning and assessment to reduce and mitigate risk. A technical control can be characterized as one that uses technology to reduce vulnerabilities. Operational controls help to ensure that day-to-day operations of an organization comply with their underlying risk management plan. Further, "testing is the process of exercising one or more assessment objects under specified conditions to compare actual and expected behaviors. Examination is the process of checking, inspecting, reviewing, observing, studying, or analyzing one or more assessment objects to facilitate understanding, achieve clarification, or obtain evidence" (Scarfone et al., 2008). In the remaining sections of this chapter, we provide a survey of technical and operational approaches to testing and examination of security control verification and validation.

Distinguishing between Testing and Examination

Examinations are the means by which security control assessment and security audit come together into a common body of knowledge. Examination activities involve the review of security documents including: policies, procedures, security plans, security requirements, standard operating procedures, architecture diagrams, engineering documentation, asset inventories, system configurations, rulesets, and system logs. Their purpose is to verify that an ICT system is documented according to organizational and industry protocol. The documentation under review should adequately ascertain the intended design, installation, configuration, operation, and maintenance of the systems and network, and provide cross-referencing that demonstrates traceability. For example, the threats and vulnerabilities identified through risk assessment should drive the documented security requirements of an ICT system. In turn, those requirements should be prevalent in the system security plan and be evident in operating procedures. The role of the assessor is to examine all plans, procedures, architectures, and configurations to ensure they are consistent with established security requirements and applicable policies identified to mitigate those threats and vulnerabilities. Moreover, examination may entail reviewing the organization's authentication ruleset to ensure its compliance with the organization's access control policies.

Alternatively, testing involves applied activities on systems and networks aimed at identifying security threats and vulnerabilities. Depending upon the organization's assessment plan, such testing can be performed on an entire ICT system and supply chain components or individual system components based on need. Testing generally uses a combination of scanning and penetration techniques capable of providing information about threats and vulnerabilities that, if not safeguarded, could induce harm to the organization's assets. Additionally, testing is also useful in predicting the likelihood that the system or network could be exploited.

NIST guidelines caution, however, that while testing does provide a clearer picture of the organization's security health then does examination, it comes at the expense of greater possibility of negative impact to the systems and networks being tested. "The level of potential impact depends on the specific types of testing techniques used, which can interact with the target systems and networks in various ways—such as sending normal network packets to determine open and closed ports, or sending specially crafted packets to test for vulnerabilities" (Scarfone et al., 2008). Ask any ICT professional, and they will tell you that any time updates or tests are performed on a system or network, there is a chance for unexpected repercussions to the extent that system outages may occur. Organizations should have resolution procedures in place, and take into consideration the potential negative circumstances that could arise, when choosing testing techniques.

It should be noted that testing should not be performed in isolation of examination. Testing does not provide a complete picture of the security state of an organization. Testing does nothing in terms of assessing management controls for example. To that extent, testing is less likely than examinations to identify weaknesses related to security policy and configuration. Likewise, organizations are often bound by constraints such as the amount of time that can be dedicated to performing the test assessments. On the other hand, attackers can take as much time as needed to exploit a system or software. The definitive answer to these issues is that combining testing and examination techniques can provide a more accurate view of an organization's security posture and its ability to protect itself from known threats and vulnerabilities.

Common Types of Operational and Technical Security Tests

Before going further, we define another security assessment term often found in guidelines and literature, the *Target*. In this chapter, we have put the assessment process into context based on the notion that tests and exams are performed on ICT components and other-related system artifacts. Most guidelines and related assessment methodology literature refer that part of the system being tested or assessed as the target. There are six general categories of testing that differ based on what the tester knows about the target, what the target knows about the tester, and the overall legitimacy of the test. In this section, we explore each of those six categories (Figure 8.7).

Blind Testing

Blind testing is performed by a tester that engages with the target but has no prior knowledge of its defenses, assets, or channels. The target is prepared for the test, knowing in advance all the details of the test. Blind testing also serves as a mechanism for evaluating the skills of the individual performing the test since coverage and depth of a blind test can only be as complex as the tester's knowledge base. Often, this type of testing is referred to as ethical hacking and generally scripted as war gaming or role-playing scenarios. Generally, this type of testing is performed by an assessment team that is external to the organization in light of the need for the tester to have no knowledge of the system.

Double-Blind Testing

Double-blind testing, again, requires that the tester engage with the target with no prior knowledge of its defenses, assets, or channels. Unlike blind testing, double-blind techniques require that the target not be aware, in advance, of the scope of the test being performed, the channels tested, or the test vectors. Like blind testing, a double-blind test measures the skills of the tester and the preparedness of the target to unknown threats and vulnerabilities. The coverage and depth of any blind test can only be as complex as the testers applicable knowledge base allows. This form of testing is also known as a black box or penetration test.

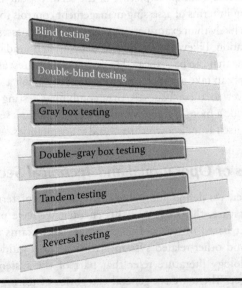

Blind testing

Double-blind testing

Gray box testing

Double–gray box testing

Tandem testing

Reversal testing

Figure 8.7   Common types of security tests.

A penetration test (often referred to as pen testing) is a proactive and authorized attempt to evaluate the security of an IT infrastructure by safely attempting to exploit system vulnerabilities, including OS, service and application flaws, improper configurations, and even risky end-user behavior. Such assessments are also useful in validating the efficacy of defensive mechanisms, as well as end-users' adherence to security policies.

Penetration testing are normally performed as part of an organization's overall security assessment process. They are typically performed using manual or automated technologies to systematically and intentionally compromise the organization's server architecture, network endpoints, web applications, wireless networks, network devices, mobile devices, and other potential points that could expose the ICT system to risk. Once vulnerabilities have been successfully exploited on a particular system, testers attempt to use the compromised system to launch subsequent exploits at other internal resources, specifically by trying to incrementally achieve higher levels of security clearance and deeper access to ICT assets and information via access privilege escalation.

Information about any security vulnerabilities successfully exploited through penetration testing is typically collected, documented, and presented to organizational management to help them to make strategic conclusions and prioritize related remediation strategies. The fundamental purpose of penetration testing is to measure the feasibility of systems or end-user compromise and evaluate any related consequences such incidents may have on the involved resources or operations.

The task of penetration testing should be performed on a regular basis to ensure more consistent ICT and network security management by revealing how newly discovered threats or emerging vulnerabilities could potentially expose the system and network to attack. In addition to regularly scheduled analysis and assessments required by regulatory mandates, pen tests should also be run whenever

- New network infrastructure or applications are added
- Significant upgrades or modifications are applied to infrastructure or applications
- New office locations are established
- Security patches are applied
- System user policies are modified

Gray Box Testing

In gray box testing, the tester engages the target with limited knowledge of its defenses and assets and full knowledge of channels. Like blind testing, the target has advance knowledge of the details of the test. Similar to blind and double-blind testing, a gray box test also measures the skills of the tester and the preparedness of the target to unknown threats and vulnerabilities. The nature of the test is efficiency. The coverage and depth of this type of test depends upon the quality of the information, about the systems or networks capabilities, provided to the tester before the test as well as the tester's applicable knowledge base. This type of test is often referred to as a vulnerability test and is most often automatically initiated by the target as a self-assessment.

A vulnerability testing process is an internal assessment of an organization's network and system security; the results of which indicate the confidentiality, integrity, and availability of the network and system. Typically, vulnerability testing starts with a reconnaissance phase, during which important data about the target and interconnected resources are gathered. This phase leads to the system readiness phase, where the target is essentially tested for all known vulnerabilities. The readiness phase culminates in the reporting phase, where the findings are classified into categories of high, medium, and low risk; and methods for improving the security posture of the organization (or mitigating the risk of vulnerability) of the target are discussed.

There is often confusion between penetration testing and vulnerability testing. Many feel that both procedures do the same thing. In reality, however, vulnerability testing is performed at a higher level of abstraction in which the goal is to identify vulnerabilities. During pen testing, the tester makes deliberate attempts to exploit the system in order to assess the organization's preparedness for protecting itself from security attack on known vulnerabilities.

Double–Gray Box Testing

Double–gray box testing is performed by a tester that engages the target and, like gray box testing, has limited knowledge of its defenses and assets. However, the tester has full knowledge of channels. In this form of testing, the target is made aware in advance of the scope and time frame of the test but has not been informed of the channels tested or the test vectors. In addition to testing the tester's skills, a double–gray box test assesses the target's preparedness to unknown threats and vulnerabilities. The coverage and depth of these types of tests largely depends on the quality of the information provided to the tester and the target before the test as well as the testers applicable knowledge base. Often, you will hear double–gray box test techniques also referred to as white box tests.

"The purpose of any security testing method is to ensure the robustness of a system in the face of malicious attacks or regular software failures. White box testing is performed based on the knowledge of how the system is implemented. White box testing includes analyzing data flow, control flow, information flow, coding practices, and exception and error handling within the system to test the intended and unintended software behavior. White box testing can be performed to validate whether code implementation follows intended design, to validate implemented security functionality, and to uncover exploitable vulnerabilities" (Janardhanudu and Wyk, 2013).

Tandem Testing

Tandem testing is an alternate form of penetration testing. However, unlike blind testing, both the tester and target are adequately prepared for the assessment. Each knows the details of the test in advance so that the appropriate preparations can be made. A tandem test assesses the protection and controls of the target. However, it cannot test the preparedness of the target to unknown threats and vulnerabilities. This type of test is best characterized by its thoroughness, as a benefit of the tester's full view of all tests and their responses. The coverage and depth of each test largely depends upon the quality of the information provided to the tester prior to the test in addition to the tester's applicable knowledge base. Tandem testing is often seen referenced as an in-house audit or a crystal box test and the tester is often part of the internal security team.

Reversal Testing

In reversal testing, the tester engages the target with full knowledge of its processes and operational security. However, the target knows nothing of what, how, or when the tester will be testing. The motivation of this type of test is to assess the preparedness of the target to unknown threats and vulnerabilities. The coverage and depth of this form of testing largely depends upon the quality of the security documentation provided to the tester and the tester's applicable knowledge base, ability to think out of the box, creative aptitude from which tests are devised. The tests performed using the reversal technique are commonly referred to as a red team exercise.

As much was the case with vulnerability testing, red team exercises are often confused with penetration testing. Red team exercises go further than penetration testing in that, these exercises have the goals of improved readiness of the organization, better training for defensive practitioners, and inspection of current performance levels. Independent red teams can provide valuable and objective insights about the existence of vulnerabilities and about the efficacy of defenses and mitigating controls already in place and even those planned for future implementation.

Common Operational and Technical Security Examination Techniques

Assessing security controls involves more than simply running a series of tests on a firewall to see which ports are open and then venturing back to your cubicle to generate a report. It is natural for security professionals to gravitate toward technology and focus on technical security control testing (i.e., penetration testing), because it is likely the "fun" part of security for anyone in the profession. Conducting a penetration test is like throwing down the gauntlet to security teams, and it gives them an opportunity to flex their hacker muscles. Assessing and auditing security as a system, however, involves significantly more than launching carefully crafted evil packets at the network to see what happens. This section discusses examination techniques assessors and auditors can use to verify and validate security controls.

Security controls are the safeguards that an organization uses to reduce risk and protect assets. Policy determines what security controls are needed, and those controls are selected by identifying a risk and choosing the appropriate countermeasure that reduces the impact of an undesirable event (such as a customer database being stolen). The examination of security controls in its simplest form validates whether or not the control adequately addresses policy, best practice, and law. Examining security controls for efficiency and effectiveness while measuring them against standards are of the best ways to help an organization meet its obligations to shareholders and regulatory responsibilities.

When examining security controls for effectiveness, three primary attributes for every control must be evaluated. All security attacks can normally be traced back to a deficiency that can be attributed to people, process, or technology. Examining these areas enables you to analyze security from a high level of abstraction, giving you a better understanding of how an organization at that moment, and recommends improvements for the future (Figure 8.8). "Following are the three facets to examine:

- People are users, administrators, data owners, and managers of the organization with varying levels of skills, attitudes, and agendas. If users are not following security policies, there might be a need for stronger administrative controls such as security awareness training or penalties for noncompliance (this is the "up to and including getting fired" clause that HR puts in the employee manual). An organization can also implement a detective/corrective control to enforce policies such as having the latest antivirus updates or operating system patches before the user is allowed on the network. People also represent the organizational structure and policies that drive security.

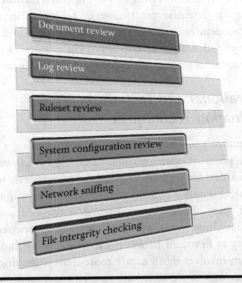

Figure 8.8   Common types of security examination techniques.

- Process represents how the organization delivers the service of IT. These are the procedures and standards that are put into place to protect assets. Processes must be up to date, consistent, and follow best practices to be effective. Process is one of the most important areas to evaluate because most attacks that result in significant loss have a component in which process has failed. Take, for example, user account creation and decommission. Someone is hired, and a request is put into IT to create the appropriate accounts, the new hire. Who is allowed to send the request? Is it any hiring manager or does it have to be one from human resources? How is the request validated as legitimate? Without strong process and the appropriate controls in place to prevent, detect, and correct, anyone can call and impersonate a hiring manager and request an account be created. This is significantly easier (and quicker) than trying to run a brute force, password-cracking tool against a server.

- Technology represents the facilities, equipment, computer hardware, and software that automate a business. Technology enables people to accomplish repetitive jobs faster and with less error. Of course, technology also enables someone to do stupid things just as efficiently (and faster). Misconfigurations and poorly implemented software can take a mistake and multiply its impact exponentially. Imagine leaving the door unlocked on a room that houses hardcopy files. Someone could potentially walk into the room and take files, but it would take a long time (not to mention effort) to hand carry those documents out to a car. Now, imagine misconfiguring a server in the demilitarized zone (DMZ) to allow for access from the Internet to a key database server. Someone could download the entire database and not even leave a trace that they were there. This is why it is so important for a business to standardize on best practices and configurations that are known to work. Best practices tend to anticipate many of these scenarios."

(Johnson, 2010)

Document Review

One of the most daunting, yet vital, tasks associated with security control assessment and audit is the determination of how effectively security policies and procedures are documented and communicated throughout the organization. This is accomplished through a document review process. The goal of documentation review is to ensure that technical aspects of policies and procedures are current and complete.

The specific documents that are chosen to be audited will vary depending upon the circumstances by which the audit is being performed. Nevertheless, at a minimum the process will consist of review of the organization's risk management plan, security policies, assessment plans, configuration management plan, system and software test plans, and any other system specifications deemed necessary for the type of audit being performed. The variety of documents assessed provides a basis from which organization builds its security posture. The assessment team will advise the organization of documents that it expects to review during the assessment process. Security teams within the organization should provide assessors with appropriate and up-to-date documentation to ensure the most comprehensive review possible.

The value that organizations get from using the document review technique is its ability to discover inconsistencies and weaknesses in terms of detail that has the potential of causing missing or improperly implemented security controls. The job of the assessor or auditor is to verify that the organization's documentation is compliant with standards and conforms to regulations, and also to look for those policies that lack depth of explanation or are no longer relevant based on the organization's current security posture. Often, the weaknesses that are discovered are found to be at the operating system level, such as outdated security procedures and protocols or nonexistent protocols that are considered necessary for the overall security of the system.

It is important to note that there is a disconnect between existing documentation and the actual implementation of security controls. "Documentation review does not ensure that security controls are implemented properly—only that the direction and guidance exist to support security infrastructure. Results of documentation review can be used to fine-tune other testing and examination techniques. For example, if a password management policy has specific requirements for minimum password length and complexity, this information can be used to configure password-cracking tools for more efficient performance" (Scarfone et al., 2008).

Log Review

In the days of mainframe legacy systems, computer operators would sit in front of black-screen terminals with green lettering watching the activity of the system. If strange activity occurred the appropriate procedures would be followed to circumvent the issue. If the crisis was taking place at 4:00 AM and could not be resolved through standard procedure, it was often the case that the operator would take great joy in waking the system administrator out of a sound sleep in order to remotely log into the system and correct the problem. We have come a long way since the mainframes of the 1980s.

Organizations now have an electronic computer operator inside most their systems called log monitoring. Log monitoring systems are intended to oversee network activity, inspect system events, and store user actions (e.g., renaming a file, opening an application) that occur within any component of the ICT system. They are constantly watching for unusual activity and have the ability to provide the data that could alert security teams to an attack. The raw log files are also known as audit records, audit trails, or event-logs.

Most systems and software generate logs including operating systems, Internet browsers, point of sale systems, workstations, antimalware, firewalls, and intrusion detection systems (IDS). Some systems with logging capabilities do not automatically enable logging so it's important to ensure all systems have logs turned on. Some systems generate logs but do not provide event log management solutions. Organizations must be aware of their systems capabilities and potentially install third-party log monitoring and management software.

It would not be an understatement that it is very likely every organization and government agency in the United States and world-wide is dealing with potential security attacks on a daily basis. Whether in the tens or in the thousands, it is crucial that they are made aware of what is happening against their system through active security log review. Such reviews should be an ongoing part of the organization's log management activities.

To establish and maintain successful log management activities, an organization should develop standardized processes for performing log management. As part of the planning process, the organization should define its logging requirements and then based on those requirements, develop policies that clearly define mandatory requirements and suggested recommendations for log management activities, including log generation, transmission, storage, analysis, and disposal. The organization must also proactively ensure that related security policies and procedures are appropriately in line with the established log management requirements recommendations. As is the case in all areas of ICT, senior management must provide the necessary support for log management planning, policy, and procedures development.

The purpose of log review, then, is to determine if security controls are logging the proper information, and if the organization is abiding by its log management policies. "As a source of historical information, audit logs can be used to help validate that the system is operating in accordance with established policies. For example, if the logging policy states that all authentication attempts to critical servers must be logged, the log review will determine if this information is being collected and shows the appropriate level of detail. Log review may also reveal problems such as misconfigured services and security controls, unauthorized accesses, and attempted intrusions. For example, if an IDS sensor is placed behind a firewall, its logs can be used to examine communications that the firewall allows into the network. If the sensor registers activities that should be blocked, it indicates that the firewall is not configured securely" (Scarfone et al., 2008).

Ruleset Review

It may be useful to begin by defining a rule set. At the most basic level, a rule set specifies what services to let through your firewall, and which ones to keep out. A rule defines the parameters against which each connection is compared, resulting in a decision on what action to take for each connection. NIST SP 800-41 Rev 1 *Guidelines on Firewalls and Firewall Policy* more formally defines rule sets as: "A set of directives that govern the access control functionality of a firewall. The firewall uses these directives to determine how packets should be routed between its interfaces." The guideline further specifies: "traffic that is specifically allowed by the security policy is permitted. All traffic that is not allowed by the security policy is blocked. Verification of the ruleset should include both reviewing it manually and testing whether the rules work as expected" (Scarfone and Hoffman, 2009).

There are two types of firewall assessments that should be performed on a regular basis. Vulnerability assessments ensure that the firewall is not vulnerable to the latest exploits. The other involves performing official audits that check for vulnerabilities, firewall software configuration, and security policy. Moreover, audits make sure that the most recent patches are installed for the firewall software and operating system. However, there is still a need for a rule review performed by the network administrator and assessor/auditor concentrating on the way rules are configured. Such a review progresses by stepping through the firewall rules one by one to make sure that they are in the proper order. An additional objective of a ruleset review is to check to ensure that rules that have been written create obvious holes, such as vulnerable services or rules that have a range of ports or all port/all protocols. An additional objective of the ruleset review is to check for obsolete rules, rules that should have been temporary, or rules that are no longer used. The individual performing the review should ensure that proper paperwork is in place for contact information and purpose of the original rule, and try to consolidate rules when possible.

The point of having ruleset reviews is largely due to the fact that many organizations must manage multiple firewalls. When responsible for a many firewalls with large rule bases, it is possible to make mistakes. It is possible to erroneously open up more than intended. Network administrators are usually the last ones to be involved in a project and are normally under time constraints to get something done to complete the project. Many times that causes a hasty decision when implementing firewall rules. Therefore, it is necessary to go back and take a look at what is there, be familiar with the connections that are allowed, make sure that the organization's security policy is being enforced, and remove unused rules.

System Configuration Review

A system configuration assessment provides in-depth details of any vulnerability, which cannot be identified using automated tools or vulnerability assessment process. During this assessment, assessor/auditor performs manual checks against predetermined system configuration settings. The process also takes into consideration the most vulnerable system access points, ICT environment, user base, and also operational procedures. This enables the assessor/auditor to be more specific in identifying the flaws and providing remediation on the basis of requirements.

NIST has developed the Security Content Automation Protocol (SCAP) under mandate of Federal Information Security Management Act (FISMA). SCAP is a standard for automating vulnerability management and policy compliance with mandated security configurations for personal computers used by federal agencies. Vulnerability scanners used by federal agencies must be validated for SCAP compliance. However, SCAP can also be a useful tool for organizations pursuing secure system configuration objectives.

SCAP incorporates six open standards for finding vulnerabilities and misconfigurations related to security. It focuses on automating these processes, scoring results, and prioritizing their impact. The goal is to automatically check the security configuration status of an agency's installed base of personal computers against the NIST Special Publication 800-53 controls framework to ensure secure computing. NIST guidelines caution, however, that "while automated system configuration reviews are faster than manual methods, there may still be settings that must be checked manually. Both manual and automated methods require root or administrator privileges to view selected security settings" (Scarfone et al., 2008).

Network Sniffing

The word "sniffer" is actually a registered trademark of Network Associates, Inc. used on their network analyzing products. However, today, sniffer has become a special name of network monitor and analyzers; it also refers to the collecting of packet level data and information. NIST defines sniffer as: "software that observes and records network traffic" (Kissel, 2002).

Typical use of network sniffer is to analyze network traffic and bandwidth utilization, so that underlying vulnerabilities in the network can be identified. There are, however, two directional usages of sniffers that have coexisted since they were first produced:

Positive usage of a sniffer is also its regular usage, which has as its objective the need to maintain the network and keep it working normally.

- Capturing packets
- Recording and analyzing traffic
- Decrypting packets and displaying in clear text
- Converting data to readable format
- Showing relevant information like IP, protocol, host or server name, and so on.

Not all packet sniffing software products have the same functions; some sniffers can analyze hundreds of protocols whereas others can only accommodate with one or two. The most common protocols analyzed by sniffer are TCP/IP, IPX, and DECNet-Ordinarily. A sniffer is used as tool of the network administrator and often used by security assessors and auditors for monitoring and analyzing a network, detecting intrusion, controlling traffic, or supervising network activity. However, it is important to note that as productive a tool as sniffers are for the purpose of identifying areas in the network vulnerable to attack, the same tools may also be utilized by hackers as a means for snooping into networks for possible attack points in ICT systems, thus forcing us to also address the negative usage dimension.

Generally, attackers will use sniffers as a means of

- Catching passwords, which is the main reason for most illegal uses of sniffing tool
- Capturing special and private information of transactions, like username, credit ID, and account ID
- Recording e-mail or instant message and resuming its content
- Modifying sensitive data stored within the system, or even cause malicious damage to the system
- Interrupting the security of a network or to gain higher-level authority

With a continuously increasing number of hackers using of network sniffers, it has become one of the most important tools in the defense of cyber-attacks and cyber-crime.

While network sniffers provide significant capabilities in the defense against attacks, they also have limitations. "Many attackers take advantage of encryption to hide their activities—while assessors can see that communication is taking place, they are unable to view the contents. Another limitation is that a network sniffer is only able to sniff the traffic of the local segment where it is installed. This requires the assessor to move it from segment to segment, install multiple sniffers throughout the network, and/or use port spanning. Assessors may also find it challenging to locate an open physical network port for scanning on each segment. In addition, network sniffing is a fairly labor-intensive activity that requires a high degree of human involvement to interpret network traffic" (Scarfone et al., 2008).

File Integrity Checking

File integrity checking, more commonly called file integrity monitoring (FIM), is a key part of comprehensive ICT security and compliance initiatives in detecting unauthorized changes to critical files by monitoring those files for change over time. In fact, regulatory and industry mandates and best practices already require FIM such as PCI DSS Section 11.5 or ITIL change management process. As we mentioned earlier in the chapter, increases in sampling requirements for security audits over time has made it necessary for organizations to automate many audit processes such as FIM. Additionally, use of FIM can be used to confirm successful completion of other ICT processes such as patch deployment or major system upgrades.

The technical details related to automated-FIM are beyond the scope of this book. However, in general, automated FIM works by using software automation to compare file attributes like file size and/or hash values over a specific period of time and at predetermined intervals. The objective of this examination technique is to ensure that critical or sensitive system-level files have not been modified or compromised. As a consequence to the system resources required to perform FIM, organizations are limited in what can be monitored. Hence, it is not possible to monitor every file on an information asset so usually a subset of files is specified for monitoring. Some system files change frequently in normal system operation so the focus should be on monitoring those files that do not change frequently to avoid creating excessive reporting and alert volume. Traditionally, a baseline is made of existing files and then an automated process periodically rechecks the file attributes and confirms that the file continues to exist in the same state as indicated by the original baseline. Important to note, though, is that the baseline approach assumes that the initial file state is acceptable so processes must be in place to ensure the original file attributes are valid.

Chapter Summary

A lot of people use the phrases validation and verification, security audit, security assessment, and security test interchangeably. An assessment is a process used to identify all potential threats and vulnerabilities that could be exploited in an environment. The assessment can be used to evaluate (using testing, examination, and interview methodologies) physical security, the user base, system controls, and network security. NIST SP 800-53A provides a four step for performing a security control assessment effectively. The first task, preparing for security and privacy control assessments, involves information gathering activities that identify the security controls to be assessed and understanding the requirements for effective assessment of each control. The second task, developing security and privacy assessment plans, includes the activities that lead to the development of a plan that the assessment team uses to guide them through the assessment process. Among other details, it provides scope, timing, and procedural details that state what should be completed before, during, and after the assessment process. The third task, conduct security and privacy assessments, uses the plan created in the second task to perform procedures that result in finding for each control, each finding is recorded as "satisfied" or "other than satisfied." Task four, analyze assessment report, involves the development of a formal report detailing how the assessment was performed, the findings identified in the third task, justification of identified weaknesses, and recommendations for improving control weaknesses and implementation of security controls that are lacking. During this forth task the report is analyzed by the organization and recommendations are acted upon.

While the NIST guidelines recommend testing, examination, and interview methodologies for assessing managerial, technical, and operational security controls, testing and examination tend to be the most effective. There are six categories of security control testing. The type of test(s) performed depends upon the underlying goal of the assessment being performed. Blind testing is used when the assessment calls for the tester to have no knowledge of the target, yet the target is aware in advance that the test is to be performed. Double-blind testing requires that the tester not have knowledge of the target, and the target not have advance knowledge of the test being performed. This form of testing is also known as "black box" testing. Gray testing is used when the assessment calls for the tester to have limited knowledge of the target, and the target has advance knowledge of the test being performed. Double-gray testing requires that the tester have limited knowledge of the target defenses and assets, while also having full knowledge of its channels. The target, in this form of testing, the target has been made aware of the test in advance, but has not been made aware of the channels being tested. Tandem testing is used when the assessment requires that the tester and target have full knowledge of the test being performed. Reversal testing techniques require the tester to have full knowledge of the test being performed, but the target has no advance knowledge of the test or channels being tested.

The examination of security controls in its simplest form validates whether or not the control adequately addresses policy, best practice, and law. Examining security controls for efficiency and effectiveness while measuring them against standards are of the best ways to help an organization meet its obligations to shareholders and regulatory responsibilities. This method assessment is also characteristic of the activities performed during a security audit. The most common examination methods include: documentation review, network sniffing, file integrity checking, system configuration review, log review, and ruleset review.

Key Terms

Assessor—in the context of security control assessment, he/she is responsible for leading the activities performed throughout the assessment process.

Ethical hacking—the process of systematically performing penetration techniques on an ICT system or network for the purpose of finding security vulnerabilities that a malicious hacker could potentially exploit.

Penetration testing—a proactive technique used during security control assessment to evaluate the security of an ICT infrastructure by attempting to exploit system vulnerabilities, including operating systems, service and application flaws, improper configurations, and risky user behavior. These tests are also useful in validating the efficiency of defensive mechanisms and user adherence to security policies.

Quality assurance—the process of checking to see whether a product or service being developed is meeting specified requirements. In the context of security controls, it is the process of checking to see whether the controls are implemented to the extent that they meet predefined requirements.

Red team exercise—an attempt to gain access to a system by any means necessary, and usually includes penetration testing, physical breach, testing all phone lines for modem access, testing all wireless and RF systems present for potential wireless access, and also testing an organization's employees through several scripted social engineering and phishing tests.

System auditor—similar to a security assessor to the extent that in the context of security audit, he/she is responsible for leading the activities performed throughout the audit process.

Target—the ICT system or system component being tested or examined through a security control assessment of security audit process.

Validation—in the context of security controls, it refers to the activities associated with ensuring that the ICT system meets the specified security requirements.

Verification—in the context of security controls, it is the process of measuring the extent to which security controls have been implemented correctly and effectively serve their intended purpose.

Vulnerability testing—a process for identifying inadequate system and network security control implementation's that cause vulnerability to security attack. Such tests also generally include methods for prioritizing and implementing additional security measures for fixing and protecting systems and networks from known vulnerabilities.

References

Janardhanudu, G. and Wyk, K. V. (2013). *White Box Testing*. Building Security In. https://buildsecurityin.us-cert.gov/articles/best-practices/white-box-testing/white-box-testing. Accessed August 2, 2015.

Johnson, C. (2010). *Network Security Auditing Tools and Techniques*. Cisco Press. http://www.ciscopress.com/articles/article.asp?p=1606900. Accessed August 6, 2015.

Kissel, R. (2002). *Glossary of Key Information Security Terms–NISTIR 7298 Rev 2* (Report). Gaithersburg, MD: National Institute of Standards and Technology.

Kissel, R., Stine, K., and Scholl, M. (2008). *Security Considerations in the System Development Life Cycle: NIST SP 800-64R2* (Guideline). Gaithersburg, MD: National Institute of Standards and Technology.

National Institute of Standards and Technology. (2014a). *Assessing Security and Privacy Controls in Federal Information Systems and Organizations–Building Effective Assessment Plans: NIST SP 800-53Ar4*. Gaithersburg, MD: NIST.

National Institute for Standards and Technology. (2014b). *NIST SP 800-53 Rev 4: Security Controls for Federal Information Systems and Organizations*. Gaithersburg, MD: NIST

Radack, S. (2009). *The System Development Life Cycle (SDLC)*—Bulletin. Gaithersburg, MD: National Institute of Standards and Technology.

Scarfone, K. and Hoffman, P. (2009). *Guidelines on Firewalls and Firewall Policy: NIST SP 800-41 Rev 1* (Guideline). Gaithersburg, MD: National Institute of Standards and Technologies.

Scarfone, K., Souppaya, M., Cody, A., and OreBaugh, A. (2008). *Technical Guide to Information Security Testing and Assessment: NIST SP 800-115* (Guideline). Gaithersburg, MD: NIST.

Shoemaker, D. and Sigler, K. (2015). *Cybersecurity: Engineering a Secure Information Technology Organization*. Stamford, CT: Cengage Learning.

Chapter 9

Control Framework Sustainment and Security of Operations

At the conclusion of this chapter, the reader will understand:

- The fundamental practices of operational control sustainment
- The processes for ensuring operational security
- The operational sensing and threat identification process
- How to implement effective change control
- The change authorization and management process
- The common types of change assurance practices
- The common types of configuration management practices for controls
- The ongoing patch management function

Operational Control Assurance: Aligning Purpose with Practice

As the name implies, operational control assurance is less involved with strategy then it is with ensuring dependable day-to-day functioning of the organization. The operational control assurance function achieves its purpose by making certain that security practices always meet specified control oversight and management goals (Figure 9.1).

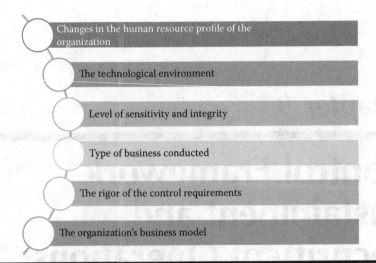

Changes in the human resource profile of the organization

The technological environment

Level of sensitivity and integrity

Type of business conducted

The rigor of the control requirements

The organization's business model

Figure 9.1 Factors that affect change.

Every organization uses some type of formal management control. That formal control must be acceptably consistent in order for the organization to be considered properly managed. However, the overall organizational controls environment is always changing as the business model and the threat horizon changes. And so those goals will change accordingly. Factors that can affect that change include

1. Changes in the human resources profile of the organization—for instance outsourcing
2. The technology environment of the organization
3. The organization's level of sensitivity or integrity requirements
4. The way the organization does business or the type of business that is conducted
5. The rigor or extent of the control requirements
6. The organization's business model

The general role of the operational assurance function is to maintain consistently correct alignment between the management goals of the business and its specific control practices. Operational control assurance is responsible for monitoring the execution of all of the controls and control systems of the business in order to ensure that they are effectively supporting the organization's business purposes.

The focus of that monitoring is on the detection of relevant deviations from intended corporate directions and purposes. Typically, this is accomplished by an identification and evaluation scheme that logs problems as they occur and the subsequent development of an appropriate response to any item of concern with respect to control set operation. The operational control assurance process is then responsible for taking the appropriate corrective, adaptive, perfective, or preventive action and then validating the effectiveness of the subsequent response.

Besides the control set itself, operational control assurance also has to routinely review, inspect, test, and audit the execution of the diverse actions that constitute the overall control architecture. As we said earlier, where problems are encountered, operational control assurance is the function that is responsible for executing the formal problem resolution process in order to correct deviations.

Operational control assurance works best when it is possible to anticipate likely meaningful control issues where there is a predefined response in place. As such, operational control assurance and risk identification/risk response might be considered to be two seamless aspects of the same larger purpose—which is to ensure that every conceivable threat to the organization is identified and appropriately responded to.

The operational control assurance process encompasses four domains. These domains represent the four primary activities of the operational security process: sensing, analyzing, responding, and improving. In the first instance, it is essential to continuously monitor the operational environment. That is because threats can arise at any point in time and can represent a range of unanticipated impacts. Thus, monitoring of the threat picture in the corporate environment must be carried out on a routine and disciplined basis. Also in that respect, it is necessary to report all incidents through a standard and disciplined process.

Threats arise out of the environment. Therefore, it is a requisite of good practice to continuously analyze those events as they take place in the operating environment in order to identify and decide how to best respond to relevant threats, exposures, vulnerabilities, and violations. The aim is to respond as effectively as possible to trouble arising from meaningful threats, malfunctions, or incidents as they emerge.

Ensuring the Long-Term Integrity of the Control Set

This final chapter looks at the everyday practices that have to be performed when the selected controls are placed into the operational environment. This is the period after deployment, which extends throughout the life of the control set. It normally constitutes the majority of the life cycle of the control system. The common term for this long period of time is "sustainment."

Sustainment entails all of the processes that are put in place to assure the continuing correctness and effectiveness of the organization's established set of controls. Controls are created and deployed in order to facilitate the organization's business goals and each goal has sustained operational performance requirements. If the control set does not meet those requirements, the organization must realign the functioning of that control set or alter the goal of the business process in order to bring the two aspects back into alignment (Figure 9.2).

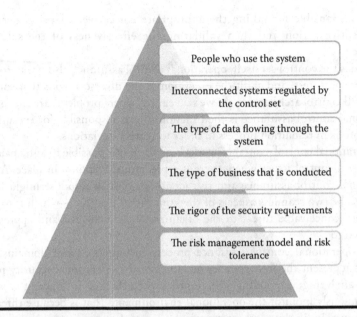

People who use the system

Interconnected systems regulated by the control set

The type of data flowing through the system

The type of business that is conducted

The rigor of the security requirements

The risk management model and risk tolerance

Figure 9.2 Environmental factors that impact effectiveness.

A systematic and uninterrupted alignment process is required because the demands of the control environment are constantly changing. Environmental factors that could impact the effectiveness of a given control include:

1. People who use the system and the changing motivations of those people
2. Different systems interconnected with the system that is regulated by the control set
3. The type of data flowing to—through—or from the involved systems
4. The way the organization does business or the type of business that is conducted
5. The rigor or extent of the security requirements
6. The organizational risk/risk tolerance model

The control set must always satisfy business objectives. If that is not the case, then the organization's management process must dictate the steps necessary to change the alignment of the control set or change the objectives for control. In general, the process for control sustainment is made up of four meta-activities (Figure 9.3).

1. Operational assurance (sensing)
2. Analysis
3. Response management (responding)
4. Infrastructure assurance

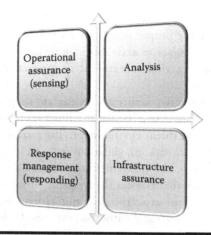

Figure 9.3   Process for control sustainment.

The sustainment process presupposes the existence and documentation of a comprehensive, correct, and unambiguous control set. This has to occur at the control system's most basic level of functioning. In addition, the interconnection between any subset of the control set and the entire portfolio of control systems must also be fully and holistically represented. The overall control system's responsibility for receiving, processing, or transmitting information must be documented as well as the status of all of the various constituencies affected by the control set, such as managers or users. The various elements of the target for control are normally understood in a top-down fashion, drilling down from the entity as a whole into each large element of that system to a more detailed understanding of the actual components and interrelationships and requirements of the control subsets of the constituent components.

The control behaviors themselves are always continuously performed in the operational space. That is necessary because risks in the threat environment and the requirements for control are continuous. Therefore, confidence in the correctness and effectiveness of the control set must be continuously renewed. In addition, because the controls themselves are increasingly interdependent, an appropriate level of confidence must also be established for the entire organizational control set.

Typically, sustainment monitors the control set's ability to ensure confidence in the continued proper functioning of the control set. Sustainment monitors the control set's ability to accurately identify and record problems, analyze those problems, take the appropriate corrective, adaptive, perfective or preventive action and confirm the restored capability of the controls. Sustainment activities also encompass the migration and retirement of the control set. The process ends when the control set or control set-intensive system is retired.

Sustainment work is either proactive or reactive. Proactive activities include identifying of threats and vulnerabilities; creating, assessing, and optimizing control solutions (within a generalized control architecture); and implementing explicit tasks to ensure the proper functioning of the control set and the information that it processes. Reactive activities include incident and threat response and the detection and reaction to external or internal intrusions or security violations.

Both proactive and reactive security activities are supported by sensing, analyzing, and responding functions. The sensing function involves monitoring, testing, and assessment of the threat environment. The goal of sensing is to identify potential intrusions (e.g., a break in), violations (e.g., an inappropriate access), and vulnerabilities (a weakness). The analyzing function facilitates the necessary understanding of the risk. Analyzing assesses the frequency of occurrence and impact. It considers and evaluates all risk avoidance, risk mitigation, and risk transfer options. The responding function selects and authorizes the remediation option. It monitors and assures the change and ensures the correct reintegration of the altered control behavior, any relevant system settings, or policies. Management must then make certain that the necessary resources are available to ensure the authorized level of risk mitigation.

With proactive assurance, decision makers have the option of authorizing a preventive, perfective, or adaptive response. With reactive assurance, decision makers have the option of authorizing corrective or emergency action. Corrective change involves identifying and removing vulnerabilities and correcting actual errors. Preventive change involves the identification and detection of latent vulnerabilities (e.g., the control set or control set-intensive system is found to be vulnerable to a particular class of intrusion). Perfective change involves the improvement of performance, dependability, and maintainability.

Adaptive change adapts the control set to a new or changed environment (e.g., a new operating system with enhanced security functionality is available). Emergency change involves unscheduled corrective action (e.g., an intrusion or violation has taken place) (Figure 9.4).

Operational Assurance (Sensing)

Operational assurance is a proactive sustainment function in essence. It encompasses the defined policies, procedures, tools, and standards that are deployed to monitor, test, and review the control set or system. Sensing is performed continuously within the operating environment. Standard operational assurance activities for the necessary risk identification and analysis are specified within the larger context of various standards of best practice discussed in this including International Organization for Standardization (ISO) 27000, National Institute of Standards and Technology (NIST) 800-53, and Control Objectives for IT (COBIT).

Operational assurance also identifies and resolves security and control vulnerabilities within the control set, the system, the data, the policies, and the users.

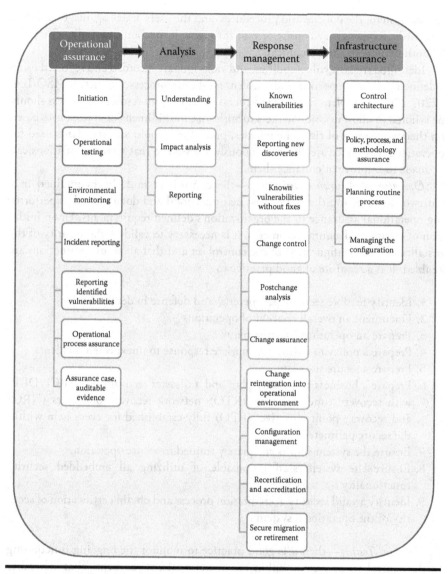

Figure 9.4   Overview of control sustainment elements.

Because vulnerabilities can be associated with everything from applications, the operating system, network or device configurations, policies and procedures, security mechanisms, physical security, and employee usage, operational assurance is not limited to the technical control set alone but extends into the operating environment that surrounds the actual electronic environment of the machine. Technical assurance practices include intrusion detection, penetration testing, and violation analysis and processing. Reviewing is a periodic activity that evaluates the control set, the system, the policies and procedures, and the users' usage against established standards. Reviews may consist of walkthroughs, inspections, or audits. They can be both managerial and technical.

Identified threats, vulnerabilities, and violations are recorded and reported using a defined problem reporting and problem resolution process, for instance ISO/IEC 12207 2008—Problem Resolution Process. The problem resolution process should be tailored to allow decision makers to authorize multidimensional responses based on their assessment of risk. The policies, procedures, tools, and standards used for operational assurance are also continuously assessed so that recommendations can be made to improve or enhance them.

Operational Assurance: Initiation—the control set must be maintained in a trustworthy state and that state must be understood and documented as performing operational assurance to the organization's defined requirements. Upon initiation of operational assurance process, it is necessary to validate the security of the installation and configuration of the control set and that all security functions are enabled. It is a requisite of good practice to

1. Identify feasible security perimeter(s) and defense in depth
2. Document an overall concept of operations
3. Prepare an operational testing plan
4. Prepare a policy to ensure appropriate response to unexpected incidents
5. Prepare a secure site plan
6. Prepare a business continuity plan and a disaster recovery plan (BCP/DRP) with recovery time objectives (RTO), network recovery objectives (NRO) and recovery point objectives (RPO) fully established for every item within the secure perimeter
7. Ensure the system staff is adequately trained in secure operation.
8. Ensure the system staff is capable of utilizing all embedded security functionality
9. Identify a valid security accreditation process and obtain certification of security of the operational system

Operational Testing—then it is good practice to monitor the ongoing functioning of the control set or system within the operational environment. That is because threats can arise at any point in the process and can comprise a range of unanticipated hazards. This testing must be done on a disciplined and regularly scheduled basis. Therefore, a requisite of good practice is to develop and utilize a continuous operational testing process to identify security threats and vulnerabilities and control violations in control set and control set-intensive systems.

Environmental Monitoring—environmental threats are always present in the real-world context that the control set functions in. In that respect, the environment represents the place where early warning of impending hazards or attacks can be best spotted. Therefore, a requisite of good practice is to continuously monitor the operating environment that surrounds the control set to identify and respond to security threats, exposures, vulnerabilities, and violations as they arise (threat identification).

Incident Reporting—incidents must be reported through a standard and disciplined process. The aim is to be able to respond as quickly as possible to any trouble arising from the exploitation of vulnerabilities, malfunctions, or incidents that might exist in the control system. The process must be both standard in its procedure and fully documented. The process also must be well understood within the organization. Therefore, a requisite of good practice is to institute a systematic procedure to document and record threat exposures and vulnerabilities.

Reporting Identified Vulnerabilities—organizations who do not actively seek to identify and report vulnerabilities in their management control systems or who do not report generic vulnerabilities that they know about, increase the chances that both the organization itself and its customers might suffer serious harm as a result, with accompanying damage to the organization's reputation or business interests. On the other hand, restricting early access to vulnerability information may be needed in practice to prevent dangerous leakage to attackers.

Therefore, a requisite of good practice is to identify and report all vulnerabilities possibly to a central entity, but not necessarily releasing them to wide disclosure: vulnerability identification takes place in operational assurance. The classification, prioritization, and development of remediation options occur in analysis.

Operational Process Assurance—it is necessary to ensure that operational assurance is carried out in the most effective and efficient manner. As such, the functioning of the operational assurance process itself must be continuously monitored. The aim is to identify and report any deviation from proper practice to management for remediation. As such, it is a requisite of good practice to

1. Assess and audit the policies, procedures, tools, and standards used for operational assurance
2. Document assessments and audits and make recommendations for improvement to the designated approving authority

Assurance Case, Auditable Evidence for Operational Assurance—a variety of evidence can be relevant to creating and maintaining an assurance case for operational assurance, including the following 11 standard elements:

1. Evidence of an organizationally standard operational procedure manual that details the required steps for every activity in operational assurance, including expected results and some way to determine that they have been achieved.
2. Evidence of a tangible set of organizationally sanctioned actions, procedures, or protocols invoked when anticipated hazards occur.

3. Evidence of a tangible set of organizationally sanctioned actions, procedures, or protocols invoked when unforeseen hazards occur.
4. Documentation of the specific method for incident reporting or requesting change and the procedures for responding to each report.
5. Documentation of the process for ensuring that the BCP is up to date.
6. Evidence that all of relevant members of the organization know precisely what activities they have to carry out in sustainment and the timing requirements for performing them.
7. Documentation of the precise steps taken to build awareness of correct practice, including a formal employee education and training program.
8. Documentation of each employee's specific education, training, and awareness activities.
9. Documentation of the explicit enforcement requirements and consequences for noncompliance for every job title.
10. Documentation and evidence of personal agreement to the consequences for noncompliance.
11. Evidence that enforcement was practiced on a continuous basis and as an organization wide commitment.

Analysis

The analysis function, which is the next applicable domain of control sustainment evaluates the consequences of an identified threat or violation and makes recommendations for mitigation along with documenting the impact of the recommended change. All control sets and control intensive systems, policies, processes, or objectives impacted by the change must be included in the evaluation. This degree of documentation is necessary to ensure a coordinated response.

Analysis entails identification of the affected control set and systems, to include cascading or ripple effects, along with affected policies or processes. Affected control set and systems elements are examined to determine impacts of a prospective change. Impacts on existing control set and systems, as well as any interfacing systems and organizational functioning, are characterized. Security and safety impacts of the change must be fully examined, documented, and communicated to the response management function for authorization.

In addition, to determining impacts, the results of the analysis are formally recorded and maintained in a permanent repository. This increases understanding of the content and structure of the portfolio of control functions. In addition, this supports retrospective causal analysis that could be undertaken to understand security and control issues that might be associated with the change.

Understanding—in order to implement a change properly, it is essential to understand all of the components and the consequences of change to the process.

That degree of understanding requires knowledge of all aspects of the design architecture and the affected business functionality. To support this change, it is good practice to

1. Document the problem/modification request and capture all requisite data in a standard organizationally sanctioned form
2. Replicate or verify the existence of the reported problem—for the sake of resource coordination, confirm that the problem really exists
3. Verify the violation, exposure, or vulnerability—understand the precise nature and implications of the vulnerability and develop an overall response strategy
4. Identify elements to be modified in the existing system—identify all system and functional components that will be changed—develop a specific response strategy for each element using good development practices
5. Identify interface elements affected by the modification
6. Estimate the impact of change to the control set on system interfaces—perform impact analysis on affected interfaces and, from that, design a specific response strategy for each interface using good development practices.
7. Identify documentation to be updated
8. Identify relevant security policies—validate recommended response strategy against relevant security and safety policy
9. Identify relevant legal, regulatory, and forensic requirements—validate the recommended response strategy against relevant legal, regulatory, or forensic requirements

These steps help to ensure proper change implementation decisions for a component or system.

Impact Analysis—as indicated in the section on understanding, in order to implement a specifically targeted response, it is necessary to know what the implications of a particular response strategy or action might be. In order to attain that level of knowledge, the organization must develop a comprehensive and detailed impact analysis. This should be based on a formal methodology ensuring a comprehensive and unambiguous understanding of all operational implications for the control set, its requirements, and its associated architecture. Therefore, for each remediation option the organization must routinely

1. Identify the impact of change on the assurance case.
2. Identify the violation, exposure, or vulnerability type—the threat is explicitly classified by type.
3. Identify the scope of the violation, exposure, or vulnerability—the extent or boundary of the threat is fully and explicitly itemized.
4. Provide a formal statement of the criticality of the violation, exposure, or vulnerability.

5. Document all feasible options for analysis.
6. Perform a comprehensive risk identification—identification of the type and extent of risk for each option.
7. Perform a detailed risk evaluation—assess the likelihood and feasibility of each identified risk for each option.
8. Estimate safety and security impacts if change is implemented—based on likelihood percentages and feasibility for each option.
9. Estimate the safety and security impacts if change is not implemented—based on the likelihood of occurrence of financial and operational impacts of each identified option.
10. Assess the impact of change on security and control architecture.
11. Perform control set understanding and design description exercise for all automated security and control features.
12. Estimate and assess the implications of change as they impact the policy and procedure infrastructure.
13. Estimate the impact of change on the business continuity/disaster recovery strategy.
14. Specify feasible recovery time, NRO, and recovery point impact estimates for each option.
15. Estimate the return on investment for each option, including total cost of ownership and marginal loss percentage.
16. Estimate the level of test and evaluation commitment necessary for verification and validation.
17. For each option, prepare a testing program—sample test cases and methods of administration.
18. Estimate the resource requirements, staff capability, and feasibility of administration of tests.
19. Estimate the financial impacts where appropriate for each option.
20. Estimate the feasibility and timelines for implementing each option.
21. Prepare a project plan for each option if detailed level of understanding required.

Once the options have been investigated, a basis for decision making exists.

Reporting

In order to support the requisite for executive decision making about the form of the response, a meaningful and valid body-of-evidence that has to be developed in the analysis phase. Then this must be communicated in a clear and understandable fashion to the designated approving authorities of the organization. That authority will then provide the actual authorization of any changes necessary to ensure the continued effectiveness of the control set.

For each change requested, the nominally correct prerequisite is to determine or designate the appropriate decision maker. This identification may be based on the results of the analysis phase or carried out as a result of predesignated contractual agreement. Decision making may also be carried out by means of a preselected control board, which is composed of the appropriate decision makers. If the decision is significant enough, it may also be decided through a process that is specifically instituted at the conclusion of the analysis phase.

The results of the analysis are reported to the appropriate manager with a full explanation of the implementation requirements for each remediation option. This report must clearly outline impacts of each option and it must be plainly and explicitly understandable to lay-decision makers. The feasible remediation options must be itemized. These must be expressed in a manner that is understandable to lay-decision makers and each option recommended must be fully and demonstrably traceable to the business case. All of this prepares the organization to develop the response that will be discussed in the next subsection.

Response Management (Responding)

Response management entails a set of processes that function within the larger context of the generic change management activities of the organization. Response management assures proper coordination and deployment of the remediation option that is selected by the decision authorities. The internal management controls development process or a necessary third-party consulting process is normally the actual agent of change. Policies, tools, and standards that are employed for response management are also continuously assessed so that evaluation recommendations can be made to improve or enhance these organizational elements.

Responding to Known Vulnerabilities (e.g., patching)—one major responsibility of the response management function is to maintain the security and integrity of the control set throughout its useful lifetime. The reality is that over that lifetime, a significant number of new vulnerabilities, which might threaten the control management process, will be discovered. Those vulnerabilities might be discovered through explicit investigation by the organization's security professionals, vendors who are external to the organization, white-hat hackers, internal members of the organization, or any other interested party, including published exploits by the black-hat community. Whatever the source, any vulnerability that has been discovered requires risk management decisions on patching or other risk mitigations (Figure 9.5).

First, it is a requirement of the process that the finder communicates in some sort of trustworthy and confidential fashion with the organization where the flaw exists. This communication process must be robust enough that it will be effective

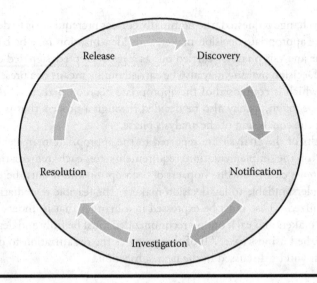

Figure 9.5   Discovery process.

throughout all phases of the patching process. In order to ensure against the general public gaining knowledge about the existence of a known vulnerability before a patch or remediation option is developed, the discovery process is likely to entail the following five stages:

1. *Discovery*—Finder discovers a security vulnerability.
2. *Notification*—Finder notifies organization's managers to advise the potential vulnerability or flaw exists. The affected manager confirms the receipt of the notification.
3. *Investigation*—Management investigates the finder's reports to verify and validate the vulnerability in collaboration with the finder.
4. *Resolution*—If the vulnerability is confirmed, management will develop an effective patch or remediation option for the control set and a change procedure will be executed in order to eliminate the vulnerability.
5. *Release*—Vendor and finder will coordinate and publicly release information about the vulnerability and remedy, including the requisite patch (if applicable).

Reporting—if a vulnerability is discovered, it is the responsibility of the response management function of the organization that has discovered it to disclose its existence to all affected parties in such a way that will ensure the overall functioning of the control set will not be affected or harmed. The risk is that, if the vulnerability is simply publically reported or reported too soon, the black-hat community will exploit the problem before the organization, can discover and implement a way to patch or mitigate it. As such, it is not correct practice to provide full and immediate public disclosure of a vulnerability without fully exploring the risk mitigation options.

That understanding is obtained through the impact analysis. Depending on the risk mitigation situation, there are three ways to disclose the existence of a new vulnerability. All three of the following entail risks, which must be considered; however, partial disclosures are considered to be more appropriate:

1. Wide public disclosure—this involves publishing a full report to a wide audience where system security experts decide on actions to take. This approach is subject to exploitation by criminals.
2. Limited public disclosure—only one organization is informed either because the remediation is only required there or to research appropriate responses, which limits the potential for exploitation.
3. Total limited public disclosure—only a selected group is informed, for example, only the security group in a particular organization, until an appropriate response is developed.

Responding to Known Vulnerabilities without Fixes—there might be operational justification for not fixing, or reporting a vulnerability at all; or for putting it on the back burner. These justifications might include such reasons as the lack of obvious harm or the amount of time and resources required to develop the fix will outweigh any potential cost should the threat happen. It might also include lack of current resources; difficulty or infeasibility of the repair or an unwillingness to take down a critical operational system. However, it is essential that known vulnerabilities are monitored and controls deployed to address them. Therefore, a requisite of good practice is to

1. Maintain continuous records of publicly known vulnerabilities.
2. Maintain a continuous record of privately known vulnerabilities.
3. Monitor operational behavior of the system to detect and recognize the signature of any attempt to exploit a known vulnerability.
4. Set automated alarms to inform of an attempt to exploit a known vulnerability
5. Maintain a systematic and well-defined response to any expected attempt to exploit a known vulnerability.
6. Ensure that the system staff understands the proper response to an attempt to exploit a known vulnerability.

Change Control

The agent performing a fix or change to the control set must understand all of the requirements and restrictions involved in making the change. Thus, a process must be established to unambiguously convey all of the technical and contextual specifications of the remediation option to the change agent. Organizationally persistent controls must be put in place to ensure that this is done in a standard and disciplined fashion. Therefore, it is good practice to

1. Identify the appropriate change agent—this may be either a managerial or a technical development entity.
2. Develop and document a statement of work (SOW) and specify the precise method for communicating this to the change agent.
3. Develop and document criteria for testing and evaluating the control set or control system to ensure successful remediation.
4. Communicate these to the change agent prior to instituting the change process.
5. Develop and document criteria for ensuring that elements and requirements that should not be modified remain unaffected.

Postchange Analysis

Changes to the control set can eliminate vulnerabilities. However, change can also create new ones. As a consequence, attackers typically examine a significant change to a control system in order to identify any new or different methods of exploitation. Therefore, the control managers must also continue to monitor and analyze the impact of a change. Focused monitoring must occur even after the change has been made. The aim is to understand all of the long-term consequences. As such, it is a requisite of good practice to

1. Perform an analysis of the changed control, or controls within its/their operational environment in order to identify potential points of future exploitation.
2. Execute pen testing, social engineering, or other forms of operational testing exercises to identify any new points of weakness or failure.
3. Continue to update the control set in order to enforce the trustworthy status and security requirements of the changed control set.
4. Modify the assurance case as appropriate.
5. Ensure that all required operational integration and testing processes have been executed on the changed control(s).
6. Ensure that all negative test results are reported to the appropriate decision authority for corrective action.

Change Assurance

Although a change is implemented through the agency of processes such as strategic planning, policy and procedure development, or operational control design and implementation, it is the change assurance process that ensures that the change meets established criteria for correctness. This assurance entails a continuous process, which involves various types of management review and problem resolution activities carried out by the organization's designated decision makers. Therefore, it is good practice to

1. Monitor the change through joint reviews as specified in the operational SOW for the change.
2. Ensure that all reviews specified by the SOW are conducted at their scheduled check points.
3. Ensure that action items issuing out of each review are recorded for further action.
4. Ensure that closure criteria are specified.
5. Perform audits as specified in the change SOW.
6. Ensure any audit specified in the change SOW is properly resourced and performed.
7. Ensure that any audit or review findings involving nonconcurrence are resolved.
8. Monitor service levels as agreed to by contract if third parties are involved in the change process.
9. If that is the case, then oversee the execution of the contract to ensure that required service levels are maintained.
10. Ensure that problems identified through joint reviews and audits are resolved
11. Baseline and track the number and type of vulnerabilities over time to verify that audit and remediation programs are demonstrating positive return on investment.

The designated manager for that control must certify that any nonconcurrences issuing out of the review process for the change are addressed and that all closure criteria have been satisfied. Then following execution of the change process, it is a requisite of good practice to

1. Perform tests to ensure correctness in accordance with the specified test and evaluation criteria.
2. Perform a verification and validation program to sufficiently ensure the correctness and integrity of operational performance of the changed control as delivered.
3. Ensure functional completeness of the control or controls against stated requirements.
4. Ensure that the change satisfies all function requirements specified in the change SOW.
5. If the change involves physical alterations in behavior or technology then ensure physical completeness against technical description.
6. Validate correctness of the change against technical description documents.

Documenting the assurance case requires an audit trail that provides traceability between the change authorization and the delivered product. For potential compliance reasons that audit trail must be maintained for a specified period of time into the future operation.

Assurance Case Evidence of Proper Response Management—a variety of evidence might be required in order to build and maintain an assurance case for the response management operation, including the following:

1. Evidence that resource considerations are factored into impact analyses and change authorizations
2. Evidence that every change has been authorized
3. Documentation of a formal schedule or timetable for each change
4. Evidence that a formal configuration management plan (CMP) exists for managing controls, which itemizes the change management, baseline management, and verification management functions, as well as documents how the control configuration identification scheme will be formulated and ensured
5. Evidence of a capable status accounting function comprising established baselines for each control set item that documents the current state of the control set at all times
6. Documentation that a baseline management ledger (BML) account exists for each controlled entity in the control set asset base

Change Reintegration into the Operational Environment

Changes must be reintegrated into the operational environment of the organization. Thus the decision maker who authorized a change must provide the formal authorization to perform the reintegration. This approval must be underwritten by the findings of the change assurance process that was described earlier. Once authorization is granted, the change is reintegrated into the operational system. It is then necessary to conduct a technically rigorous process to assure that this reintegration has been done correctly.

This reintegration is supported by a comprehensive review, audit, and testing program. The reintegration assurance program is specified at the point where the change agent prepares the plan to perform the work. The testing certifies that the reintegration is satisfactory and that all interfaces are functioning properly.

Configuration Management

In addition to certifying of the correctness of the re-integration, it is necessary to fully document the new control set's baseline configuration and then maintain it under strict configuration control. The documentation is kept as a current baseline configuration description. That baseline is stored in an organizationally designated repository. Therefore, it is good practice to

1. Confirm reintegration maintains correct level of integrity and security. This confirmation is certified by the results of the testing program.
2. Ensure documentation is updated at the requisite level of integrity and security (including the assurance case). This is assured by confirming that the new baseline has been satisfactorily represented in a controlled baseline repository.
3. Ensure changed items maintain backward and forward traceability to other baselined states. This is assured by maintaining a repository of prior baseline states that is typically called a static library or archive.
4. Ensure the configuration record is securely maintained throughout the life cycle and archived according to good practice.

Recertification and Accreditation of Change

In the case of certain regulatory requirements, such as the Federal Information Security Management Act (FISMA, 2002), it might be necessary for the control set and related systems to be assessed and authorized by an appropriate third-party evaluator using a commonly accepted process of assessment. The findings of that process are typically accredited by formal third-party certification, such as the Approval to Operate issued by the General Accounting Office (GAO) in the case of FISMA. Or in the case of commercial ISO 27000 control assessments, the ISO 27000 certification is issued by a notified body of the ISO.

In the case of FISMA and ISO 27000, reaccreditation of initial certification is obtained periodically from a third-party certification and assessment body. In both cases, the aim is to ensure continuing confidence in the performance of the control system. Intervals for reaccreditation are typically specified by organizational policy and/or external regulation, therefore

1. A legitimate third-party agency must be employed to conduct certification audits—the audit standard should be established by regulation or contract.
2. Assessments for certification/recertification of accreditation must be performed by properly certified lead auditors.
3. Adequate resources must be provided to ensure the effectiveness of the audit process.
4. The independence of the auditing/accrediting agency must be assured.
5. Consistent use of a standard audit method must be assured.
6. Recertification audits must be performed timely enough to ensure continuing confidence in the performance of the system.

Secure Migration or Retirement of a Control System

Overall operations of an organization will change over time. Therefore, the migration and retirement of the associated control set or control system must be overseen and controlled by organizationally standard and rigorous processes. This level of rigor ensures that major changes to organizational functioning are managed using a rational and secure systematic process.

The rigor also ensures that the overall portfolio of organizational controls will continue to meet its intended purpose. Therefore, it must be ensured that migration and retirement risks and impacts are known. And that knowledge is developed and obtained through the agency of a well-defined and systematic organizational analysis function.

A transition strategy must be developed that assures the desired level of control will be maintained during the transition from one form of the organizational function to the other. And the assurance aspects of the transition must be fully and explicitly studied, characterized, and understood. Finally, the appropriate decision maker must authorize the migration or retirement strategy prior to the implementation of an organizational change. Then tests and inspections must be executed to explicitly assure the following:

1. The transition of the control set or system is accomplished in a safe and secure fashion.
2. The transition process is confirmed effective and correct.
3. The proper functioning of the control set or system after transition is confirmed.
4. The effectiveness of the transition is confirmed and certified by a satisfactory verification and validation procedure.
5. The results of the transition process are documented and retained.
6. The integrity of the control set or system is confirmed after transition [ISO04, p. 33].
7. All control set operations and data integrity are confirmed by an appropriate set of measures.
8. The results of the program and data integrity checking process are documented and retained.
9. Control set or system documentation accurately reflects the changed state.

Operational Oversight and Infrastructure Assurance of Control Set Integrity

The oversight and assurance of the control infrastructure calls out processes that establish, coordinate, and sustain the operational assurance, analysis, and response management functions. Establishing and maintaining a control architecture ensures tangible management oversight over the interrelationships among the various control responses. Control infrastructure assurance ensures that the organization has a planned and documented assurance case and a comprehensive control architecture as well as tangible policies, processes, and methodologies that establish everyday operational assurance, analysis, and response management work.

The organization's control architecture is the composite of all of the tangible behavioral and technical controls that the organization has established to provide tangible threat identification, analysis, and response services. The entire control architecture must be holistic and complete. Standard policies, processes, and methods are necessary to establish and then ensure that the actions of the organization in that respect will be appropriate.

Because change is inevitable, those policies, processes, and methods will have to be altered from time-to-time in order to maintain a correct response to threats that emerge in the contextual situation. This has to be a formal oversight process in order to maintain alignment between security objectives and the control(s) set(s).

The policies, processes, and methods that are imposed to ensure a properly running control infrastructure comprise the tangible elements of the sustainment process. Besides enabling a tangible sustainment infrastructure, policies, processes, and procedures also ensure continuous coordination between the sustainment function and the business processes of the organization.

Control Architecture

Control architecture involves the development, deployment, and continuous maintenance of the most appropriate and capable set of behaviors, tools, frameworks, and components. The aim of control architecture is to maintain a dynamic management response to threats and changes to the organizational environment. To accomplish this

1. Standard control oversight and assurance processes must be planned, designed, administered, and maintained. The aim of this is to ensure that effective leadership vision, expertise, and the correct technology solutions are available to ensure security and control of applications and infrastructure.
2. Standard procedures are in place to assess, integrate, and optimize the control architecture—the control architecture must be assessed regularly and systematically to ensure that it remains effective.
3. Organization-wide evaluations must be done to ensure the continuous integrity and performance of the control architecture within the enterprise. The control architecture must be evaluated to ensure that it remains effective in that respect.
4. Future control requirements and trends must be evaluated in order to define a long-term control architecture strategy. Threats must be assessed as they impact the evolution of the control architecture of the organization.

5. Subject matter expertise and consultation and strategy resources must be made available to ensure the effectiveness of the control architecture. Expertise is provided to lay-managers in order to ensure a minimum acceptable awareness of the implications and requirements of the overall control architecture.

6. Directions must be evaluated as they relate to the acquisition of specific control elements with the architecture. From this evaluation, rational decisions are made on the most effective purchase of components and services and the in-house development of monitoring and assessment tools.

7. The control aspects of third party and outsourcing process must be continuously ensured to be in conformance with all control practices that have been defined by the organization to address third-party control issues.

8. On-call technical support must be provided for control maintenance. Any questions or concerns raised in the day-to-day execution of any given control in the control architecture must be responded to on a priority basis.

9. Enterprise management and control lessons learned must be maintained as a readily available knowledge base. This must be kept in an information store that will preserve, as well as make necessary control architecture knowledge available to all levels in the organization.

Policy, Process, and Methodology Assurance—in order to ensure appropriate management control at all times, the most effective and capable set of policies, processes, and methodologies must be defined, assured, deployed, and sustained. The aim of this part of the process is to maintain a dynamically effective management controls architecture. Modeling of application and infrastructure must be done from a control perspective in order to ensure targeted application. The goal is to ensure that the most current security methodologies, processes, and associated documentation have to be investigated, designed, and deployed and that they will be maintained in an organizationally standard and appropriately correct form for use across the business.

In order to ensure effective use, a cross-organization collaboration must be established to communicate security practices through the implementation and use of training materials. These materials must be organizationally standard. Their coordination and application in the practical operational environment must be underwritten by a formal process. Then appropriate security metrics must be developed and collected. Those security metrics must be standard. They must be used for causal analysis and to optimize the ongoing security process.

In addition to organizational level measures, operational control management teams must be established and coached in how to best apply the organizationally standard methodologies and processes that have been developed to ensure smooth running control. And management control awareness, knowledge of policies, procedures, tools, and standards must be championed and promoted. This item also assists with assessing compliance. Metrics to improve methodology and process efficiency, usage, and results must be defined and analyzed.

Assurance Case Evidence for Infrastructure Assurance—Ongoing certification of the controls and the control sets that exist within the overall control infrastructure must be obtained where regulatory requirements demand it. A variety of evidence is relevant to creating and maintaining an assurance case for certification of control correctness, including the following:

1. Evidence of sustainment function's role in formulating strategic security requirements
2. Evidence that sustainment operational plan exists and is current
3. Documentation of assumptions about current, known risks, and threats
4. Documentation of organization-wide standards or standard practices
5. Specification of the technologies and products that will be utilized during the planning period, along with the method for installing, maintaining, and operating them on a secure basis
6. Evidence that all updates to controls have been verified, tested, and installed in a timely fashion
7. Evidence of organization-wide information sharing processes
8. Evidence that the information sharing process is revised and updated as the security situation changes.

Planning—Establishing the Routine Control Operations Process

Control assurance is founded on an organization-wide, standard set of policies, procedures, and behaviors. The role of controls of control operations is to maintain the relevance and effectiveness of that system. Controls of control operations are embodied through an operational plan. That plan delineates the requirements necessary to ensure a robust and persistent process. The operational plan is a particularly useful support to the organizational budgeting process because it allows decision makers to align their controls with available resources.

The operational plan organizes and focuses the deployment of those resources in a way that allows them to be used most effectively. The operational plan organizes the technical and procedural response in a way that the right countermeasures are in place to address the right controls requirements. Like the organization's strategic plan, the operational controls plan should be easily understood by all participants. Typically, operational planning is carried out on an annual basis. However if the situation warrants, it can be done as often as required. For instance, if the circumstances are particularly fluid, this type of planning might be necessary on a quarterly, monthly, or even weekly basis.

The first step in the operational planning process is an assessment of the current status of the organization. This assessment is done (usually annually) to characterize the near-term threat picture and the controls situation and specify the resultant controls requirements. The concrete outcome of this process is a baseline or bench-mark status for control. That baseline documents the current controls state and specifies the ensuing set of control requirements.

After the current status has been established and documented, any necessary change requirements are defined. These could be internally focused and only apply to a particular unit. Or they might be global recommendations for the entire organization. The purpose of the global recommendations is to provide a road map for executing the generic controls function. This road map documents all of the issues and priorities that will define the conduct of the operational controls function organization-wide during the specific planning period.

The road map also provides a management framework for the technical and procedural control behaviors that will be adopted for that period. In order to accurately determine the feasibility of these approaches and the resources required, these decisions ought to rest on a thorough understanding of the risks involved and be filtered through the threat prioritization process.

The road map is then used to develop the controls architecture. Once the direction is decided on, planners document an appropriate infrastructure of operational control procedures. The aim is to create a secure and stable day-to-day operational controls function. The outcome of this stage is a set of defined practices and work instructions that dictate operational controls practice. The aim is to ensure understanding of the procedures required to support every aspect of day-to-day controls functioning. This is typically communicated through a policy and procedure manual. Because that manual publicizes the controls of operations function to the organization at-large, it must be kept current.

Once tangible controls procedures and technical countermeasures have been captured and publicized in the policy and procedure manual, the organization uses that manual to build awareness. That typically involves focused employee education and training programs. It is obviously not sufficient to simply have a set of procedures in place without making the user community precisely aware of their personal responsibilities with respect to any defined practice that involves them. Therefore, proper education and awareness is one of the cornerstones of the implementation process. The educational program is deployed and administered as part of overall operations planning.

The maintenance of staff capability is a continuous responsibility. The specific education, training, and awareness activities that are implemented are always directly referenced to the procedures that they are meant to support and are always developed for the particular period. The staff capability plan also contains a detailed specification of the knowledge required to operate the technologies and products that will be used during the planning period. Technology alone will not secure the organization, but it is obviously a critical aspect of the process. Therefore the staff capability plan should specify the controls-related technology knowledge, skills, and abilities that will be required and their specific application.

Generic corrective action procedures are responsible for bringing the operational controls execution process into line with any change in conditions or other unanticipated circumstances. Because conditions are always changing the precise execution of the corrective action function has to be established in the yearly operational plan. The specific method for reporting the need for corrective action and the procedures for responding to each report must be specified in that plan. Without formal accountability, it is impossible to guarantee that procedures will be followed correctly. As such, the organization must also assign personal responsibility for execution of the steps in the plan.

Those responsibilities have to be itemized and unambiguously assigned to each individual participant. Once these have been itemized, the appropriate measures have to be defined to enforce them. Enforcement is a critical success factor. In order to ensure controls, explicit enforcement requirements and consequences for noncompliance have to be designated for every job title. Consequences for noncompliance have to be explicitly understood and personally agreed to this is necessary to ensure that employees will faithfully carry out their assigned controls duties. Then enforcement has to be practiced on a continuous basis and as an organizational commitment from the top of the organization.

The organization's continuity planning process establishes the overall approach that will be taken to ensure operational continuously. However, it is the responsibility of the everyday controls operation to make certain that all preplanned responses remain appropriate and that the organization is able to identify, report, and respond to incidents in a timely and effective manner.

Therefore one important duty of controls operations is to assure that the organization is always protected by a well-defined operational response. The duty of the operational response process is to always be prepared to resolve problems as they appear. That operational response is established and maintained by a plan. It integrates the sensing, analyzing, and responding principles into substantive procedures that meet the controls' needs of the organization.

The operational response function follows the same basic sensing, analyzing, and responding steps that are a fundamental part of the controls' operations process. These principles apply no matter whether the event was foreseen or unforeseen. The only difference is that, if the event was anticipated, the response is determined in advance. For example, there are always a set of operational contingencies aimed at responding appropriately to a fire. And most organizations execute a regular drill to ensure that the response is understood and reliably executed. The presence of that predefined response ensures that an optimum solution is provided in as timely a fashion as possible.

However, many events are unforeseen and they can often be the most dangerous. If the incident is unforeseen, the aim of the controls' operations process is to ensure a coordinated and appropriate response. The difference is that, because the incident was unforeseen there is a much greater emphasis on timely analysis leading to a rapid and intelligent response. Timeliness is underwritten by effective incident reporting.

Incident reporting triggers the operational response process. Incident reporting ensures that every meaningful event that might threaten the organization's information is identified and reported. These incidents are not just limited to events that make the six o'clock news, like the occasional Internet-wide denial of service attack. They include everything from major time sensitive attacks all the way down to routine reports of vulnerabilities spotted by the staff.

The incident reporting function kicks in when an incident is identified. It provides a description of both the type and estimated impact of the event. The primary success factor for effective incident reporting is timely detection. Therefore a successful reporting function is founded on a range of sensing measures. These measures are placed around the organization, both on the perimeter and embedded within operational practice.

The goal is to identify controls violations, or attempts to exploit controls vulnerabilities, or even inadvertent breakdowns in controls functioning in as timely a fashion as possible. Sensing measures can be as varied as output from automated intrusion detection (IDS)/intrusion prevention (IPS) systems, software driven scans, such as malware and virus checkers, or tips or direct reports from guards, law enforcement officials or other outside sources.

If the incident was foreseen, the incident report would typically recommend the management and/or technical resolution specified in the incident response plan. This recommendation would be transmitted to the operational response team for implementation and coordination. Proper control practices dictate that incident reports go to a single central coordinator for confirmation analysis and subsequent action. Central coordination is necessary because attacks and compromises do not usually present themselves in a single neat package. Instead, a series of suspicious events begin to form the signature of an impending attack.

Consequently, a single coordinating entity has to be in place to collect and analyze the information. Once an incident can be confirmed, its impacts must be (at least minimally) understood in order to set the right response in motion. The role of the staff of any central coordinating agency is to continuously work to connect the dots.

In practice, incidents are either potential or active. Potential incidents include such things as preattack probes, unauthorized access attempts, denial of service, or infrastructure vulnerabilities identified by the staff. One other potential source could be the notification by an outside entity, such as Microsoft or the Computer Emergency Response Team Coordination Center (CERT/CC) at Carnegie Mellon University.

The reports of potential incidents are typically generic and usually result from routine data gathering activity and analysis. For instance, there might be a wide array of similar reports that a virus incident has, or is likely to occur. Potential incident reports can also result from analyses performed by the makers of the software themselves. Manufacturers can send out a notice that vulnerability has been reported as a result of operational use of the product.

Most potential incident reports are generated by the various intrusion detection devices. One of the most common methods is called operational event logging. It is necessary to the controls operation because it monitors events that are taking place within the system itself. Most operating systems provide an event-logging function. Automated event logging is typically executed as a subsystem within the operating system.

That typically consists of a software agent that is set to capture events, which are typically recorded and stored for further retrospective analysis. That agent allows people who oversee the system's operation to determine whether it is being used properly. It also helps them to diagnose undesirable events such as controls violations and intentional or unintentional misuse. The purpose of an automated history such as an event log is to provide an audit trail. The function of that trail is to support the analysis of system performance that is a critical part of the overall controls' operational planning process.

Active incidents always require operational control. If it is possible to confirm that an unauthorized access, denial of service, or successful vulnerability exploitation has occurred, then the appropriate corrective actions must be undertaken. Since those actions are dictated by the circumstance, they cannot be characterized. However, they can range from

- Applying a technical patch, such as a reconfiguration or reinstallation of the system
- Changes in policy and procedure
- Implementation of new enforcement mechanisms for the entire organization

Configuration management then ensures that the recommended change has been properly requested, analyzed, authorized, executed, and assured. Where a change to organizational policy and/or procedure is needed, the operational control team does the coordination and documentation activities. These ensure that the change has been persistently established within the target system and is being followed.

Every organization has to compile, distribute, and update a procedure manual. The purpose of this manual is to detail all requisite procedures to ensure continuous control operation. At a minimum, there should be simple checklists within that provide clear direction for employees performing routine housekeeping activities. The checklists prevent the people who are executing a controls process from omitting something important. At a minimum, every documented control procedure manual should ensure that

- The required steps are specified.
- The expected results are specified.

- The criteria that will be used to determine that the goals of the procedure have been met.
- Finally, there should be a clear statement of the interrelationship between related procedures.

Rationally Managing the Configuration of the Control Set

Since in the mid-1980s, the practices that describe how we control any form of abstract process or product has come to be lumped under the generic heading of "configuration management." Configuration management defines and enforces the requisite management control over the technological and business practices of the entire organization. The type of configuration management that we will discuss here is meant to be a formally organized and implemented organizational process for the rational management of necessary changes to the control set and its related artifacts.

Rational management of the control set is an essential part of ensuring comprehensive management control over the control infrastructure as a whole. In that respect, configuration management functions as a general oversight and regulatory process for the management function of the business. Configuration management is based around well-defined methods for efficient and effective identification and monitoring of threats and weaknesses in the operation of the general business. And it applies throughout the complete life cycle of a given management process.

In concept, configuration management refers to the organization and maintenance of control objects. Its purpose is to rationally control changes that are made to the control set. This must be done in a way that preserves the overall integrity of the control system. As we said earlier, configuration management provides a basis to measure quality, improve the entire control set functioning, and make the testing and quality assurance part of the process easier because it provides traceability into all associated control problems for a given function, which enables automated problem tracking.

Configuration management incorporates two processes: (1) configuration control and (2) verification control. These are implemented through three interdependent management activities. In actual practice, these activities must be fitted to the needs of each project. These activities are: change process management, which is made up of change authorization, verification control, and release processing; baseline control, which is composed of change accounting and library management; and configuration verification, which includes status accounting to verify compliance with specifications.

The "configuration manager" insures that the requirements of change management are properly carried out. The configuration manager's general role is to process all control set change requests, manage all control set change authorizations, and verify that the change is completed correctly.

The organization also defines and appoints a baseline manager who is responsible for ensuring that all configuration items (CIs) defined by the project CMP are identified, accounted for, and maintained consistent with a specified identification scheme. This individual establishes a change management ledger (CML) for each controlled product and records all changes and promotions and maintains all libraries associated with a given product.

The baseline manager accounts for product CIs. To do this, the baseline manager, together with appropriate development personnel, set ups and maintains a CML. This ledger represents a complete accounting of control set CIs for each controlled product, including CI descriptor label, promotion/version level, and change activity. Since items not in the ledger are by definition not CIs, the baseline manager is responsible for keeping the ledger up to date. The baseline manager maintains records sufficient to reflect the current state of all valid configurations of the control set and the baseline manager is responsible for the authorization of entries into the CML.

The verification manager has the responsibility for ensuring that management control and control set integrity is maintained during the change process. The general role of the verification manager is to confirm that items in the CML conform to the identification scheme, verify that changes to control operation have been carried out, and conduct milestone reviews after the fact. The verification manager also maintains documentation of all reviews for the purpose of lessons learned. The verification manager must guarantee that items maintained in the CML reflect the true status of the control set at any given point in time.

The cornerstone of control configuration management is the control set configuration identification scheme. This scheme is a prerequisite for the management of the control configuration because it sets up the "day one" baseline. As such it is usually established during the initial identification, design, development, and deployment of the control set.

All targets for control and their control components are identified and uniquely labeled. The control targets and their associated controls are arrayed as a baseline centered on their interrelationships and dependencies. This array then depicts the basic structure (configuration) of the control set. It must be noted here that the decisions that determine the shape of this configuration are made outside configuration management, usually by business process owners but sometimes by upper management. Nonetheless, a precisely defined baseline is an absolute prerequisite for managing control configurations since the baseline is the structure which is maintained in the CML.

Once established, the control set identification scheme is maintained throughout the life cycle. Items defined at any level within the control hierarchy must be given unique and appropriate labels, which are typically referred to as control identification numbers [CINs]. Generally, CINs are associated with the structure itself. They can be used to designate and relate the position of any given item in the overall "family tree" of the control infrastructure. Change occurs when new control baselines are created either through the promotion or release of new controls. If there are changes to the items in the evolving structure such that it represents a new baseline, the identification labeling is modified to reflect this.

The management level authorized to approve change for each baseline must be explicitly defined. Authorization is always given at the highest practical level in the organization. It is assumed that as the control set evolves it will be necessary to increase the level of authority required to authorize a change. Changes at any level in the basic structure must be maintained at all levels.

The configuration control board (CCB) executes configuration control at defined levels of authorization. CCBs are hierarchical and composed of managers with sufficient authority to direct the change process. At a minimum there are three control boards within an organization, one composed of top-level policy makers and one for each of the major organizational processes, for example, the management control processes CCB and the technical control processes CCB.

The practical realization of the control board assignments is a panel comprising members who are at the optimum level of authority to oversee the policy and managerial processes of the organization. This means that, generally it is not a good idea for policy makers to be placed on technical boards and technology wizards to serve on top-level CCBs. The scope of the board's oversight must be formally and explicitly defined, usually in the general CMP.

Configuration management is specifically defined and formally implemented through a CMP. Commitment to this plan must be rigorously enforced throughout the business operation. At the minimum, this plan should specify the change management, baseline management, and verification management roles, as well as the control configuration identification scheme. Also, the basic structure of the discrete CIN and how it will be assigned must be provided, including the specific format of the CIN.

The hierarchy and composition of the CCBs must also be defined and each board must have its authority, scope, and responsibility for decision making. In addition, the mechanism must be defined for monitoring baselines and releases, providing timely information to management to support the authorization function, and for verifying and validating changes. Finally, the rules for the dynamic, controlled, and static libraries must be defined.

Chapter Summary

As the name implies, operational control assurance is less involved with strategy then it is with ensuring dependable day-to-day functioning of the organization. The operational control assurance function achieves its purpose by making certain that security practices always meet specified control oversight and management goals.

The general role of the operational assurance function is to maintain consistently correct alignment between the management goals of the business and its specific control practices. Operational control assurance is responsible for monitoring the execution of all of the controls and control systems of the business in order to ensure that they are effectively supporting the organization's business purposes.

The sustainment process presupposes the existence and documentation of a comprehensive, correct, and unambiguous control set. This has to occur at the control system's most basic level of functioning. In addition, the interconnection between any subset of the control set and the entire portfolio of control systems must also be fully and holistically represented. The overall control system's responsibility for receiving, processing, or transmitting information must be documented as well as the status of all of the various constituencies affected by the control set, such as managers or users. The various elements of the target for control are normally understood in a top-down fashion, drilling down from the entity as a whole into each large element of that system to a more detailed understanding of the actual components and interrelationships and requirements of the control subsets of the constituent components.

Typically, sustainment monitors the control set's ability to ensure confidence in the continued proper functioning of the control set. Sustainment monitors the control set's ability to accurately identify and record problems, analyze those problems, take the appropriate corrective, adaptive, perfective, or preventive action and confirm the restored capability of the controls. Sustainment activities also encompass the migration and retirement of the control set. The process ends when the control set or control set-intensive system is retired.

In order to implement a change properly, it is essential to understand all of the components and the consequences of change to the process. That degree of understanding requires knowledge of all aspects of the design architecture and the affected business functionality. To support the requisite for executive decision making about the form of the response, a meaningful and valid body-of-evidence that has to be developed in the analysis phase. Then, this must be communicated in a clear and understandable fashion to the designated approving authorities of the organization. That response manager will then provide the actual authorization of any changes necessary to ensure the continued effectiveness of the control set.

Changes to the control set can eliminate vulnerabilities. However, change can also create new ones. As a consequence, attackers typically examine a significant change to a control system in order to identify any new or different methods of exploitation. Therefore, the control managers must also continue to monitor and analyze the impact of a change. Focused monitoring must occur even after the change has been made. The aim is to understand all of the long-term consequences.

Although a change is implemented through the agency of processes such as strategic planning, policy and procedure development, or operational control design and implementation, it is the change assurance process that ensures that the change meets established criteria for correctness. This assurance entails a continuous process, which involves various types of management review and problem resolution activities carried out by the organization's designated decision makers.

Changes must be reintegrated into the operational environment of the organization. Thus the decision maker who authorized a change must provide the formal authorization to perform the reintegration. This approval must be underwritten by the findings of the change assurance process that was described earlier. Once authorization is granted, the change is reintegrated into the operational system. It is then necessary to conduct a technically rigorous process to assure that this reintegration has been done correctly.

In addition to certifying of the correctness of the reintegration, it is necessary to fully document the new control set's baseline configuration and then maintain it under strict configuration control. The documentation is kept as a current baseline configuration description. That baseline is stored in an organizationally designated repository.

The organization's control architecture then is the composite of all of the tangible behavioral and technical controls that the organization has established to provide tangible threat identification, analysis, and response services. The entire control architecture must be holistic and complete. Standard policies, processes, and methods are necessary to establish and then ensure that the actions of the organization in that respect will be appropriate.

Key Concepts

- Sustainment is a continuous function.
- Sustainment is executed by plan.
- Sustainment comprises four domains—sensing, analyzing, authorizing, assurance.
- Sustainment is a standard activity of several large frameworks.
- There are two types of responses—proactive and reactive.
- Proactive assurance is best because it responds to events prior to occurrence.
- Controls are sustained for both processes and technologies.
- Staff capability and accountability are key issues in sustainment.
- Sustainment ensures confidence in the control set.
- Infrastructure assurance is based around configuration control.
- Configuration control is a management discipline based around authorizations.
- Controls are managed in hierarchical baselines.
- Baselines are assured by formal reviews, tests, and audits.

Key Terms

Adaptive change—alterations in control behavior due to new understanding of threat

Assurance case—statement of correct outcome of a response to a threat

Baseline—collection of assurance behaviors associated with a given target of control

Change management—structured and disciplined process to rationally manage a baseline

Controls—behaviors designed to assure performance to designated criteria

Control board—designated authorization agent for change

Control management ledger—organizational record of baseline configuration

Control set integrity—assurance that control set functions as intended without weaknesses

Control target—the entity to which a control objective applies

Incident reporting—the formal statement of an adverse occurrence

Monitoring—routine assessment of control set performance during normal operations

Operational assurance—continuous practices to confirm correct performance

Proactive assurance—identification and response to a threat prior to occurrence

Procedure manual—record of the specific actions to be taken in the case of a foreseen event

Reactive assurance—actions taken to respond to an unforeseen threat

Response planning—establishing the best possible reaction to a foreseen threat

Sensing—continuous investigation of the internal and external threat environment

Threat understanding—formal process to analyze an adverse occurrence

Validation agent—certifier of correctness of a change

Reference

Federal Information Security Management Act of 2002 (FISMA). Title III, Information Security, pp. 48–63.

Index

Printed in the United States
by Baker & Taylor Publisher Services